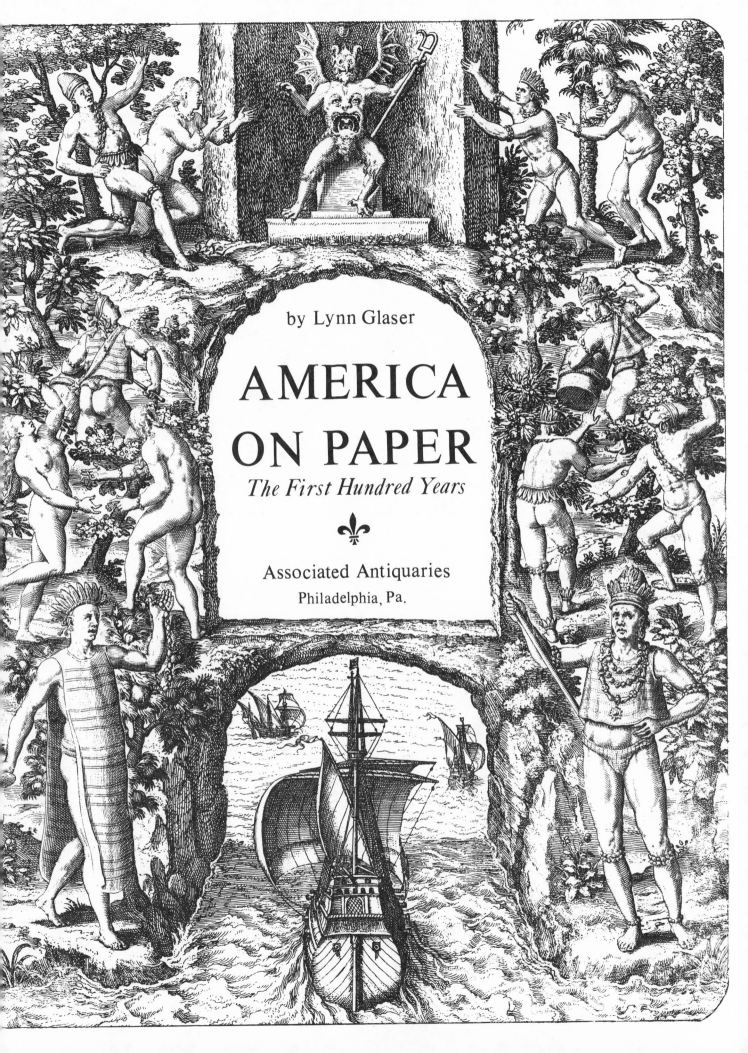

by Lynn Glaser

AMERICA
ON PAPER
The First Hundred Years

⚜

Associated Antiquaries

Philadelphia, Pa.

Columbus' ship sailing among the new islands from Sebastian Munster's cosmography.

Published by Associated Antiquaries
P.O.Box 42896
Philadelphia, Pa., 19101

Library of Congress Cataloging in Publication Data

Glaser, Lynn.
America on Paper
Bibliography: p.
Includes index.
1. America - - Early accounts to 1600. 2. Indians - - History - - 16th. Century - -
Sources. I. Title.

E141.G58 1989 970.01 89-6846
ISBN 0-929769-00-7

Contents

INTRODUCTION 1

PARTNERS IN DISCOVERY 4

FILLING IN DISCOVERY 23

NATURE IN OR OF THE NEW WORLD 81

INDIAN ORIGINS AND THEOLOGICAL PROBLEMS 118

ALL SORTS OF INDIANS 138

THE QUEST 191

THE BLACK LEGEND 214

THE COLONIAL IMPULSE 229

AFTERWORDS AND AFTERTHOUGHTS 243

NOTES 250

INDEX 251

This charming pen and ink wash drawing done by Marten de Vos about 1594 was copied and recopied into the 18th. Century to make it the commonest allegorical depiction of America.

An age shall come, ere ages end,
Blessedly strange and strangely blest,
When our Sea far and near oppressed
His shore shall farther yet extend.

Described then shall a large land be,
By this profound sea's navigation,
Another World, another nation,
All men shall then discovered see.

Thule accounted heretofore
The world's extreme, the Northern bound,
Shall be when Southwest parts be found,
A nearer isle a neighbor shore...

Nothing now more to discover,
No place is now left to surprise,
Towns now that for defense devise,
With new fortifications cover.

All in the world turned round about,
Nothing in place as was enured,
Nothing unseen, nothing assured
This circle universe throughout.

The Indian, whom at home heat fries,
Drinks of Araxis waters cold:
The Persian, rich in gems and gold,
Wash in the Rhine and Elbe likewise.

- Seneca in *Medea*, ca. 50, A. D.

"This prophecy was fulfilled by my father, the Admiral, in 1492."

- Words proudly written against this passage by Ferdinand Columbus
in his own copy of Seneca.

Introduction

BACK around 1575 a writer named Louis le Roy equated the development of the printing press with geographical discovery as the greatest accomplishments of his age. This is the story of the effect of one upon the other.

The tide of discovery rose on an ocean of ink. As the New World slowly emerged from the mists that had hidden it for so long stories of fantastic kingdoms, already in print, combined with curiosity and avarice to broaden the map. In the process strange things were found stimulating new publications which in turn encouraged further discovery. In short America was history's first media event. By 1800 a body of literature from conquistadors, missionaries and stay at home armchair philosophers reached 50,000 items and everyone who took up a pen or burin had his own idea about what America looked like, its shape and size and a vision of what it all meant. The books can be touching as Ferdinand Columbus' biography of his father, gut wrenching as Bartolome de las Casas' passionate plea for the Indians, pompous as a conquistador's braggadocio, speculative as a confused cartographer or quaint as a treatise in which one Leon Pinelo discusses the momentous question of whether Catholic priests can eat chocolate on Friday and still save souls from perdition.

Nobody would have suspected this plenitude from the little pamphlet that showed up in the streets of Barcelona and Rome in the spring of 1493. It began:

> *THE LETTER OF CHRISTOPHER COLUMBUS to whom our age owes a great debt, on the recent discovery of the islands of India beyond the Ganges, to look for which he had been sent eight months before under the auspices and at the expense of the most invincible Ferdinand and Isabella, sovereigns of the Spains; sent to lord Gabriel Sanchez, treasurer of the said most serene sovereigns. . .*
>
> On the thirty-third day after I left the Canaries I reached the Indian sea, there I found many Islands, inhabited by numberless people, all of which I took possession without opposition in the name of our most fortunate king by making formal proclamation and raising standards: and to the first of them I gave the name San Salvador, the blessed Savior, through dependence on whose aid we reached both this and the others. . . I gave each one of the others too a new name; to wit, one Santa Maria de la Conception, another Fernanda, another Juana [Cuba - in honor of the future Queen of Spain, Juana the Mad].
>
> When we first put in at the island I said was named Juana I proceeded along its shore westward a little way, and found it so large (for no end to it appeared) I believed it to be no island but the continental province of Cathay. . .

The pamphlet goes on to describe simple natives eager to swap gold for trinkets, beautiful islands with lush fields ripe for cultivation and flora and fauna which he tries to describe in terms understandable back in Spain. Astonished readers learned Columbus "did not find any monsters among them, but men of great dignity and kindness." He mentions the island of Mateunin which was inhabited solely by women and "two more provinces which I did not visit, one of which is called Anan whose citizens were born with tails." There were also cannibals about but Columbus had not seen any of those either.

Apparently Columbus had discovered a sea route to the Indies. Naturally more expeditions would be required before their Catholic Majesties presented an ambassador to the Great Khan but it would simply be a matter of organization and planning. The admiral concludes:

> Indeed the outcome was manifold and marvelous and fitting not to my own claims to merit but. . . to the holy Christian faith and the piety and religion of our sovereigns, for what the human mind cannot comprehend the divine has granted to men, for God is accustomed to listen to his servants and those who love his commandments, even in impossible circumstances, as happened in the present instance, for we have succeeded in that which hitherto mortal powers have in no wise attained. For if others have written or spoken of these islands, they have all done so by indirection and guesses; no one claims to have seen them, whence it seemed almost a fable. Therefore let the King and Queen, the Prince, their happy realms, and all other provinces of Christendom give thanks to the Savior, our Lord Jesus Christ, who has granted us so great a victory and reward; let processions be celebrated; let solemn Holy rites be performed; and let the Churches be decked with festival branches; let Christ rejoice on Earth as he does in Heaven when he foresees that so many souls of peoples hitherto lost are to be saved. Let us too rejoice, both for the exaltation of our faith and the increase in temporal goods which not only Spain but all Christendom are to share. As these things were done, so to have they been briefly narrated.
> Lisbon, the day before the Ides of March,
> *Christopher Columbus*

Columbus was rightfully proud having, he thought, largely accomplished his objective. All that remained was the simple task of sending missionaries, establishing settlements and organizing a government for the Indies while he went on to find the Great Khan. His letter asked no questions nor did it bring up any issues. Soon it would raise many that resulted in the discovery and conquest saga that makes up the Americana library because the simple act of bumping into America was no mere nautical achievement. Instead it was the discovery of a new race, a diametrically opposed religion, a natural history totally unheard of and a new cosmology. During the period this work examines none of the issues discussed here were resolved. Originally seen in the context of the late medieval and renaissance mind they changed form from century to century in a way that largely determined the early history of our hemisphere and in the process produced a new type of man.

For twenty-five years I have been handling browned bits of paper, usually bound in calf with ridged spines and gold stamping that somehow survived into the late 20th. Century. Sometimes, even if I could not read a work in the original, simply handling it made me imagine I was in touch with the time. To convey the feeling I offer a discussion of most of the major works of the period, books, prints and maps, in an effort to let the people who lived it tell us where and what they were and what they were doing. I have confined myself as much as possible to works that saw the printing press during the century on the assumption the media is the message. To the extent I varied from that rule it is because what was suppressed or considered of insufficient interest to print at the time sheds light on what appeared. As far as space permits maps and prints are reproduced in their entirety in an effort to paint a pandemic picture, complete with nuances.

This is no story of actions and deeds but one about the thoughts and feelings of a long forgotten time which can be more interesting than the accomplishments of conquerors and discoverers. At least I hope I have made it that way.

ACKNOWLEDGEMENTS

Although America is the only place in the world to have its early history written down by contemporaries sorting out an incredibly complex and contradictory mass of material has required the labors of scores of scholars and I am indebted to every one, from pioneers like Henry Harrisse and Justin Winsor to the last writer to go to press before I typed my final word. They reduce me to the proverbial ant standing on the shoulders of giants. Among those I most owe are: Patrica Olive Dickason, J. H. Elliot, Antonello Gerbi, his translator Jeremy Moyle, Lewis Hanke, Margaret Hodgen, Benjamin Keene, Hugh Honour, Howard Mumford Jones, Samuel Morison, Henry R. Wagner and his collaborator Helen Rand Parish and Wilcombe Washburn. The reader can praise or damn Diane Sholander for encouraging me to write what follows and James Galbraith for raising me to such literacy needed to punch it out.

Partners in Discovery

THE letter quoted in the introduction was actually a second draft. On February 14, 1493 the returning caravels, *Nina* and *Pinta,* ran into a storm off the Azores. (The *Santa Maria* had run aground off Haiti.) Columbus, fearing the loss of both ships and his news of discovery, committed a record to parchment which, according to his log, he "enveloped in waxed cloth, and tied it very securely, and ordered a large wooden barrel brought, and placed the parchment in the barrel without any person knowing what it was, as they all thought it was some act of devotion, and thus had it thrown into the sea."

The following day the storm abated, giving Columbus an opportunity to prepare another account during a brief stopover in Lisbon before returning to his home port of Palos. This he sent to Luis Santangel, keeper of the privy purse and one of his early supporters, for presentation to Their Catholic Majesties at the proper moment.

The earliest edition of *De Insulis Inventis Epist. . .* appeared in Barcelona where the peripatetic Spanish court was then sitting. Its rarity suggests a small printing, probably for circulation among officialdom.

News apparently traveled fast because the Barcelona folio was soon followed by three Latin quartos published in Rome, one of which bares the date April 29. The Rome editions show Gabriel or Raphael Sanchez, treasurer of the Kingdom of Aragon, as the recipient but this was probably a mistake on the part of the translator who assumed Sanchez, rather than Santangel was the treasury official referred to as the addressee.

The sensation spread quickly with a Latin edition of the "Letter" coming out of Antwerp and another from Basil - this one containing eight woodcuts (one a repetition), which however fanciful provided Europe with its first visual impression of a New World. Three more Latin editions from Paris and a German translation appeared in 1493.

Still in 1493 and back in Rome a mitered sycophant named Giuliano Dati (d. Bishop of St. Leone in Calabria, 1524) was grinding out a bit of doggerel with the, englished, title: *A History of the Discovery of the Canary Islands in the Indies; Extracted from the Letter of Christofano Columbo and Translated into the Common Language.* This literary effort, in addition to being a little vague on who Columbus was, where he went and even when he got there is also not a translation but a paraphrase of sixty-eight stanzas, the first fourteen of which are a full and vapid preamble praising, among others, Alexander VI (father of Lucretia Borgia). The following is a fair sample of his poetry:

And in the future men shall read the fame
of Alexander Sixth of that great name;
Of his election pure of every guile,
Hailed by the world with an approving smile,
Walled about from his first papal year
With general love and reverential fear;
Benign to all, Pope Borgia son of Spain,
In judgement righteous, and in heart humane!

Columbus shows up in the fourteenth stanza with the same drivel:

Back to my theme, Oh listener, turn with me
and hear of islands all unknown to thee!
Islands whereof the grand discovery
Chanced in this year of fourteen ninety-three,
One Christopher Colonbo who's resort
Was ever in King Ferando's court,
Bent himself still to rouse and stimulate
The king to swell the borders of his state.

Dati's paraphrase added no new information. He had none to add, but his account was the most popular probably because its ballad-like quality provided entertainment. It saw two more printings in Florence in 1493 and another two in the same city in 1495. It was probably sung in the streets by itinerant singers.

¶ La lettera delli fole che ha trouato nuouamente il R e diſpagna.

Title cut for Dati's Poem (First printing.) It suggests the importance of Ferdinand, seated in the foreground gazing across the ocean at the heathen he has subdued. A tiny Columbus, his standard bearer, sits in his ship in the distance.
    Variations of this cut were used in other editions of Dati as well as an edition of Vespucci.

TOP: Illustration from Dati's poem. BELOW: Title cut from EIN SCHON HUBSCH LESSEN
PAGE 7: These famous woodcuts from Johannes Besicken's Basle edition of Columbus' letter are
the first visual impression Europe received of America. Note that Hispaniola appears as a
castellated island and Columbus is rowing ashore in a Venetian galley. The caravel had previously appeared in other items of incanabula and Besicken used it twice in his account of
Columbus. The Venetian galley may also have appeared elsewhere. Other plates in the pamphlet
include a portrait of Ferdinand, apropos of nothing a cut of Granada, and escutcheons of Castile and Leon.

In 1494 the story was appended to a Latin work by Verardo lauding Ferdinand for expelling the Moors from Spain as if Columbus was playing Roland to Ferdinand's Charlemagne. Another printing of the original letter came from Valladolid in 1497. Again rarity suggests a small edition for circulation to appropriate officials, perhaps to give them an idea of what to expect from Columbus' third voyage. Although his second had been completed and altered the picture somewhat Spanish bureaucracy apparently felt no need to promulgate its results. The same years saw a Strassburg translation into German. This, one of the few versions in the vernacular may, like Dati's, have been prepared more for entertainment than informative value as suggested by the title: *Ein Schon Hubsch Lessen. . .* ("Nice Pleasant Reading"). The title cut showing Ferdinand and his entourage approaching Christ implies the publisher was impressed with the religious implications of the discovery.

Who got this remarkable news and how was it received?

It would be a long time before Americana assumed the bulk of the religious and philosophical tomes and reprints of classical authors that occupied printers of the period. The various versions of Columbus' story were short, unbound and probably issued in editions of 200 to 500 copies. They are comparable with broadsheets or newspapers of the day. Their rarity, combined with the number of editions (eighteen known before 1500) suggests they were received as a sensation and thrown away. But it was a sensation. Assuming average printings of 350 pamphlets per issue 6,300 copies circulated. A best seller for the Century.

How was it understood? Probably not very well. Dati's reference to the Canary Islands is indicative of the contemporary ignorance of geography. Furthermore Verardo's attachment of the letter to his celebration of Ferdinand along with the frequent appearance of woodcuts of Ferdinand in various issues implies a greater fascination with the last crusader's feats than Columbus.

At least in some cases. Ten printings in Latin were produced for the learned. In Italy powerful Mediterranean houses like the Medici and Capponi had every reason to take note. As the news spread to Germany the Wessers and Fugger commercial interests probably perused the pamphlet. Spanish officials certainly had reason to give it consideration along with some schoolmen.

For those that did understand the message the general impression was that Columbus had not discovered anything more than a sea route. Despite the title: "The New Islands" affixed to various issues of the admiral's message its readers already knew about them. Marco Polo described a passel of islands off Cathay, including an island of women and the Chinese province of Anan while the ancient authority, Pliny, not only described cannibals but included a bestiary of oriental humanoids in his natural history. A few, Vespucci and Martyr, for instance, expressed confusion but could not understand alternatives.

But Columbus was the man of the hour. He had discovered a short route to the Indies to replace tedious caravan treks, largely severed by the Turks. Necessary spices and occasional luxuries could flow into Europe and now there would be no middleman. As he prepared for his second voyage the man who had been scrounging jails a year before was so overwhelmed by would be adventurers he was turning them away.

Within a month of his return Columbus negotiated a contract with the Spanish sovereigns to lead a new expedition for the purposes of 1) converting the Indians, 2) establishing a colony on Hispaniola and 3) exploring Cuba on the assumption he would find a road to the golden cities of Cathay. He sailed in August, 1493, a bare six months after his triumphant return. Now he commanded seventeen vessels carrying at least twelve hundred men.

The reading public got an account of the second voyage even before the admiral got home. Running short of supplies, he dispatched the major part of his fleet home with a request for more of everything, men, munitions, livestock, food, wine, clothing and shoes. With it sailed Guglielmo Como who wrote a letter to his friend Nicolo Scillacio, a doctor and teacher at the University of Pavia, who tried to explain where Columbus was and what he was finding in a ten leaf quarto entitled: *De Insulis Meridiani Atique Maris Nuper Inventis* which appeared, probably in Pavia, late in 1594 or '95. It was no best seller but more of Scillacio later. Considering the level of his achievement it seems strange that Columbus was already fading into obscurity, at least as far as the media was concerned.

Four other participants in the second voyage prepared accounts but they all lay in manuscript for years. Those authors were Diego Chanca, the fleet surgeon Michele de Cueno, a childhood friend of Columbus and Bernardis Buell, a monk who later became a caballer against the admiral. In 1504 Peter Martyr's first decade appeared with information derived from a forth participant, a former Spanish diplomat, Melchior Maldonado and perhaps Columbus himself.

A few independent references to Columbus appeared but nothing new about the new islands. Sebastian Brant's *Das Narrenschiff* ("Ship of Fools," Basel, 1497) mentions a land previously unknown until Ferdinand discovered innumerable people, presumably idiots, in the great Spanish Ocean. Zacharias Lilio has two allusions to Columbus in his *De Origine et laudibus scientiarm...* (Florence 1496) and a funeral oration printed in Rome, again lauding Spanish (Ferdinand's) valor makes a reference to the overseas discovery. But it was just a matter of a few words here and there.

Then everything changed.

ENTER THE NEW WORLD

In 1496 Columbus complained, "There is not a man down to the very tailors who does not beg to become a discoverer." One of the interlopers on what he considered his exclusive domain was Americus Vespucci who burst into print in or shortly before 1504 with a four leaf quarto entitled *Mundus Novus.* The verso of the title page tells us what it is all about. It is a letter from "Alberic" Vespucci to his friend and patron Lorenzo de Medici which:

> The interpreter Giocundus translated... into the Latin language, that all who are versed in the Latin may learn how many wonderful things are discovered every day, and that the temerity of those who want to probe the Heavens and their Majesty, and to know more than is allowed

to know, be confounded; as not withstanding the long time since the world began to exist, the vastness of the Earth and what it contains is still unknown.

Like everything else associated with Vespucci and his publications even the identity of the mysterious translator is argued to this day. One candidate is Fra Giovanni Giocando, an Italian architect who worked on the Notre Dame bridge. Several others have been unearthed. Another possibility is that it was a pseudonym since Giocundus in its various spellings contains the Latin for "joke."

Mundus Novus certainly was a joke on traditional schoolmen. It was no simple announcement of the arrival on the other side of the traditionally understood Earth by sailing West. Instead it was a proclamation of a land in the middle of the Sea of Darkness, cut off from the world, beneath the Equator and teeming with people and lush plants where none were supposed to be. Of course da Gama had impugned ancient authority when he sailed into the Southern Hemisphere but he had only circumnavigated a region already partially perceived. This was different. Vespucci himself was amazed. In his original letters to Medici he, at least once, used the expression, "I whisper this" for fear of his truth turning into heresy. It may be "Giocundus" thought Vespucci was the jokester and not taking any chances used a pseudonym. Supporters of this theory point out that early editions of *Mundus Novus* appear without dates and sometimes printer's names, a curious omission for a publisher putting out a letter to the powerful Medici.

In any event *Mundus Novus* boldly announced:

> These regions which we found and explored. . . may rightly be
> called a New World. Because our ancestors had no knowledge
> of them. . . this transcends the view held by our ancients. . .
> that there was no continent beyond the equator, but only the
> sea which they named the Atlantic. . . In those southern parts
> I have found a continent more densely peopled and abounding
> in animals than our Europe, Asia or Africa. . . Part of this
> new continent lies in the torrid zone beyond the equator
> toward the antarctic pole. . .[1]

The dialogue of discovery was now on. *Mundus Novus* was an instant success and promptly eclipsed Columbus' message about some islands off China. Between the first appearance of *New World* and 1529 some sixty accounts of Vespucci's exploits came from presses all over Europe except England and Iberia, first individually, then as part of Martin Waldseemuller's *Cosmographia Introductio.* . .

What was so astonishing about Vespucci's little book or for that matter the man himself that he should have an entire hemisphere named after him?

He was born the third of four sons to an upper class Florentine family on March 9, 1454. His relatives included a banker, an ambassador and a bishop, all friends of the Medici. He was related through a cousin to Simonetta Vespucci, the model for Botticelli's "Birth of Venus" and "Primavera." Amerigo attended school at the Convent of San Marco which was conducted by an uncle. There a schoolmate was Pier Soderini who rose to become the gonfaloniere of Florence and apparent recipient of the infamous "Soderini Letter."

Lettera di Amerigo vespucci
delle isole nuouamente
trouate in quattro
suoi viaggi.

Quarto Viaggic.

LEFT: Title page from an early anonymous
edition of Vespucci's FOUR VOYAGES. ABOVE:
Illustration from the same work. King
Emanuel seems to be bidding Vespucci bon
voyage in an awfully small ship.

Amerigo entered the establishment of Lorenzo de Medici who sent him, in 1491, after twenty years of service, to Seville where he rose to become head of the Medici affiliated firm whose main businesses were merchant banking and ship chandlery. In that capacity he helped outfit Columbus' fleet for his third voyage - the one that finally touched the American continent. For this service he earned the admiral's rare praise - in 1505, well after the fat was in the fire - as an honest ship chandler.

Until now Amerigo seems pretty uncontroversial but from here on things get sticky. The number of times he went to sea and where he went are as far from certain as his complicity in naming a hemisphere, the duplicity of his publishers and the credulity of his readers.

His maiden voyage was probably with Alonso de Ojeda, one of Columbus' more malfeasant lieutenants on his second expedition. Ojeda having gotten a peek at the admiral's description of the pearl fisheries around Margarita set out on his own in May, 1499 to make his fortune. Ojeda's proclivities for robbing and pillaging may have been a little too much for Amerigo who jumped ship in Hispaniola and returned home ahead of his captain. From there, on July 18, 1500, he wrote to Lorenzo de Medici the first of three known letters on which his legitimate posterity rests. This letter, along with one from Cape Verde dated July 4, 1501 and another from Lisbon in 1502 were discovered and printed in 1745, 1827 and 1789 respectively.

The first letter describes a landfall near the Gulf of Paria (calling it by the name Columbus had given it when he sighted the mainland), sailing East to-

Woodcut from a 1505 Strasburg edition of
Vespucci: DE ORA ANTARCTICA.

Cut from an undated account of Vespucci, COPIA
DER NEWEN ZEYTUNG. (Probably after 1514)

ward the tip of Brazil then turning West to trace the coast of South America to
the approximate area of Cartagena. From there they sailed to Hispaniola where
Amerigo parted company with Ojeda. In his message to his patron Vespucci says
he "has discovered a very large country of Asia." He admits confusion, quoting
Ptolemy as giving the earth a circumference of 24,000 miles and complains he
has spent many sleepless nights and taken ten years off his life trying to
reconcile his landfall with Ptolemy's longitude. (Vespucci for all that he may
never have made an Atlantic voyage before was a fine mathematician, an astute
astronomer as well as a careful pilot but Columbus' "Asian landfall" seemed to
make the planet smaller than it was to the confusion of Vespucci and everybody else who crossed the Atlantic for fifty years.)

While Amerigo was at sea King Emanuel of Portugal dispatched Pedro
Alvares Cabral on a voyage to India in the footsteps of Vasco da Gama who had
returned from around the Cape of Good Hope in 1499. Cabral's fleet, deflected
from its optimum course by a shift of wind or a current stronger than expected,
wound up sighting Brazil about seventeen degrees South latitude. After coasting
far enough North to determine he had at least sighted a large island he dispatched a ship back with the news, then continued toward his original objective.

King Emanuel acted quickly. He assembled an expedition under the command of Goncalo Coelho to reconnoiter the new island. Amerigo was invited
along for the ride. The fleet sailed in May or June, 1501, stopping off at Cape
Verde where they ran into Cabral on his return journey. Vespucci took the

Vespucci's ship in the Rio de la Plata with Indians (Giants?) on shore, from
G. Stuchs Nuremberg edition of 1505 - '06.

opportunity to write his second letter to de Medici. This message is largely
devoted to what he learned from Cabral interspaced with some severe Italian
chauvinist criticism of Portuguese navigation.

Coelho reached the eastern tip of Brazil and sailed to a (disputed) point
probably below the Rio de la Plata. Then he turned home entering the Tagus in
September, 1502. Shortly afterward Vespucci dispatched a third letter describing
a lengthy voyage in the language of a surprised but careful observer.

He again describes the discovery as "a new land" which based on the experience of two voyages was obviously of continental proportions but presumably
an Asian peninsula extending further South and East than anything that could
be understood from reading Marco Polo and Ptolemy. In no instance does he use
the words "New World."

In substance these three letters may be understood as a coherent, deliberate
description of the physical nature and inhabitants of the Brazilian coast and the
region Vespucci himself gave the name Venezuela as he had seen a whole city
of houses built on water there, like a miniature Venice. His eyes were also
turned to the sky, contemplating movement of stars in the other pole, reminding

Wild man and his wife
from an edition of MUNDUS
NOVUS printed in Rostock,
ca, 1505

some of Dante's "Oh widowed world of the North forever deprived of the sight of them." According to *Mundus Novus* they were "manifold and much brighter than those of our pole."

Vespucci's original letters and the history books make it clear he was not the first to see or discover anything, nor was he ever a fleet commander as he had claimed for him in print. His accomplishment, sailing under two captains and two standards was the demonstration of a continuous littoral reaching from Cartagena to, according to *Mundus Novus*, fifty-two degrees South (the Approximate latitude of Tierra del Fuego). Meanwhile Columbus had been sailing around the Caribbean almost aimlessly.

On his third voyage, approaching the Gulf of Paria, into which the Orinoco empties Columbus heard "in the dead of night an awful roaring" and saw "the sea rolling from West to East like a mountain as high as a ship, and approaching little by little; on top of this rolling sea came a mighty wave roaring with frightful noise." Entering the gulf and seeing it was filled by a great river he was convinced it was rushing down from the summit where the Lord planted the earthly paradise, in the midst of which was a fountain whence flowed the four great rivers of the world, the Tigris, Ganges, Euphrates and Nile.

Now the medieval Christian transformed into modern geographer reverted to what he believed and what experience was showing him. He wrote back to his sovereigns that the earth was not a perfect sphere, as pagan philosophers would have one believe; but rather like "the form of a pear, which is very round except where the stalk grows, at which part it is most prominent; or like a round ball upon one part is a prominence like a woman's nipple, this protrusion being the highest and nearest to the sky, situated under the equatorial line and at the

Dye figur anzaigt vns das volck vnd insel die gefunden ist durch den chustenlichen künig zü Portigal oder von seinen vnterthonen. Die leüt sind also nacket hübsch braun wolgestalt von leib ir haüber. haiß arm scham füß frawen vnd mann ain wenig mit federn bedeckt. Auch haben die mann in iren angesichten vnd brust vil edel gestain. Es hat auch nyemand nichts sunder sind alle ding gemain. Vnnd die mann habende weyber welche in gefallen es sey müter schwester oder freündte dye jnn haben sy kain vnterscheyd. Sy streyten auch mit ainander. Sy essen auch ainander selbs die erschlagen werden vnd hencken das selbig flaisch in den rauch. Sy werden als hundert vnd fünfzig iar. Vnd haben kain regiment.

     This anonymous German woodcut of ca. 1505 is the first serious effort to depict New
World natives. The inscription based on Vespucci reads: "This figure represents to us the
people and island discovered by the Christian King of Portugal or his subjects. The people are thus naked, handsome, brown, well shaped in body; their head, necks, arms, private
parts, feet of men and women are a little covered with feathers. The men also have many
precious stones on their faces and breasts. No one has anything, but all things are in
common. And the men have as wives those who please them, be they mothers, sisters or friends; therein they make no distinction. They also fight with each other; and they eat each
other, even those who are slain, and hang the flesh of them in the smoke. They become a
hundred and fifty years old and have no government."

eastern extremity of the sea." In short he had reached the Mountain of
Purgatory at the top of which lay Eden. Columbus, preferring biblical to ancient
authority, did not need help from pagan philosophers who held that the top of
the world was under the polar star. He had made voyages along the African
coast and noticed the further South he got the darker the people. That was
Ptolemy, but here he noticed, on the southern most point he reached, there was
no change in skin color furthermore he was in a mild climate instead of a torid
one - also Ptolemy. The implication? He was sailing upwards, approaching the
sky at a point higher than anywhere else; where the first rays of the sun lit
gold and crimson on the day of creation. He offered as further evidence that

sailing away from the Mountain of Purgatory, which he considered himself unworthy to ascend ("whither no one can go without God's permission," he said), his ships traveled faster - they were going downhill.

Columbus has been easily and unfairly twitted on this sort of medievalism but given the mind set he had to work from he had no reason to assume any different. His expression "situated under the equatorial line" suggests he at least knew he was approaching it but nobody had crossed it and for all his courage Columbus was probably as afraid of it as everybody else. Peter Martyr also speculated that benevolent climate in the tropics, hitherto considered impossible, might have something to do with the particular relation of New World earth to the sky. Columbus' mistake was, instead of exploring the coast in either direction, sailing back to Hispaniola with a set mind.

His account of this voyage which seemed to confirm medieval maps but confute Polo, who he accepted fervently, did not appear until 1504 with publication of Martyr's *Libretto de Tutta Navigatione*... and then only as a brief digest along with two insignificant voyages by Pedro Alonzo Nico and Christobal Guerra in 1499 and 1500.

Columbus' mental picture of the Asian coast began with Cuba, which he forced the entire crew of his second expedition to swear was the "Mangi" peninsula of Cathay on pain of having their tongues cut out. (There would also be a fine.) Having explored most of its southern coast he returned to his original idea that it was too big to be an island and besides the peninsula appeared on all his maps. Where else could he be? (Obviously he could have saved himself a lot of trouble if he had sailed another fifty miles but he did not.) From there he envisioned a littoral stretching down behind the clutter of islands reported by Marco Polo culminating in the Malay peninsula around which Polo sailed into the Indian Ocean. Now Vespucci had presented him with a coast of almost unimaginable dimensions. If the 13th. Century traveller sailed from China to India there had to be a strait.

With this in mind he set out on his forth voyage of May, 1502 to November, 1504 complete with a letter of introduction to da Gama who he expected to meet in India. Using Cuba as a jumping off point he sailed Southwest to strike the northern coast of Honduras. He followed it eastward until it turned South causing him to name the point "Cape Gracias a Dios" in the belief he should thank God for finally allowing him to reach the Malay peninsula. He followed the Central American coast until he reached the Gulf of Uraba and South America. He was within a few miles of Vespucci and Ojeda's western most reconnaissance and had he turned East to examine the coast he might have realized it but again he did not, probably because his expeditionaries were worn out. He sailed back to Jamaica apparently without realizing his hope of following Polo into the Indian Ocean was dashed forever.

On July 7, 1503, Columbus, back in Jamaica and sick in body and spirit, wrote a rambling incoherent letter to his sovereigns suggestive of mental aberration or at least unwillingness to give up his conviction that he had reached the Orient.

Everything had gone wrong on his final voyage and the admiral filled his account with a superfluity of self justification and unconvincing "proofs" he had reached Malaysia. Among them was information that he heard of gold nearby which had to be the mines of "Ciamba," the southern most province of Polo's Golden Cheronese (Malaysia). He still insists Cuba is "Mangi" and that he was only ten days journey from the Ganges.

PAGE 16: This world map which appeared in a work entitled
RUDIMENTUM NOVITRIORUM in 1475 illustrates Columbus' idea.
Maps in this format with the Mountain of Purgatory at the
top were printed well into the 16th. Century so although
Columbus was convinced of a spherical earth he had plenty
of authority for his idea.

This letter was translated into Italian by one Constanzo Bayuera and published in Venice in 1505 under the title: *Copia de la Letter per Colombo Mandata*. It is extremely rare indicating that it did not see much circulation. Compared with the hardly suppressed ecstacy of the Santangel Letter of a mere decade before this unhappy little epistle reads like the denouement of a Greek tragedy.

Nothing more was heard from or about Columbus for the rest of his life and very little for years after.

While Columbus was languishing in Jamaica Vespucci was back in the South Atlantic, sailing again under Coelho. This time they had a fleet of six ships "in quest of an island toward the East called Melaccha [the Moluccas - the Portuguese still hoped to reach the Spice Islands by sailing West] of which we have information that it is very rich."

That the voyage was made there is little doubt but since the only account of it is the Soderini Letter the details are suspect. All this expedition managed to accomplish was lose four ships "all through the pride and folly of our admiral," says Vespucci, reconnoiter the already discovered coast and build a fort somewhere near the present Rio de Janeiro. They loaded up with Brazilwood and left a garrison to cut more for future export. Then Coelho and Vespucci sailed home with their two remaining vessels reaching Lisbon in June, 1504.

At this point Vespucci could have been relegated to a mere footnote in history, like his commander Coelho but after a combination of confusion and

This incident occured on Vespucci's voyage of 1501 when a young sailor went ashore to charm some women gathered at the water's edge. They clubed him to death and ate him within sight of his shipmates.
- From a German translation of Vespucci done in 1509.

literary chicanery the die was cast. When the printing press came into play Amerigo, the astute, eloquent honest ship chandler became a hero of romance and a lying semi-literate braggart apparently without even knowing it was happening.

Lorenzo the Magnificent died in 1502. Since the first editions of *Mundus Novus* appeared without dates it is unclear whether he authorized publication or not. In any event Vespucci's letter describing his first voyage with Coelho fell into the hands of an anonymous printer who by affixing the words "New World" to a story about antipodal lands across the Sea of Darkness inhabited by naked savages and cannibals, further embellished by Giocundus' hyperbole, created an instant best seller. It appeared in Florence, Venice, Antwerp and Nuremberg by 1507.

To make matters worse Vespucci allegedly wrote a letter to his equally alleged "old school friend" Pier Soderini who had replaced Lorenzo as gonfaloniere. It was dated September 4, 1504. Although the original has never turned up internal evidence suggests that some such letter must have been sent. For instance: It describes Coelho's flagship striking a reef off "an island in the midst of the sea" which Vespucci's reckoning would make Ascension Island, previously unreported. Furthermore to the extent the text bears any semblance to Vespucci's inquisitive style, which it hardly does, it contains a number of insults directed towards Coelho although he does not mention him by name. As we have seen in the case of Cabral Amerigo was not above some well deserved Italian chauvinism in his criticism of Iberian seamanship.

As a postscript to *Mundus Novus* Vespucci's account of his second voyage with Coelho makes dull reading but when the Soderini Letter hit the streets around 1505 under the title: *Lettra di Amerigo Vespucci delle Isole Novamente Trovate in Quatro Soui Viaggi* it was anything but. It was twice as long as the earlier work (a quarto of sixteen leaves) including not only the Brazilian voyages but details from the Ojeda voyage of 1499 which now becomes two with Vespucci, writing in the first person, clearly the hero of each. Ojeda gets no credit as captain but this omission is insignificant compared to the claim that the first voyage to touch the New World was moved back two years to 1497 when the honest ship chandler was in Andulusia fitting out vessels for the very voyage of Columbus that would make the landfall.

According to *Four Voyages* Vespucci discovered quite a lot. Not only had he sailed to an almost impossible fifty-two degrees South but on his Caribbean travels he accomplished even more. We hear he made land at a point that could only be Cape Gracias a Dios, then proceeded along the coast constantly Northwest for 3,100 English miles on a course which would have let him sail across Mexico and Arizona to someplace in California. We also learn that "near the equator in the month of June it is winter," among a handful of other ingenious contradictions and guileless absurdities.

But as Vespucci's nautical achievements increased his language deteriorated. Both *New World* and *Four Voyages* were "translated" into a sort of bastardized

Spanish-Latin-Italian in a style very unlike the thoughtful letters he composed to de Medici. They make him half bombastic and half puerile such as a claim in *Mundus Novus*, "I was more skilled than all the ship masters in the world."

But literary style is not the criteria of a best seller and Vespucci's books certainly were. Assuming the same average printing of 350 copies per edition we gave Columbus the sixty accounts of his exploits to appear over approximately twenty-five years resulted in 21,000 descriptions of his adventures in circulation. Enough at least to attach the expression "New World" to the new hemisphere.

To begin understanding implications of the Columbus/Vespucci experience and incidentally the naming of America we must move to the village of St. Die in the province of Lorraine and a coterie of monks intensely interested in the progress of geography. They had a printing press and were in the process of preparing a new edition of Ptolemy which, when it finally appeared in 1513, was the first to include modern maps in addition to Ptolemaic models. One of this little band of scholars was Matthias Ringman who happened to be in Paris at the same time as Fra Giocondo, the architect. If the architect and Vespucci's translator were one and the same Ringman may have imbibed his enthusiasm for Vespucci from the Italian.

In either event Ringman translated *Mundus Novus* into German and added a Latin poem in tribute to the discoverer of a land unknown to Ptolemy. In April of 1507 the group, under the leadership of its professor of geography, Martin Waldseemuller, published their *Cosmographiae Introductio* or to give its full English title: "An Introduction to Cosmography together with some principals of geometry necessary to the purpose. Also four voyages of Americus Vespucius. A description of universal cosmography, sterometrical and planometrical together with what was unknown to Ptolemy and has recently been discovered."

Waldseemuller had a fondness for making up names as evidenced by his signature Hylacomylus, a hybrid of Greek for wood (German: wald), Latin for lake or sea followed by the Greek for miller (German: muller). Indulging his name coining propensity he introduced this famous passage into chapter nine:

> Toward the South Pole are situated the southern part of Africa recently discovered, and the islands of Zanzibar, Java Minor and Seula. These regions have been more extensively explored, and another or forth part has been discovered by Americus Vespucius, as may be seen by the attached charts; in virtue of which I believe it may be very just that it should be named Amerige ["eg" in Greek meaning "of"], after its discoverer, Americus, a man of sagacious mind; or let it be named America, since both Europe and Asia bear names in the feminine form.[2]

Europe was developing a bit of nascent curiosity after a millenium of orthodoxy and Waldseemuller's book on geography with the appendage of Vespucci's account of a different world saw immediate popularity, going through four Latin printings in 1507, two more in 1509 and two in German the same year.

To accompany the cosmography Waldseemuller prepared a set of globe gores and an enormous woodcut map measuring thirty-six square feet, entitled: "A

Map of the World According to the Traditions of Ptolemy and the Voyages of Americus Vespucius." Now both survive as single copies but they were extremely influential at the time. Waldseemuller claimed he sold a thousand of the maps. It features the work of the two great geographers dramatically demonstrated by an inset in the cartouche with Ptolemy facing East and Vespucci West.

While other map makers placed a mysterious land mass on southern portions of their charts Waldseemuller knew the results of Columbus' third and forth voyages and something of the discoveries of Cabot and Gaspar Corte Real to the North. Until the discovery of his map in the early years of this century this was not understood. Because he included Vespucci's "first voyage" with its prior date in the *Cosmographiae.* . . he was generally assumed to be Vespucci's or his overly helpful publisher's dupe, in making him the discoverer of a New World.

Of course Waldseemuller was working from secondhand information but he did no discourtesy to Columbus. His map places a Spanish standard right above the mainland on the spot Columbus touched with the inscription: "These islands were discovered by Columbus, an admiral in the service of the King of Spain." He was even more explicit on the "Admiral's Map" of 1513 where he wrote "Terra Incognita" across the South American portion along with the inscription: "This land and adjacent islands were discovered by Columbus on order of the King of Castile." In the cosmography he comments on the surprising fact of a continent South of the equator continuing "Now it proves clearly to be true: There is a land discovered by Columbus, a captain of the King of Castile, and by Americus Vespucius, both men of great ability which though a great part lies beneath the path of the year and the sun and between the tropics nevertheless extends about nineteen degrees beyond the Tropic of Capricorn and the Antarctic Pole."

Columbus never entered the Southern Hemisphere although Waldseemuler's map places his landfall below the Equator. Vespucci had penetrated deep and his remarkable message made it into print. Waldseemuller had no reason to question or verify Vespucci's mysterious first voyage. It was unimportant to his purpose. He places "America" well down on his map indicating Vespucci's ventures deep into the antipodes might have more to do with the shape of the earth than Columbus' earlier achievement. This suggestion is reinforced by his omission of Vespucci's name from the Admiral's Map which does not extend far enough South to make his discoveries applicable.

So,· Columbus insistence that he had reached the Golden Cheronese, an anonymous Florentine literary hack and a stay at home philosopher/geographer conspired to affix the names "New World" and "America" to a hemisphere.

On May 20, 1506 Columbus with his relatives and faithful friends gathered around his bedside received his final mass and died after uttering the words of his Lord and Saviour, "Into Thy hands O Lord I commend my spirit." During his last years he retained his relationship with Vespucci who helped him with some legal problems. He may or may not have seen the Soderini Letter with its boastful claims. If he did he probably did not care, nor would he have cared if he lived long enough to see Americus' name applied to his discovery. For him it was just another "island beyond the Ganges."

Columbus' objective was never the discovery of land. Instead it had been a quest which would spread the gospel to the Great Khan, increase the might of his masters so they could crush infidels, liberate the Holy City and bring on the millennium. Although the world had forgotten him he must have died believing he paved the way.

Vespucci's career took a different turn. For a decade after his death in 1512 the purple prose attributed to him remained the commonest description of America in print. Florid and stressing the exotic, these vivid accounts provided great scope for the imagination of artists, geographers and even philosophers. It was only when more exciting news came in from Mexico that printers broke down their fonts to set up new books.

From then on Vespucci's image went downhill. As early as 1515 Sebastian Cabot, son of the man who actually did make an American landfall in 1497, questioned the authenticity of the first voyage "which Americus says he made." (Sebastian was no mean fabricator of voyages himself. In the course of a checkered career he pushed the idea that he, not his father, discovered the American mainland.) Thus began a lively, vicious and idle debate which spilled enough ink to sail Vespucci anywhere he wanted to go. But best we not dwell on it here. For our purposes Vespucci's "New World" and Columbus' "Asia" created two images which lasted past mid century. The impact their concepts had on geographers is clear and traceable. The philosophical impact is a little harder to grasp, but versions of both ideas, sometimes overlapping, crop up here and there as an underground stream occasionally producing a spring.

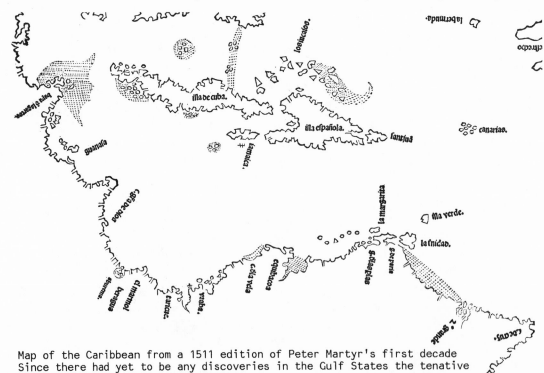

Map of the Caribbean from a 1511 edition of Peter Martyr's first decade Since there had yet to be any discoveries in the Gulf States the tenative islands in the North are speculative.

Filling in Discovery

THE dialogue begun by Columbus and Vespucci was exacerbated in their lifetime by other explorers, notably John Cabot and Gaspar Corte Real.

By 1497 news of discovery reached England. John Cabot, an Italian, probably from Genoa, who had settled in Bristol - a major center for Atlantic fishing fleets and home of Britain's most knowledgeable mariners - approached Henry VII with a plan to reach Cathay. Presumably he pointed out that sailing in northern latitudes, where a degree of longitude is shorter, he could reach Asia faster than Columbus.

Although the Pope had already assigned overseas lands to the Iberians Henry knew a good thing when he saw it and had no intention of giving Spain and Portugal a monopoly on the Orient. Accordingly the first Tudor, niggardly at the best of times, furnished a "navicula" (little ship) with which the Italian departed Bristol in May, 1497. He made Newfoundland a month later, explored for another month and was back home in August with news he had reached land on or near the Asian coast. Encouraged, Henry provided another ship to which the merchants of Bristol added four more, laden with "coarse cloth, caps, lace, points and other trifles," supposed to be proper trading stock for Orientals. The ships departed Bristol in 1498 only to have one promptly put into an Irish port in distress. The other four were never heard from again prompting contemporary London chronicler, Polydore Vergil's, snide remark that Cabot "found his new lands only at the ocean's bottom."

While Vergil may have been Cabot's only eulogist he had one other pathetic posterity. The Portuguese, learning of Cabot's discovery, realized it was in the hemisphere assigned to them by the Pope. At least two of them, Gaspar and Miguel Corte Real sought to claim it. Gaspar may have already made a voyage before 1500 when he received a patent from King Emanuel "to search out discover and find. . . some islands and a mainland. . ." With commission in hand he sailed with three ships from Lisbon in May of 1501. Two ships returned in October to announce Gaspar's craft had disappeared. Forever.

It took more than maritime disaster to discourage the search for a convenient route to Cathay so in January, 1502 Emanuel assigned half the territory Gaspar discovered to his brother Miguel, who, with two ships, embarked toward Newfoundland. Again the flagship was lost. The other ship returned with nothing new to report and since the venture came to nothing the printers made little of it. Such contemporary notice it received was confined to a mention in Damiano de Goris' *Cronica do Felicissimo Rei D. Manuel*. It fell to the cartographers to deal with the discoveries.

For the historian of discovery making sense out of early maps is frequently as enlightening as watching a political campaign but our purpose is to see the world through 16th. Century eyes so for us they can be informative.

The earliest extant map to include America is generally considered to be a portolan world chart discovered in 1832 in a Paris bric-a-bric shop by the Dutch ambassador to France who purchased it and presented it to Alexander von Humboldt for authentication. Drawn in ink and watercolor on oxhide and bearing the name Juan de la Cosa along with the date 1500 it both informs and confuses. Even the identity of the maker is subject to debate but the most likely candidate is the great Basque cartographer of that name, owner of the *Santa Maria*, companion of Columbus on his first and second voyages and signer of the affidavit insisting Cuba was the "Mangi" peninsula.

La Cosa's map covers the area between Capricorn and the Arctic Circle. Europe, Asia and Africa are finely rendered with artful symbols of cities, kings trade caravans and so on with Asia running off the sheet without a coastline. Cuba and the other Antilles are also neatly drawn in but apparently la Cosa did not take his oath overly seriously for Cuba appears as a shrimp shaped island and recovers its original name, "Cuba." The Caribbean sits in the middle of a huge C, presumably the eastern littoral of Asia, which bisects a meridian drawn through the Azores both at the top of the sheet and below the Equator, then veers sharply back midway between the Equator and Capricorn. The Brazilian bulge seemingly records the discoveries of the Pinzons who had briefly crossed the Equator shortly before Cabral and possibly news from Cabral himself. This is suggested by the presence of two ships with Spanish standards and another on the mainland all beneath the Equator. Cabot's discoveries are commemorated at the top of the C by five English flags and the phrases "mar descudieta por yngleses" (sea discovered by the English) and "cavo de ynglaterra" (Cape of England). The Central American coast which Columbus searched two years later is obscured by a portrait of the admiral's name saint exactly where he expected to find his strait.

Although there is no reported circumnavigation of Cuba before 1508 it would be a mistake to make much of a case for its appearance as an island; others rendered it the same way. More interesting is the appearance of a continous coast (save for the possible strait) from above the Arctic Circle to below Capricorn. This coast is cluttered, North as well as South with randomly placed capes, rivers and lakes. They have no significance nor appear on later maps. They are simply a case of a cartographer saying more than he knew, a common enough practice for the next three centuries. One other feature creates confusion. While everything from the Antilles eastward is beautifully and meticulously rendered the C shaped littoral in the West is carelessly splotched in with bilious green suggesting the work of a later hand filling in or altering an East Asian littoral la Cosa might have been unprepared to commit to. Marco Polo's Cipango or Zipanngo (Japan) supposed lying 1,500 miles off China has disappeared along with an assortment of mythical islands. The implication is that la Cosa or whoever finished the map for him speculated that places reached might have been some of these Islands.

The date and provenance of the second map to display America, the Cantino Mappemonde or Plainisphere, is easier to establish. Cantino, in Lisbon ostensibly to buy horses for the Duke of Ferrera but probably to collect information the Portuguese wanted kept secret commissioned an unknown cartographer to prepare a map which he sent from Lisbon on November 19 1502. It remained in the ductal collection in the Palace of Modena until it was thrown out of the palace window during a republican riot in 1859. It did duty as a screen in a butcher shop until 1870 when it was recognized and rescued by the librarian of the ductal collection.

The Cantino Mappemonde is a lovely ink and watercolor manuscript on vellum. Unlike la Cosa's it extends slightly beyond Capricorn and the Arctic Circle. Cantino's meridian is moved 370 leagues West of the Azores to represent the Tordesillas Line. A Portuguese flag is placed on an ice covered Greenland noting it is "a point of Asia" (as it was depicted on contemporary ptolemaic maps, arcing out from behind Scandinavia). Newfoundland is an Island labeled "Terra de Rey Portugall" and a futher inscription attributes the discovery to Gaspar Corte Real. It is conveniently separated from another unnamed island by the meridian. Asia gets an eastern littoral running constantly Northeast to the Arctic circle and then veers straight East to run off the sheet.

South America shows Vespucci's discoveries extending several degrees below Capricorn. The coast is liberally embellished with trees and parrots but the cartographer is prudent enough not to indicate a western border. Like la Cosa he makes Cuba an Island and like him mistakenly places it well above Cancer. It sits on a Northwest/Southeast slant with a bay at the top making it look like a nasty dog about to bite the foot of a mysterious island that runs off the edge of the map. Florida? That was not supposed to have been discovered till 1512. It could represent Japan which he otherwise ignores or an earlier discovery of Florida than has been recorded. In any event it runs to the latitude of Newfoundland although much further West and carries place names which would seem to indicate landfalls although none are informative. Cantino refers to the Caribbean islands as "Las Antilles del Rey de Castella," and "Colombo almirante" ("Columbus the admirable one") is credited with their discovery.

The trouble with both planispheres is that they run off one side of the sheet and unto the other. La Cosa seems fairly clear cut. The Antilles are tightly nestled in an Asian gulf but we get no idea of the length of Asia. In fact he places almost all his location designations West of the Ganges. Cantino refuses to commit himself on how wide the Pacific is (not that the Pacific was actually known to exist). Since both tend to omit islands described by Marco Polo the suggestion is they both accepted a small world with America laying somewhere in Asian waters.

There are a few other manuscript world charts of this period which tend to follow Cantino but from these two seminal efforts we can pass to the first printed maps to deal with America. The oldest is a world map by the Italian Giovanni Matteo Contarini engraved by Francesco Roselli in 1506. This map, known from a single copy, represents a transition in the ptolemaic form. The ancient geographer had little need to extend his world beyond 180 degrees. Contarini's is the first attempt to add the remaining half of the world to a sheet of paper and still represent it as a sphere.

Contarini still has Greenland as a peninsula arcing off Russia but it may find an echo of itself on the North American coast which reaches almost to Europe and carries the legend "Terra de Caramella" ("Land of ice). Moving South and West this lengthy peninsula merges with Newfoundland which is inscribed "Hanc Terram Invenere nave de Lvsitano Regis" ("Land discovered by sailors of the King of Portugal"). From there the coast moves due West until it hits China and turns South. Contarini accepts Columbus' description of his forth voyage at face value. He ignores Central America, places the Antilles off Japan and adds an inscription near China that "Columbus, after leaving the West Indies sailed to the land of Ciamba; that is, the Chamba described by Marco Polo on his return from Indochina." (From looking at their own map Contarini/Roselli must have concluded that Columbus was no mean sailor.) Meanwhile South America appears as a huge empty blob with a vaguely delineated West coast extending off the bottom of the chart.

The Contarini/Roselli map has an affinity with or shares a lost original with one prepared by Johannes Ruysch which first appeared in the 1508 Rome folio Ptolemy, but is occasionally found in the 1507 edition as a later insert. Little is known of Ruysch except that he was born in Antwerp and is believed to have visited America, possibly with Cabot but more likely with an Anglo-Portuguese exploration between 1501 and '05. This gives him the distinction of being the first New World visitor to prepare a printed map of it.

His "Universalior Cogniti Orbis Tabula" generally follows the Contarini format, creating a Greenland-Newfoundland peninsula as an extension of Asia. He adds the names: "Gruenland" and "Terra Nova" but severely truncates it serving the dual purpose of removing the discovery from the Portuguese domain and placing it right around the corner from Cathay. He also adds the helpful information that sailing the gulf between Greenland and Newfoundland demons assaulted the ships but were avoided without peril.

In the process of shortening the Greenland-Newfoundland peninsula Ruysch kept the Antilles directly South of it along with Contarini thereby pushing them closer to Asia. He omits Japan but makes up for it by letting Cuba be an unnamed mass truncated by a scroll with the inscription: "Huc usque naves Ferdinandi Regis Hispanie venerut" (As far as the ships of Ferdinand, King of Spain, have come). The implication was either a very large island off the coast of Cathay, maybe Japan or even Polo's Mangi but Ruysch was not going out on a limb. Vespucci's New World appears below, again as a landmass of continental dimensions with a scroll in the West leaving the viewer to wonder where it all ends.

1507 brought *Cosmographia Introductio* along with Waldseemuller's map and globe gores. Now North America and the entire hemisphere is clearly separated from Asia with Japan between. Relying on Ptolemy, Vespucci and his own mathematics Waldseemuller realizes American landfalls are too far East to be Polo's Orient, but however much of an advance his map makes it still leads to confusion. He follows Cantino's delineation of Cuba (finally bisected by cancer) with its jaw like bay still nipping at a Florida peninsula connected by land to "Parias" (Mexico or Central America) and traces a Gulf of Mexico, filled with Islands, down to, apparently Honduras. He continues Florida to the latitudes of Scandinavia where he places a Spanish flag and indicates a passage on his main map and gores in the approximate area of Panama but connects the continents on his cartouche inset.

How did he know all this? He places Japan far enough off China to satisfy anything he learned from Polo and may have understood Cabot and Corte Real touched land too far West to be oriental and the narrowness of land around Panama could have been suggested by reading Columbus between the lines. Thickening South America came from reports of rivers (the Orinoco for instance) too large to emerge from an island. How he managed to identify a Florida peninsula and connect it to Mexico and Newfoundland is anybody's guess.

However speculative he might have been Waldseemuller did not go overboard. He cuts off western North America with a mountain range and draws a straight line down the West coast of South America knowing he has no more to say. In any event his book plus the map with its continental hemisphere sitting in the middle of the Atlantic definitely confirmed the existence of a new world.

Sylvanius' 1511 ptolemy contains a beautiful world map printed in two colors but adds nothing new except for the label "Regalis Dommus" on North America. Then, in 1513, Waldseemuller was back in the act this time sowing confusion wherever he went. His ptolemy of that year includes two vaguely similar world maps in addition to obligatory ptolemaic world of the second century (in case he was wrong) and a chart of the Atlantic. One of the planispheres: "Orbis Typus Universalis Ivxta Hydrographam Traditinen" and the Atlantic chart: "Tabula Terra Nove" are traditionally ascribed to Columbus on the strength of a passage in the introduction: "Charta autem Marina, quam Hydrographiam vocat, per Admiralem quondam serenissmi... regis Ferdinandi, ceteros denique lustratores verissimis per agrationibus lustrata." ("The Carta Marina or Hydographia was drawn by a certain admiral of King Ferdinand and other authors, based on true voyages of discovery.")

Waldseemuller could have gotten the map(s) from Columbus because it is commonly believed the St. Die coterie was working on their ptolemy while the admiral was still alive. They could have also gotten it from his son Diego who inherited his father's title. The problem is they are wildly contradictory and do not seem to represent Columbus' thinking. They are also at considerable variance with his superior chart of 1507. For all Columbus harping on the subject

ABOVE: Western portion of the
Johannes Ruysch world map of 1508.
PAGES 30 - 31: Contarini world map
of 1506. PAGES 32 - 33: Waldseemuller,
1507. PAGES 34 - 35: Waldseemuller, 1513.

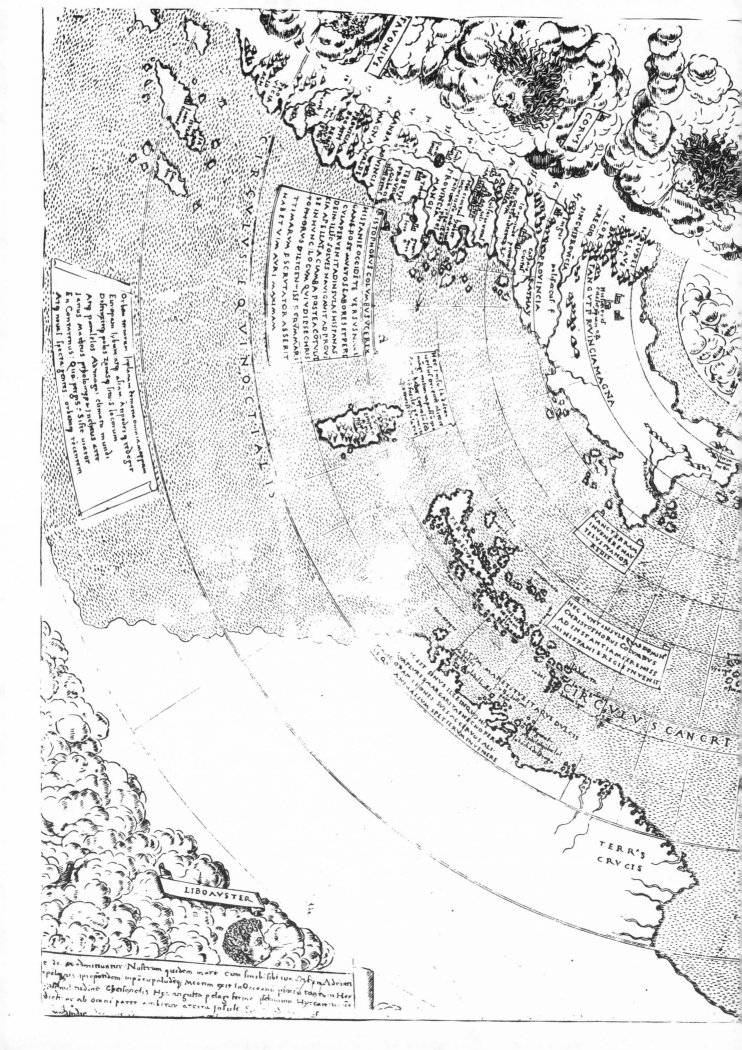

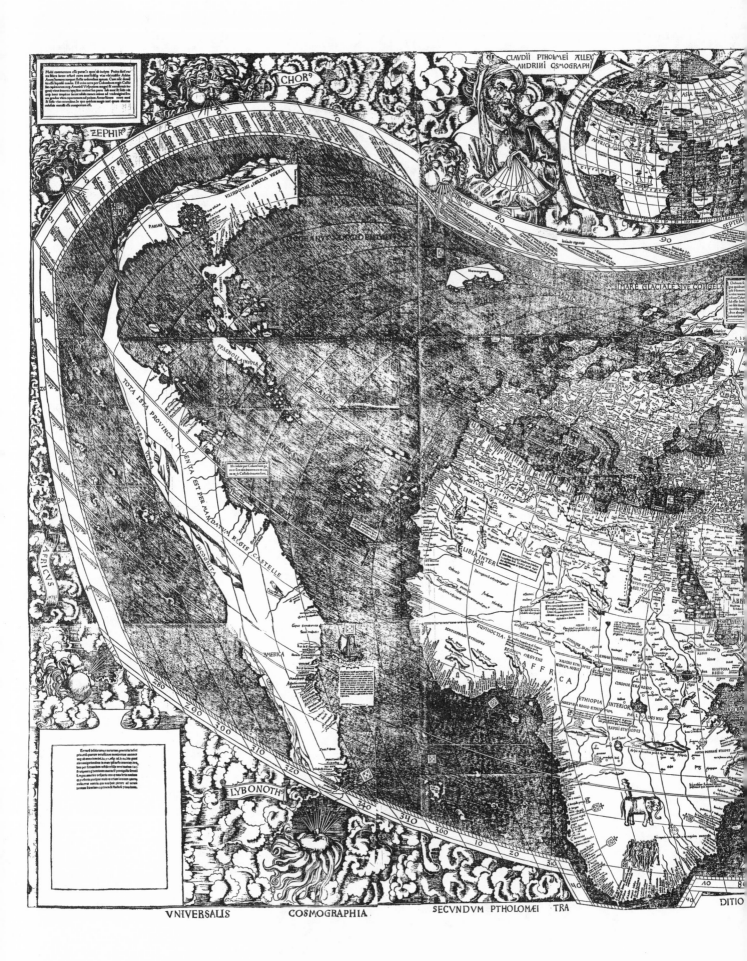

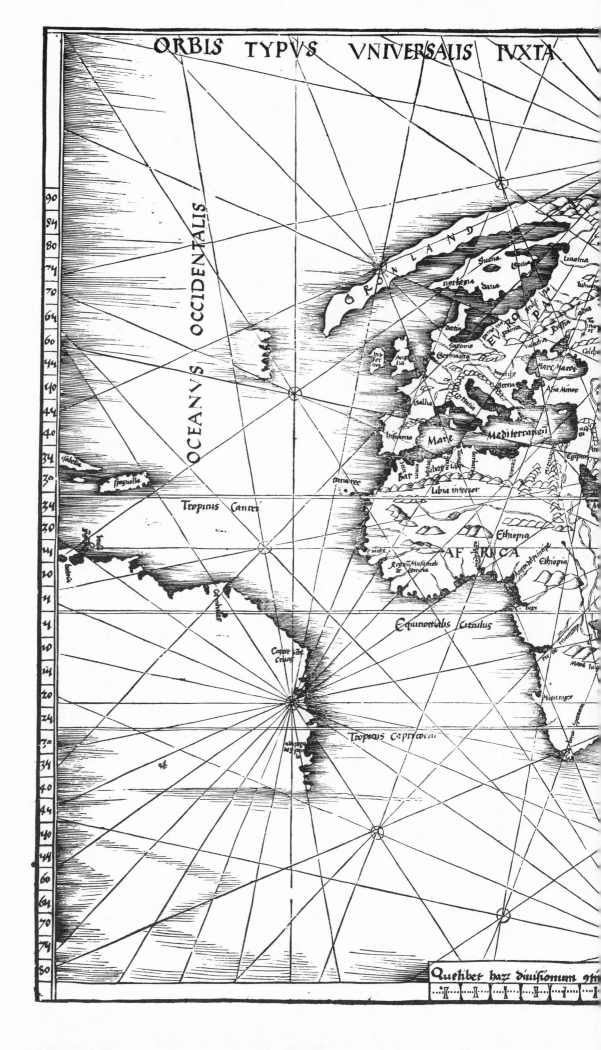

90
84
80
74
70
64
60
44
40
44
40
34
3n
34
30
44
10
11
4
10
14
20
24
70
34
40
44
40
44
60
64
70
74
80

OCEANVS OCCIDENTALIS

GROWLAND

Suena
nothena
datia
Spilia
Linonia
EVRO PA
Sagonia
Germania
Russia
Polonia
Frislia
Marc Maior
Colch
Asia Minor
Gallia
Witalia
Mare Mediterraneii
Egipt
Infunana
bar
Canarie
Libia interior
Ethiopia
AFRICA
Ethiopia
Regnu Musameli
Genoia
purde
C. lupi
Equinottialis Citatilus
Tropitus Cancer
Isabella
Spagnolla

Tropitus Capricorni

Caput ster
Crunis

Fic de Triumphe
Maris Tug
Mons niger

Quelibet bazz diuisionum qti

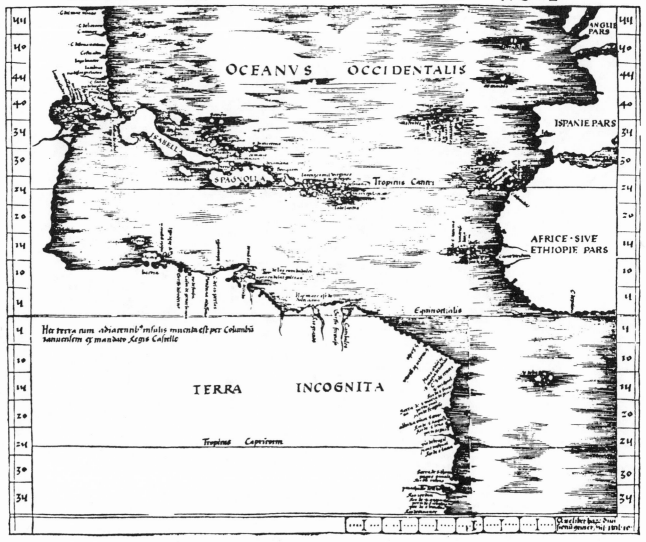

ABOVE: Waldseemuller's map of the Atlantic (1513). LEFT: Drawing of of the western portion of Schoner's globe of 1515. He tends to follow the 1507 Waldsemuller save for separating Newfoundland from a northern continent and adding an inscription along the western border that it is "terra incognita." He does the same for the western portions of North and South America. On his 1520 globe Newfoundland becomes "Terra de Corte Real" and North America "Terra de Cuba." South America bears the inscriptions, "America," Brasillia" and "Papagalli." (This last a corruption of "Cannibal.") PAGE 37: Four of twelve gores bound in a Lugduni, 1514(?) edition of COSMOGRAPHIA INTRODUCTIO which closely follow Waldseemuller's 1507 gores. (Reproduced from Judsin Winsor's NARRATIVE AND CRITICAL HISTORY... Vol. II, p. 120).

Cuba is an island on the Atlantic map. On the mappemonde he acknowledges English/Portuguese discoveries with a one sided Island but is no longer sure if they extend down to meet South America as they did on his 1507 chart which was probably more prophetic than dependent on available information. He drops out Japan which appeared on the earlier chart as if he has changed his mind about what Columbus found. The third elongated Asian peninsula of the 1507 map reappears. This could be a holdover from Ptolemy who assumed the Indian Ocean was enclosed combined with reading of Columbus' failure (assuming he made it as far as he and Contarini claimed he did) to reach the Indian Ocean. Cuba and Hispaniola appear on one of the world maps but not the other while Vespucci's America, now unlabeled - it would regain its name in the 1522 edition - runs off the left of the sheet.

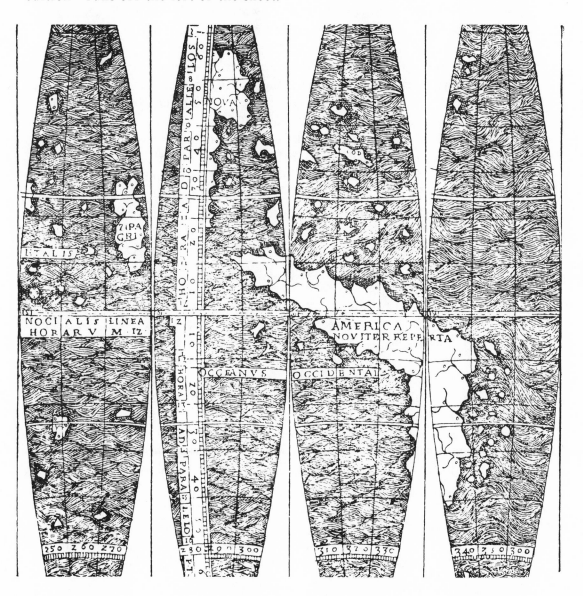

Waldseemuller knows he is in trouble though. He marks the side of his world map with degrees stretching to the poles but confines himself to placing twelve unnumbered longitude markers in the center of the bottom border. The markers each standing for ten degrees should cover a third of the map but they fall short by an inch or so. He had a lot of space to fill in but does not know where to put it so he leaves the width of America and the oceans to the viewer's discretion.

Waldseemuller provided the cartographic prototype for the next twenty years. Jan ze Stobincy was content to break the cartouche insert of the 1507 map in half for the only two charts in his Cracow ptolemy of 1512 and Peter Apian reduced the main part for his map of 1520. Globe makers, till the late 1520's, were content to follow Waldseemuller's gores.

A couple of interesting exceptions are worth noting. One is the large antarctic land mass on a pair of globe prepared by Johann Schoner in 1515 and 1520, carrying the respective designations, "Brasille Regi" and "Brasillia Inferior." They seem to anticipate Magellan or a discovery of Antarctica. In fact they are merely the antipodes of the ancient cartographer, Pomponius Mela who we will meet shortly. Even more interesting is the label "Zona Mela" Gregory Reisch put on the American portion of his world map of 1515.

Waldseemuller remained busy. In 1516 he issued a twelve sheet "Carta Marina Navigatoira Portugallen Navationes" which like his 1507 map survives in a single copy. It resembles his map of the Atlantic of three years before with North America defined as "Terra de Cuba Asia partis." He was obviously confused by what he was reading, changing his mind regularly but doing the best he could. The chart embellishes South America with the first depiction of an American mammal, an opossum, along with the infamous cannibals.

In 1520 his ptolemy was reprinted with the same blocks used in 1513. Two years later, Laurent Fries got out a new edition in a slightly smaller format, although still a folio. Although the blocks were recut the three contradictory maps reappear with little change, but Fries was no slavish copyist. To demonstrate his originality he makes Scotland an island on one of the two world maps, separates Iceland from Greenland and renders an elephant in the upper left corner to let his readers see what one looked like. He throws Waldseemuller's opossum, sans cannibals, onto South America while adding Spanish standards to the Caribbean.

Fries' blocks were used for subsequently ptolemys of 1525 and 1535. The latter was edited by Michael Servetus who John Calvin ordered burnt at the stake for various heresies, including a remark in the ptolemy that Palestine was not as fertile as generally believed since modern travellers found it quite barren, and another expressing doubts about the terrestrial paradise. A final printing from Fries' woodcuts appeared in 1541. Although a few manuscript maps and fewer globes appeared during the period Waldseemuller's view, as expressed in 1513, was the commonest picture of American and world geography during this era of robust expansion.

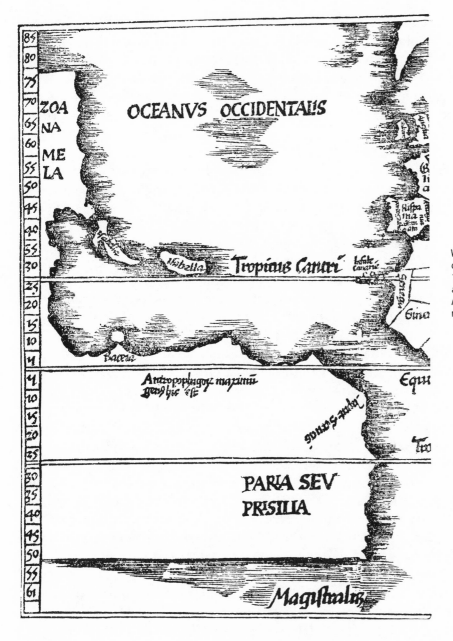

Western portion of Gregory Reisch' world map of 1515. The inscription across the top of South America refers to cannibals living there.

THE MENTAL MAP

Though Ptolemy measured the globe with considerable accuracy medieval scholars ignored him. During the full retreat from the tactile into spirituality even essential subjects, like medicine, were relegated to Jews because it was considered unseemly to concentrate on the corporal when the spiritual was so much more important. Christian physicians were suspected of witchcraft.

In 1451, the year usually given for Columbus' birth, most world maps were not maps at all but diagrams indicating a tripartite world divided among the sons of Noah. Schoolmen realized these were not accurate descriptions but they satisfied theology.

The best of the few world maps to survive before publication of the second printed ptolemy (Bologna 1477) - the first to contain maps - look like a pancake which somebody took a bite out of to form the Mediterranean. They are cluttered willy-nilly with nation names culled from the Bible, possessing a spiritual rather than geographical quality. The extreme East is usually at the top with Jesus enthroned above the Mountain of Purgatory beneath which lay the Garden which tradition gave to a classical age noble savage who lived in a state of natural Christianity.

From this mountain the four great rivers flow to irrigate Earth. The ocean is given short shrift, appearing as a thin band around the edge of the map. Out of necessity it might be dotted with a few nearby islands but the concept of places out of "the world" was unpopular suggesting alienation.

For practical purposes there were localized maps and charts of the Medierranean, necessary for crusaders and trade and even manuscript Portuguese maps from Henry the Navigator's day prepared by mariners who passed the "Ne Plus Ultra" Pillars of Hercules to explore the African coast but Western Christendom was largely insular, uninterested in lands beyond and dependent on Byzantium for trade and cultural resources.

This attitude was evident as late as 1493 in the *Nuremberg Chronicle* which ignored recent maps that added Scandinavia and Greenland and extended Asia to include information derived from Marco Polo. The *Chronicle* included a world map which, although using Ptolemy's projection, presented the world just as it had emerged from the flood without bothering to update it. On the other hand the same volume includes a modern carefully drawn map of Europe for benefit of pilgrims traveling to the Holy Land.

The fall of Constantinople to Islam three years after Columbus' birth changed all that. Suddenly Europe was on its own. Fortunately during that same decade Johann Gutenberg came to the rescue, culturally at least, by developing moveable type. Classical works, preserved in monastic libraries and carried West by Christian refugees started rolling off presses all over Europe. For Columbus' purpose the most important of these was Ptolemy.

The appearance of the first printed ptolemy in 1475 rekindled interest in the size and shape of the world. Seven editions were issued by 1490. Its influence was so great that until Abraham Ortelius published his atlas of 1570 a "ptolemy" was the only place to find a uniform bound collection of maps. Over sixty editions were published by 1730. Ptolemy, who died in the 2nd. Century succeeded, thirteen hundred years later, in reintroducing a spherical earth.

Ptolemy divided the globe into five zones, two frozen and uninhabitable, two temperate and habitable and one torrid or fiery, uninhabitable because the Sun circling the Earth at the Equator beat directly on it. He had been impugned as early as the 13th. Century when Marco Polo disproved his idea of an enclosed Indian Ocean by sailing into it and by 1500 when the Portuguese sailed into the same sea crossing the fiery zone in the process. Still European experience with the burnt North African desert, cold northern regions and the obviously (once it was pointed out) spherical world made Ptolemy the penultimate authority.

Except, perhaps, on the circumference of the Earth.

The Portuguese sailing South and East depended on costal rather than celestial navigation. Consequently they had no idea of how far or how fast they were sailing. This allowed Martin Behaim, a Nuremberg geographer who visited Portugal, to prepare a globe in 1492 which, relying on information derived from the Portuguese and Marco Polo, showed the coast of China 4,400 nautical miles from the Canaries. He was also able to include the gaggle of islands off the coast described by Polo, Zipagu, Java, and assorted other Indonesian islands (probably prompting Columbus' brag that he had discovered 1,400 islands).

Drawing of the Atlantic portion of Behaim's golbe with America
traced in with relation to its actual location.

Behaim largely agreed with Columbus' mentor, the Italian geographer Toscanelli, who made the distance 5,000 nautical miles. Columbus, largely by underestimating Ptolemy's measurement of a degree, optimistically reduced this to 3,500. There was powerful authority for his optimism which can be largely summed up by marginal notes he placed in his copy of Piere d'Ally's *Imagio Mundi* which survives in the Cathedral of Seville among some of his other papers. One is "Aristotle [says] between the end of Spain and the beginning of India is a small sea navigable in a few days." Another: "Esdras [says] six parts [of the Earth] are habitable and the seventh is covered by water. Observe that blessed Ambrose and Austin considered Esdras a prophet." (*Esdras* 2, vi 42, "Six parts hast Thou dried up." - Roger Bacon also cited Esdras as an authority for the size of the Earth). The result of this speculation was that when Columbus touched Cuba after sailing about 3,500 miles from the Canaries he was exactly where he expected to be. China!

But America was too big and too different to easily absorb into a millenium
old geographic and cultural framework and it would take a while to straighten
out. The geographical and ethnological (a word coined centuries later) naivete
of the time which depended on biblical orthodoxy and rediscovered classical
authority is easily evicenenced by Columbus. Remember he at one point considered himself within ten days of the Ganges and would not be surprised to
met the centuries old African prince, Prester John, for whom he was actually
looking. Another example of this naivete is Luis de Torres, a *converso*, "who
knew how to speak Hebrew, Chaldean and even some Arabic" who Columbus
took on his first voyage as a translator. It is unclear from history books how this
linguist made out but he probably did about as well as many who followed.

Illustration from the title
of an edition of Marco Polo
(Seville, 1518). It shows a
familiar looking European city
on Hispaniola.

During the twenty years after discovery the only navigators to report back
in print were Columbus, Vespucci and the Pinzons (these last in Martyr) all of
whom, despite *Mundus Novus*, assumed they were in Asian waters. Martyr was
unable to make up his mind if Columbus traveled as far as he claimed and Rod-
rigo Ferandez de Santaella asked the same question in his 1503 edition of Marco
Polo. But where else could they be?

Even before Columbus and long before they rounded the tip of Africa the
Portuguese secured papal bulls confirming their rights to occupy (for the holy
purpose of Christianization - a prerequisite to expansion into heathen lands
dating from centuries before) all the way to the mythical Christian Kingdom
of Prester John ("as far as the Indians who are said to worship Christ"). When
it began to look like Spanish sailing West and Portuguese sailing East were
entering the same heathen infested waters and it became incumbent for Alexander VI to do something about it. The result was the famous bull *Inter cetera* or
Alexandrian Line of May, 1493 which placed all discoveries 100 leagues West
of the Azores in the hands of Spain and assigned the other half of newly found
portions of the globe to Portugal. Apparently this line was proposed by Columbus himself. He claimed as you approached his mysterious East just beyond that
hundred league mark the climate suddenly changed, "as if you put a hill below
the horizon," the temperature became mild "and no change winter or summer."
And "Up to the Canaries and 100 leagues beyond. . . many are the lice that
breed; but from there on they all commence to die, so that on raising the first
island there be no man that breedeth or seeth one."

Perhaps because of its patent absurdity *Inter cetera* had a short life. Spaniard, and duplicitous as he was, Alexander was still faced with the fact that by arriving first the Spanish had prior claim so in October he issued a new bull attempting to wipe Portugal's claims out of existence. This resulted in a conference between Spain and Portugal at Tordesillas to settle the question of soverreignty over the Moluccas. The outcome was a purely secular treaty giving the Portuguese a line 370 leagues from the Azores and the other half of the world to Spain to discover and Christianize.

This vague vision of distant lands can be partially understood by looking at the table of contents in *Paesi Novamente Ritovati et Novo Mondo. . .* which first appeared at Vicenza in 1507. This partial plagiarism of Martyr's *Liberetto di tutta la Navigazione. . .* of three years before, was attributed by Martyr to one Aloisio de Cadamosto who he scathingly denounces for the piracy in the seventh book of his second decade. Evidently popular *Paesi Novamente,* the first printed collection of voyages, saw Milan, Paris and Basel editions in 1508. It begins with an account of a Portuguese voyage to Cape Verde and Senegal in 1454 - '55 and another to Senegal in 1462. Vasco da Gama's epic journey follows. Then Cabral appears followed by the first three voyages of Columbus, the voyage of Alonso Negro and the Pinzons' expedition to the Spanish Main. Vespucci comes next then more information on Cabral, a notice of Corte Real and further information about voyages to the East Indies. The problem? The full englished title is: *Countries newly discovered and the New World of Alberico Vesputio, called the Florentine.* There are two ways to read this. The first and most prosaic is a modernized version of Marco Polo and Sir John Mandeville's descriptions of a jumble of exotic lands remote from Western Christendom which could be read by the man on the street like a science fiction novel about a distant solar system. This attitude is vividly expressed by the noted humanist Cochlaeus' introduction to a 1512 edition of Mela where he remarked:

> In our lifetime Amerigo Vespucci is said to have discovered that New World with ships belonging to the kings of Spain and Portugal: he sailed not only beyond the torrid zone but far beyond the Tropic of Capricorn. He says Africa stretches as far; and that this New World is quite distinct from it and bigger than our Europe. Whether this is true or a lie, it has nothing. . . to do with Cosmography or the knowledge of History. For the peoples and places of that continent are unknown and unnamed to us and sailings are only made there with the greatest dangers. Therefore it is of no interest to geographers at all.[1]

So much for America! Despite exciting accounts of the new and the strange the New Hemisphere still had a long way to go before it would enter European consciousness as much more than a novelty.

But for those who were paying attention there was a second way of reading the title of *Paesi Novamente. . .* which can summed up by Alexander von

Humboldt's cynical remark, "There are three stages in attitude towards any great discovery. First men deny its existence, next they doubt its importance, and finally they credit it to someone else." The New World ran this gamut very fast. Skipping over innumerable claims of pre-Columbian discovery for the time being we can let ancient authority tell us all about "The New World of Alberico Vesputio," so neatly set off from the rest of the title of *Paesi Nouemente. . .* Vespucci by committing the virtual heresy of sailing below the Equator had rediscovered the Antichtones or Antarctica Pomponius Mela drew on his map in the early years A. D.

The first modern edition of Mela appeared at Milan in 1471. It was followed by Venetian editions of 1478, 1482, 1502 and a Paris edition of the next year. In 1512 his text came under a new influence. A circle of geography students in Vienna were studying Mela and a writer of the third century named Solinus. Their work appeared in that city in 1512 under the title: *De Situ Orbis. . .* The same year saw the Nuremberg Mela in which Cochlaeus found speculation on America so idle. Editions came from Vespucci's home town in 1517, 1519 and 1526, suggesting affinity between an ancient philosopher and Florence's favorite navigator.

Meanwhile in Switzerland, in the village of St. Gall, another geography buff, Jochim Watt (latinized Vadianus), wrote to a colleague, Rudolfus Agricola, seconding Waldseemuller's suggestion that Americus' name be applied to Brazil. This appeared in Vienna in 1515 as *Habes Lector, hoc libello, Rudolphi Agricolae* appended to Watt's own edition of Mela. Three years later he published another edition of the work. In 1520 a combined edition of Solinus and Mela appeared

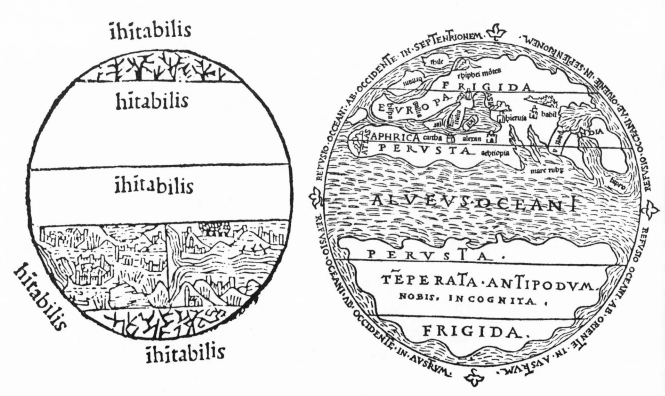

under the direction of Peter Apian (Apianus). It contained a modern world map derived from Waldseemuller's 1507 chart bound between the two authors while, as noted above, Gregory Reisch boldly placed the words "Zona Mela" on the American portion of his map of 1515. Mela enjoyed popularity through the remainder of the century and saw print well into the 1700's. In the process the ancient philosopher succeeded in providing a description of a place he never heard of.

Such vague but effortful attempts to depict the Earth ran in an anachronistic manner through the 16th. Century. As late as 1557 Andre Thevet referred to Brazil and Canada as "France Antarctic." Another book carrying an apparently equally naive title is Tamara's *El Libro de las Costumbres de total las Gentes de Mundo y de las Indias.* (Antwep 1556). It would seem that we are talking about two different worlds. It would be dangerous to read too much between the lines but the suggestion of another world was lurking around.

The message of Mela welded to Vespucci appears in an anonymous little book printed by John Gruniger in Strasbourg, 1509: *Globus Mundi,* the title page of which breathlessly explains is an:

> Exposition or description of the world. . . constucted as a round globe similar to a solid sphere, whereby every man, even of moderate learning, can see with his own eyes there are antipodes whose feet are opposite to ours; and how men may lead a healthy life in every part of the globe the sun shining upon the different parts thereof, which seems to be suspended in the airy vacuum, supported only by God's will; together with things concerning the forth part of the earth recently discovered by Americus.

Globus mundi

Declaratio fiue defcriptio mundi

et totius orbis terrarum, globulo rotundo comparati vt spera solida. Qua cuiuis etiã mediocriter docto ad oculũ videre licet antipodes esse, quox pedes nostris oppositi sunt. Et qualiter in vnaquaq orbis parte homines vitam agere queunt salutare, sole singula terre loca illustrante, que tamen terra in vacuo aere pendere videtur, solo dei nutu sustetata, alijsq permultis de quarta orbis terrarũ parte nuperab Americo reperta.

PAGE 44; left: Ptolemy's view of the World with it's impassable torid zone from Johannes de Sacra Bosco: SPHERA MUNDI (Venice, 1499) Right: Mela's view of the world. This map, with minor variation appeared in most issues of Mela.

ADJACENT: Title page of GLOBUS MUNDI.

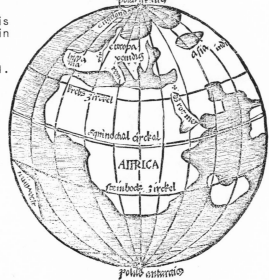

Sounds a bit naive but even Peter Martyr had to explain to the Pope there was sun in the Southern Hemisphere and:

> Each year the Portuguese arrive at the antarctic antipodes, and carry on commerce with those people. I say the antipodes; yet I am not ignorant that there are learned men, most illustrious for their genius and science, amongst whom there are some saints who deny the existence of the antipodes. No man can know everything. The Portuguese have gone beyond the fifty-fifth degree of the other pole where. . . they could see throughout the heavenly vault certain nebulae similar to the Milky Way.[2]

THE EARTH GETS (MUCH) LARGER

Twenty-five years after Columbus things seemed to be slowing down.Hispaniola was still producing gold. There was some agriculture in the Antilles and a nascent die wood trade in Brazil. Tentative probes in the North had found nothing except fishing grounds off Newfoundland. In 1512 Ponce de Leon explored Florida as far as Cape Canaveral to discover mosquitos and swamp. The rest of North America was a void. There were pearl fisheries at Paria and even the first permanent settlement on continental soil near Panama. The coast between was given over to slavers. Balboa discovered the Pacific but mountanous Central America did not lend to easy exploitation. America was little more than an annoying obstacle blocking the route to Cathay. Even effervescent Martyr, the Livy of American history, was bored. He began his forth decade, a letter to Pope Leo, with an apology for not having written since 1516 because, "Our Royal Council for Indian Affairs daily receives letters devoid of interest written by correspondents bereft of intelligence from which I could draw little material." Now something exciting had occurred.

Martyr says Darien explorers had encountered Indians who claimed they formerly occupied a country with temples of stone, streets properly laid out for commerce and books. Now the Spaniards had discovered that place. A slave catching expedition under the command of Francisco Hernandez de Cordoba sailing around western Cuba was driven Southwest by contrary winds until they hit a coast where they were amicably received by the natives.

> When they demanded by signs and gestures the name of the country, the latter replied "Yucatan" a word which in their own language means "I do not understand you. . ." The Spainards discovered a fortified town on the bank [coast] of such importance that they named it Cairo, after the capital of Egypt. It possesses houses with towers, magnificent temples, regular streets, squares and market places. The houses are built of stone or brick, held together by mortar and skillfully built. . . The natives wore clothing. . . made of a thousand different kinds of cotton dyed in divers colors. The women are covered from waist to heels, and envelop their breasts in several veils, and take modest care that neither their legs nor feet shall be visible. . . They have laws and are extremely honest in their trading which they carry on without money.[3]

Of course Martyr's news had already reached Diego Valasquez, governor of Cuba, who immediately prepared another expedition under the command of his nephew, Juan Grijalva. His ships made a landfall at Cozemel where they again encountered civilized natives. From there Grijalva reconnoitered the coast westward to Campeche trading trinkets for gold. Naturally they asked where the gold came from and the Indians pointed West. Having filled their hulls with loot the ships returned to Cuba.

At this point Hernando Cortez comes on the scene. He was about thirty-three, *alcalde* of Santiago and a man of courage and agile mind. Even before Grijalva returned from the Yucatan Valasquez was preparing another expedition under his leadership. With about 600 men he set sail on February 18, 1519 on a mission that for better or worse made his name immortal.

Martyr reported Cortez' adventures as the news came in but by September 1522 he had something more exciting. He told his correspondents, "While these writings lay in my cabinet awaiting the absent secretaries. . . pregnant Ocean produces a new recently born progeny." He was referring to the arrival of a ship at Seville, under the command of Sebastian del Cano, carrying eighteen men who left that port three years before with four other ships and at least 237 sailors. The ship was the *Victoria* carrying all those who had not died, including its commander, been executed for mutiny or deserted in the course of a tragic and glorious round the world voyage. The next day, sick and ragged, the eighteen walked barefoot to churches to fulfill vows made during hours of peril.

Peter Martyr relegated the task of interviewing these survivors to a secretary who returned with information that the eighteen who made it were completely illiterate. Fortunately one was not because Martyr's account was lost during one of those periodic sacks of Rome. Only a fragmentary description of Magellan's epic voyage appears in his decades. It fell to thirty-two year old Antonio Pigafetta of Vincenza to present the story in all its incredible detail.

Pigafetta, anxious to secure his niche in history, as he reveals in the dedication of his book, did not show Martyr's lackey the journal he kept on his voyage. Instead he took it to Charles V and presented it in homage explaining he was not bringing "gold or silver, but things that will be highly prized by such a Lord."

Late in 1524 or early 1525 he drafted two more accounts, one for the Marquis of Mantua and another for the Pope himself. The printed book, edited and condensed by Antoine Fabre showed up in Paris about 1525 with the title: *Le Voyage et Navigatioin facit par les Espanigolzes Isles de Molluques.* A subsequent version appeared in Venice and in Ramusio's collection. A grossly abbreviated description was englished by Richard Eden in 1555 but the full story waited until 1800 when it was printed from the original manuscript in Milan's Ambrosian Library.

For purposes of describing America the significance of Magellan's voyage was the demonstration of an enormous ocean between the tip of South America and the Orient, a serious blow to the small Earth theory. But before leaving him we should recount an amusing anecdote that sheds a little light on the cosmology of the time.

When the *Victoria* reached Cape Verde the crew realized it was Thursday rather than Wednesday. Peter Martyr makes much of his, speculating the sailors might have lost a day in prayer or missed the twenty-ninth of February during the leap year of 1520. He also records the crew's distress over celebrating holy days and fasts on the wrong day. Pigafetta, who Martyr never mentions, claimed he had never been sick and made an entry in his diary every day. To Martyr this was a matter for grave consideration but after giving the matter much thought concluded with Pigafetta, who apparently had no trouble figuring it out, that by sailing continually West they had come back to the same place as the Sun.

ANOTHER COUNTRY HEARD FROM

Gomora provides a story about the Portuguese delegation enroute to Tordesillas to negotiate the famous treaty. They passed a child guarding laundry on his mother's clothesline who asked these notables if they were on their way to divide the world in half. They answered they were at which point the brat pulled up his shirt displaying his bare behind and said, "Draw your line through this place!" Some of the outraged Portuguese wanted the child whipped but the rest "turned it into a joke and laughed it off."

Francis I probably thought as much of the papal bull of 1493 and the subsequent treaty as the kid. And, when he wasn't expending energy on love affairs and money fighting Charles V he may have had enough leisure to peruse Waldseemuller's ptolemy which made the Iberians look like bunglers for their failure to find a viable route to Asia.

The French had been invidiously reading Columbus and Vespucci since the first French printing of Columbus' letter of 1493. And, as one of her leading 16th. Century historians, Henri Lancelot-Voisin wrote: "The French above all were spurred by a desire to do likewise in areas that had not been reached by them [the Spanish] for they did not esteem themselves less than they, neither in navigation, in feats of arms nor in any other calling. They persuaded themselves that they had not discovered all and that the world was large enough to reveal even stranger things than those already known."

French interest in exploration evidenced in 1523 when the Queen Mother invited Pigafetta to her court where he presented her with "certain things from the other hemisphere." The same year a group of Italian bankers in Lyon, center of the French silk industry, desirous of reducing the price of their main product found a thirty-eight year old Florentine pilot, Giovanni da Verrazano, who they hoped could romp across the Western Ocean to "those happy shores of Cathay."

With the patronage of the syndicate and the king Verrazano assembled a fleet of four ships, two of which were dispersed by a storm shortly after departure. The remaining two headed South for a little pirating before getting started on the main project. Having taken a few prizes one of the ships peeled off to escort the loot back to France leaving Verrazano with one ship, *La Dauphine*, to continue the voyage. Wishing to avoid Spanish fleets protecting treasure ships he set a course parallel to Columbus but several degrees North making a landfall around Cape Fear, North Carolina in March 1524. From there he sailed South, probably as far as Charleston. Then he turned North again "in order not to meet Spaniards." It was on this league of the journey he made his great geographical error. He was a deep water sailor, careful to avoid breakers and shoals. The result? As he sailed distant from the outer banks of North Carolina and gazed across them into Pamlico Sound he perceived the sandbars as "an isthmus a mile in width and about 200 long, [from] which we could see the Oriental Sea. . . " This sea he says, "is the same which flows around the shores of India."

Unable or unwilling to tempt the banks Verrazano continued North staying well out to sea, thus apparently missing the Chesapeake and Delaware bays but making it to New York Harbor. But he recognized the river flowing into it for what it was. He was looking for salt water not fresh, so after a brief boat ride around the harbor he raised anchor and headed North again. Reaching Maine he applied the name Orambega to the general region which Ramusio, printing his message thirty some years later, labeled "Terra de Norumbega."

Sailing North and East *La Dauphine* finally "approached the land that in times past was discovered by the British," so the discouraged sailors, "having spent all our naval stores and victuals and having discovered 700 leagues and more of new country we topped off with water and wood and decided to return to France."

They anchored at Dieppe in July 1524 when Verrazano dispatched the letter to King Francis on which his posterity rests. He regretfully explains, "My intention on this voyage was to reach Cathay and the extreme eastern coast of Asia not expecting to find such a barrier of new land as I did find; and, if I did find such a land, I estimated that it would not lack a strait to penetrate to the Eastern Ocean." Instead he found a place he compared with the "wild wasteland of Scythia," adding optimistically "it was not without some properties of value since all the hills showed signs of minerals." He prayed that God and His Majesty "may help him bring this initial step to a perfect end, so that in the words of the Evangelist (*Romans* IX, 18), 'Their sound went into all the earth, and to the ends of the world.'"

This was not exactly the case. Verrazano made two more voyages both to the South apparently looking for his strait in regions the Spanish had fruitlessly explored. On the first he zipped across the Atlantic narrows only to load up a cargo a Brazilwood which he returned to France. (The Florentine had a penchant for making exploration pay off, either through commerce or piracy).

1528 found him with a flotilla of two or three ships which raised the coast of Florida, then shaped a course for Darien. Stopping at one of the Lesser Antilles Verrazano with his brother Girolamo rowed shoreward in one of the ships' boats where a crowd of cannibals waited at water's edge licking their chops at the prospect of human lunch. While Girolamo and the boat crew kept the dingy behind the breaker line Verrazano waded innocently ashore where the cannibals slaughtered him, sliced him up and ate him while his brother looked helplessly on, seeing the "sand ruddy with fraternal blood. . . To so miserable an end came this valiant gentlemen," Ramusio lamented.

Verrazano died without realizing the contribution he made to the progress of discovery. Like Columbus he erred in the belief he sailed much further West than he had (about fifty degrees) but insistence on having repeated Balboa's achievement as far North as Carolina combined with evidence of a continuous coast from Florida to Newfoundland proved America was no mere southern peninsula jutting off Asia but an entirely new world. This information did not circulate in print for three decades but it was taken up by the map makers.

Interest in a northern passage was not confined to France. Charles V, apparently hearing of Verrazano's departure dispatched Esteban Gomez on the same quest in 1524. Gomez had mutinied against Magellan after the discovery of the southern strait and sailed back to Spain where Charles had him clapped in irons. In his defense Gomez argued Magellan's discovery was too far South, too treacherous, involved and too long a voyage to be practical. On reading the official report of the expedition the emperor decided Gomez might have a point (and he did - the southern passage saw little use until the California Gold Rush). He released the mutineer and sent him West but Gomez did little more than reconnoiter what Verrazano had already accomplished. The Spanish made further ventures in the South, exploring the Plata hoping it would open a passage in the process of which they found a route to inland empire.

One other venture of this period deserves attention, not so much for the voyage but the manuscript that inspired it. In 1527 Robert Throne, an English merchant residing in Seville, wrote "A Declaration of the Indies" to Henry VIII and a "Booke" supporting the same theme for Edward Lee, British ambassador to Charles V. The Iberians monopolized more than their fair share of the fruitful parts of the earth by sailing South, East and West he explained to Henry. Here "now rest to be discovered the sayd North parts, which it seems to mee, is onely your charge and duety." And to Lee he made the bold suggestion there was "no land uninhabitable, no sea innavigable." He supported his contention with a map extending from pole to pole which at first glance must have looked a little discouraging. It shows America running off the top. However, according to Throne, nothing prevented "sayling Northward and passing the Pole," then dropping down on the other side of the globe halving the distance sailed by the Portuguese to reach Asia. He pointed out that in summer "perpetual clereness of the day without any darkness of the night" would make navigation safer by this route than those of the Iberians which were fraught with "dangers or darknesse."

King Henry was apparently impressed by Thorne's memorandum for he promptly outfitted two ships under the command of a Master Grube and John Rut. Apparently wise enough counsel prevailed to discourage a polar route so when Grube and Rut sailed from Plymouth in July, 1527 they followed the tracks of earlier voyagers from Bristol.

Rut later reported he parted from Grube in "a marvailous great storme." He was never seen again. Rut continued on to Newfoundland where, losing taste for polar exploration, he turned South. The next we hear of him is in November when he turned up in Santo Domingo only to be chased out of the Antilles by the Spanish. He was back in England in the spring of 1528 having accomplished nothing more than aggravating Anglo - Iberian tension.

In 1534 it became Cartier's turn to search for the passage. That year he sailed into the St. Lawrence as far as Quebec. On a second expedition the following year he reached the Huron settlement of Hochelaga (now part of Montreal). Climbing to the top of a hill he christened Mont Royal he spied, to his dismay, a series of rapids which nothing larger than a canoe could pass, but in the process he heard the river extended so far no man had reached the end. This suggested an interesting possibility. Anything flowing from that far East might well rise in the heart of China, or at least that is what Cartier or Francis must have convinced themselves, for in 1540 the king issued a new commission to "our dear and good friend Jacques Cartier, who having discovered the great country of the lands of Canada and Ochelaga, constituting a westward point of Asia." Although the purpose of this expedition was a combination of prospecting and settlement the implication was that settlers, if they passed the rapids, could continue the voyage to Cathay.

Between 1520 and 1550 the world grew like Jack's beanstalk. European maritime nations covered immense amounts of territory in a hemisphere that had mysteriously and unaccountably risen out of the Sea of Darkness. This lead to wildly contradictory and confusing theories of where it all started and ended. Peter Martyr examples the confusion when he mentions Cortez' landfall at San Juan de Ulloa, explaining, "They imagined the land sighted was part of the 'supposed continent' or was joined to the southern part of the coast of Baccalaos [Labrador]."

But the map did slowly and agonizingly fill out. In his fifth decade Martyr describes the voyage of Alonzo Alvarez de Pineda, who searching for a western passage, sailed along the Gulf coast where he discovered "a great river" (the Mississippi) then sojourned down the Mexican coast until he ran into Cortez who told him to turn around and go back the way he came. Martyr explains this expedition determined Florida was no mere island: "We know this from a painted map he brought back. This map represents a bow; starting from Temistitan [he confuses Mexico City with the country] the line is traced towards the North as far as the bend of the arch; then inclining slightly towards the South in such wise that if it were prolonged to the extreme point it would approach the island of Fernandia."

In Mexico Cortez, in the process of making himself master of the country and searching for the strait he assured Charles V he spared no effort to find, sent lieutenants West. An expedition under the Spanish explorer Cabrillo sailed along the coast, probably further North than present Los Angeles, to give North

America a western littoral.

The 1540's saw the Coronado expedition into New Mexico and de Soto's meandering through Florida to South Carolina, the Gulf states and Arkansas. Although chronicles of the latter's route are too vague to indicate actual East - West distances and Coronado moved more or less on a North South axis their information tended to confirm a broad contiguous land with a western coast. In Peru the Spanish used that miracle of engineering, the Royal Road of the Incas, to carry them as far as Chile and in the process fill in the hemisphere.

All this should have given a reasonable estimate of the shape and position of America and finally it did, but not without fifty years of confusion.

There were five problems. The first: classical authority. Europeans were so fascinated with what they were discovering from ancient authors they could not get it out of their heads that a collection of countries clustered around the Mediterranean did not understand the entire world. This was exacerbated by the second problem; the serious underestimation of longitude and overextension of Asia that Columbus introduced and demonstrated to the satisfaction of some. Third was the insistence of a contiguous, uninterrupted "Island of Earth" albeit one which had dramatically changed shape. Christian theology (as espoused by Augustine and others) would have nothing less. This sentiment is expressed in an exchange between Ramusio and Oviedo when the former sent a map by Olas Magnus published in Venice in 1539 from which Oviedo learned with pleasure that Labrador was "joined to and one land with Europe, leaving Iceland and Scotland and England and many other notable islands surrounded by land" with the significant consequence that "All the world. . . is one same land and coast, without sea dividing it." In other words the Atlantic was nothing more than another Mediterranean Sea. (By way of compensation Oviedo sent Ramusio an iguana but believing the creature subsisted solely on dirt packed it in a box of earth so the iguana arrived dead.) This problem can be labeled the iguana for a map or Augustinian problem. There could be no "Terra Mela" or "Novus Orbis."

The forth problem was Verrazano's identification of Pamlico Sound with the "Eastern Ocean" suggesting a narrow northern continent to confute Soto and Coronado. He was in turn contradicted by the fifth problem. The western littoral of America runs continually Northwest from Panama to a point above San Francisco, and since nobody had yet traveled further, presumably continued to do so. Taken together these issues created a very confusing picture.

ANOTHER LOOK AT THE MAP

In 1524 Juan Vespucci engraved an indecisive world map of a circle and two semi-circles to show the new discoveries. His vagueness suggests information was being suppressed and the only copy I know of gives the impression the plate was never even completed.

Globes of the 1520's and 1530's attempt to record the discoveries of Verrazno and de Pineda. The Bailly Globe of 1530 shows North America much as

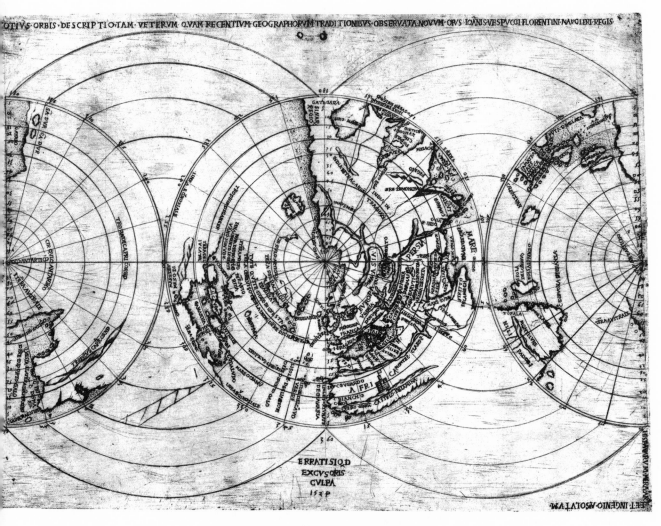

Juan Vespucci's world map of 1524.

it would be drawn by Michael Lok in 1582, except that it thins out Mexico and omits Baja California. More interesting are the Paris Guilt Globe of about 1528 and the Nancy Globe of 1535. They ignore the "Sea of Verrazano" and make his costal discoveries a simple extension of Asia. On both the Florida Peninsula is separated from Cathay by the Gulf of Mexico. The Gobi desert is across the "R. de S. Spirito" (as de Pineda called the Mississippi) from "Terra Francesca" which is reported as newly seen. Gog and Magog, those flesh devouring arch enemies of Christianity planning one day to besiege Jerusalem who Johannes Ruysch, in 1508 placed a tad East of Cabot's landfall, now live west of the Gobi, presumably in California where many believe they still are. Mexico is right under Tibet. Both globes pepper North America with names from Polo and Mandeville and sit the Spice Islands off Mexico. Variations of these configurations appear on a handful of manuscript and small printed maps of the 1520 - 1540 period.

❧ DE ORBIS

SITV AC DESCRIPTIONE. AD RE-
*uerendiſſ. D.archiepiſcopum Panormitanum, Fran-
ciſci, Monachi ordinis Fraciſcani, epiſtola ſanć quā
luculenta. In qua Ptolemæi, cæterorumq̃; ſuperiorū
geographorum,hallucinatio refellitur, aliaq̃; præte-
rea de recens inuentis terris,mari,inſulis. De ditio-
ne Papæ Ioannis. De ſitu Paradiſi ,ꝯ dimenſione mi
liarium ad proportionē graduum cœli, præclara ꝯ
memoratu digna recenſentur.*

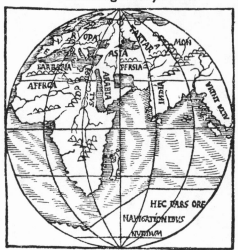

CVM PRIVILEGIO INVICTISSI-
*mi Romanorum imperatoris Caroli quinti, ad quin-
quenniū,ne quis uel typis excudat, uel excudendos cu
ret hos codices geographicos,una cū globis,ſub mul
čta amittendorum exemplariū , aliáq̃; pœna Principis ſeueritate inferenda.*

A 2

Title page and first page of Franciscus Monarchus' DE ORBIS SITU... ca. 1527

Verbally we find the same Schoner who boldly placed Vespucci's name on globes of the teens and early twenties changing his mind and deciding the navigator had not discovered much of anything. His *Opusculum Geographicum* of 1533 maintains Mexico is in fact China and Templistan is Marco Polo's Quinsay. Old ideas die hard and the identification of America with Asia would continue for a long time. As late as 1590 it appears so on a map in Myritius' *Opusculum geographicum rarum...* and in 1638 a French priest, Jean Nicolet, setting out to visit the Winnebago provided himself with a robe of Chinese damask in case he should meet a mandarin!

Returning to maps we find the first chink in Waldseemuller's strangle hold on the big picture in Benedetto Bordone's *Isolario...* (Venice, 1528). It enjoyed considerable popularity and was reissued several times over the next fifty years. However as a prototype its world map is a bit of a flop. Bordone confidently gives Asia a coast and since he is writing about islands remembers Japan. He joins Newfoundland to North America connected by a narrow Central America to a bulging southern land. He apparent!y never heard of Magellan, de Pineda or Balboa. South America truncates at Capricorn while the entire hemisphere slips off the edge of his oval projection to - who knows where?

A rare heart shaped map by Peter Apian appeared in 1530. As in 1520 he largely follows the 1507 Waldseemuller with the interesting exception that he places a convenient strait in the Plata region. (On the other hand he does not seem to have much confidence in Magellan whose strait is missing.) Sebastian Munster prepared a world map for Johann Huttich's *Mundus Novus*. . . (Basel, 1532). This is also a throwback to Waldseemuller's 1507 chart projected as a planisphere. He follows the earlier cartographer's outline of the Americas, if not verbatim at least closely enough to make it clear he had been looking at it. He includes the Central American strait despite the fact that by now it was excruciatingly obvious it was not there and exacerbates his anachronisms by labeling an Atlantic island "Terra Cortesia" (Land of Corte Real) and North America "Terra de Cuba." The Basel edition was popular and saw subsequent printings (which must have been large for the book is common) in 1535 and 1550. So for many this was the world picture through mid-century.

Mundus Novus appeared in Paris the same year it came out in Basel but it contained a radically different map drawn by the French cartographer Orince Fine. He uses a double heart shaped projection (allowing for a better concept of relative space) and the most up to date information. He connects America and Asia with a Labrador-Newfoundland peninsula stretching way into the Atlantic

Gemma Frisius' world map

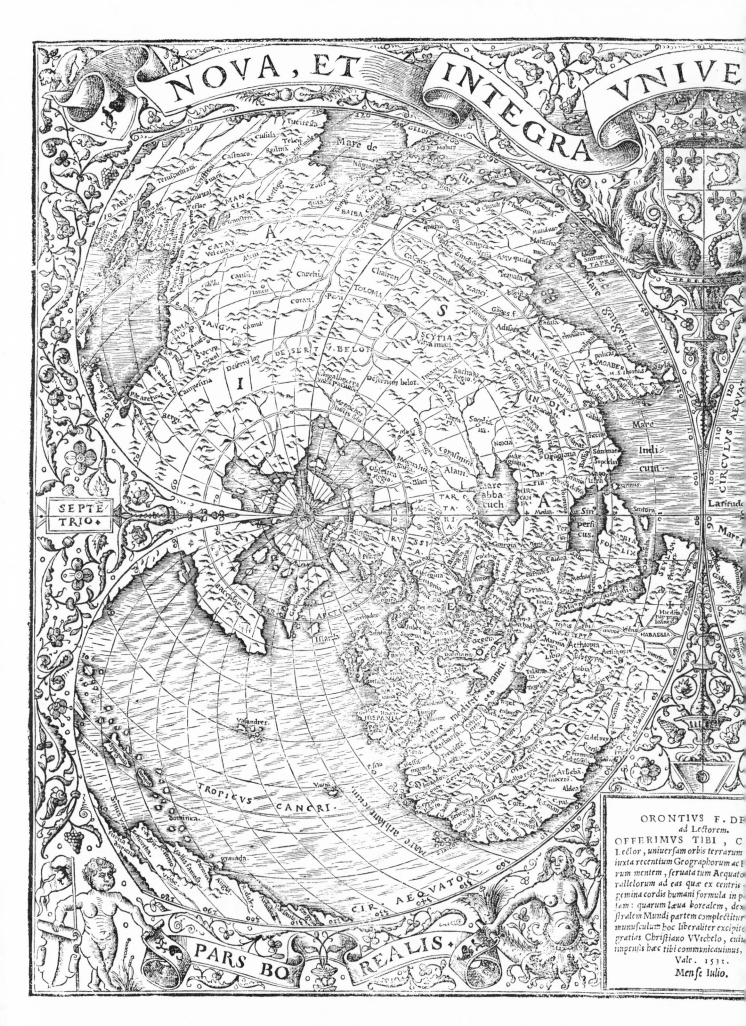

NOVA, ET INTEGRA VNIVE

PARS BO REALIS.

ORONTIVS F. DE
ad Lectorem.
OFFERIMVS TIBI, C
Lector, vniuersam orbis terrarum
iuxta recentium Geographorum ac F
rum mentem, seruata tum Aequato
rallelorum ad eas quæ ex centris
gemina cordis humani formula in p
sam: quarum læua borealem, dex
stralem Mundi partem complectitur
munusculum hoc liberaliter excipite
gratias Christiano VVechelo, cui
impensis hæc tibi communicauimus,
Vale. 1531.
Mense Iulio.

ADJACENT: Orince Fine's
world map of 1531 from
NOVUS ORBIS. PAGES
58 - 59: Munster's map
from the same work.

Latitudo 80 Septentrionalis

Cirag

SEP

Islandia

Ibernia

Moscouia

Anglia

Dacia

Germania Sarmatia

EVRO

PA

Terra
de
Cuba

Terra Cor
teria

OCEANVS
MAGNVS

Gallia

ta
lia

Grecia

Borsint

Chozus

Hispa
nia

Mare
mediterra
neum

isabella

Insulæ
Antigliæ

Portus sanctus

Medera

Barbaria

Atlas mons

Aegyp
tus

Spagnolla

TROPICVS CANCRI

Insula Canariæ

Terra alba

Getulia

NIGRITAE

Zi
pan
gri

Dargin
Alba
Gazara

Caput album

Hodeni

Caput uiride

Aethiopia

Sanga flu.

APHRICA

Me
roe

Insula boni visus

Sinus magnus

Gambra regnu

AETHIOPIA
interior

Fr

Sagres

Besigne

Fanonig

Parias

Sinus fra
tres

Ginega

Canibali

AEQVINOCTIALIS

Regnum
Melli &
Nebeorum

Origo
Nili

AMERICA

270   280   290   300   310   320   330   340   350   360   10   20   30   40   50   60

TERRA NOVA

Prisilia

Terra psi
tacorum

TROPICVS CAPRICORNI

Lips

Caput bo
ne spei

CANIBALI

OCEANVS MERIDIONALIS

Aphzicg

Latitudo 80 meridionalis

PIPER

SCATA

CARIOFILI

Aquilo seu
Boreas

CONGELATA

SCYTHIA

Regnū Cassae

Scythia intra Imaum

Scythia extra
Imaum

Imaus
mons

Regnum Cu
maniae

Desertum
Belgian

TARTARIA MAGNA
Terra Mongal

ASIA

Regnum
Corasine

Cambalu

Aria

Emodij mōtes

Regnum
Tharsae

Regnū Cathay

Indus
flu.

Drangiana

Gan
ges
flu.

Regnum
Turquestran

Caerins

Gedrosia

TROPICVS CANCRI

India extra Gangem

Prouincia Syn

INDIA INTRA
Gangem

INDIAE
regnum

Cale
chut

Sinus
Gangeticus

Sinus
aureus magnus

Ciamba
prouincia
magna

Ta
bana

Bubsolang

Cherfone

Sinaru
regio

Regnum
Mursul

INDIA ab Indo flu. sic appellata, oppidis adeo
exculta dicitur, ut quidam 5000. in ea esse dicāt.
Terra est saluberrima, bis in anno metit fruges.
Fert cynnamomum, piper, & calamum aromati-
cum. Ebenum arborem sola producit. Psitacū auē
& monoceron bestiam habet. Beryllis, adamanti-
bus, carbunculis, margaritis, & alijs gēmis pre-
ciosis abundat. Centum & triginta annorum euū
ob temperatum cœlū quidam agunt. Cultus prae-
cipuus cum gēmis: alij laneis, alij lineis peplis ue-
stiuntur: pars nudi, pars obscœna tantum amici-
lati. Niger uulgo corporis color, ex materno ute-
ro sic nati. Potum ex riso & hordeo conficiunt.
Aetati senū praerogatiuā nullā tribuunt, nisi pru-
dentia excellāt. Sunt tamen Indorum multae gentes, diuersae formā & lingua, nec eisdem niuen-
tes moribus.

Regnum Pego

Iaua

Regnum
Malacha

Vultuzng

SCYTHARVM natio primo parua &
contempta fuit, sed postea in magnum imperiū &
gloriā peruenit, agros ampliās usq; ad Tanaim
flauium, à quo Scythia ipsa longo tractu uersus or
tum protensa, Imao monte per medium uelut in
duas Scythias diuiditur.   Tartaria quae &
Mongal, maiorem Scythiae occupans partem: regio est plurimum montosa, & ubi campestris est,
admixta est glarea harenosa, multis patens deser
tis. Aër & cœlum intemperatum, tonitrua & ful
gura in aestate adeo horrēda sæpe fiunt, ut prae ti
more homines intereant. Iam calor magnus est,
mox frigus & densißime niues cadunt.

Euro auster

Latitudinis meridionalis

VARTOMANVS.

and traces Verrazano's reconnaissance without his "sea" showing up. Fine along with others identifies the other part of Magellan's strait as an antarctic continent noting it has been "recently discovered but not explored." This does not stop his cavalier tracing of its contours nearly to Capricorn in the void of the Pacific, adding mountainous topography and labeling some mythical kingdoms. Fine's map although far rarer than Munster's saw service in a couple of other books into the early 1540's. It clearly influenced Mercator's initial effort to depict the world in 1538 although Mercator optimistically separated the continents, holding out the possibility of a passage.

About the same time *Mundus Novus* appeared Gemma Frisius got out a new edition of Apian's cosmology including a reduced version of his own wall map (now extinct). Totally different, it encompasses information gathered from Corte Real and Verrazano. Frisius imagines a narrow stretch of land, not far from Cathay, extending from above the Arctic Circle until it bulges into South America. He inscribes the entire northern continent with the name "Baccallarum" ("Land of Codfish" - the name Portugal assigned her discovery). Frisius' inexpensive octavo was popular, enjoying several editions until 1584, long after everything on the map was proved wrong.

Meanwhile, back in Basel, Sebastian Munster had been brushing up on his geography. When, in 1540, he produced a new ptolemy to replace the outdated Waldseemuller - Fries renderings he included a new world map and another of America. They show the continent as a single, fairly well roughed out entity scrunched under an eastern extension of Asia and a Greenland peninsula, called "Bacallos." He includes Verrazano's sea and places the New World a short boat ride from Japan. With the publication of these two maps, first in the 1540 ptolemy and subsequently in his *Cosmology* of 1544 and later Munster gained two distinctions. The first, not uncommon for cartographers of his day, was having mutually contradictory maps in print at the same time, the *Novus Orbis* one and the two just described. Second was the renown of printing the first separate map of America, forty-seven years after its discovery.

Many navigators would later rue Munster's "advances." By the time the last printing came out in 1650 the *Cosmography* had gone through forty-six editions in six languages, some having press runs going into five digits. This enormous popularity made the American related maps, complete with their "Sea of Verrazano" the commonest of the era. The result? As late as 1651 John Farrer with a copy of Munster or Frisius in hand is drawing a map of Virginia which has a narrow plain West of the Appalachians labeled "Nova Albion" (the name Drake had given California). Beyond Nova Albion lies "The Sea of China and the Indies," and Farrer confidently inscribes his plate with the message that the Pacific coast is a scant "10 days march over hills and rich adjacent valleys."

Munster made another even costlier mistake. By underestimating the size of North America he paints in a strait, complete with an inscription that it is the passage to the Mollucas, that makes it look like clear sailing along a latitude at the approximate level of England to "India Superior." That strait would remain the bane of navigators for another century.

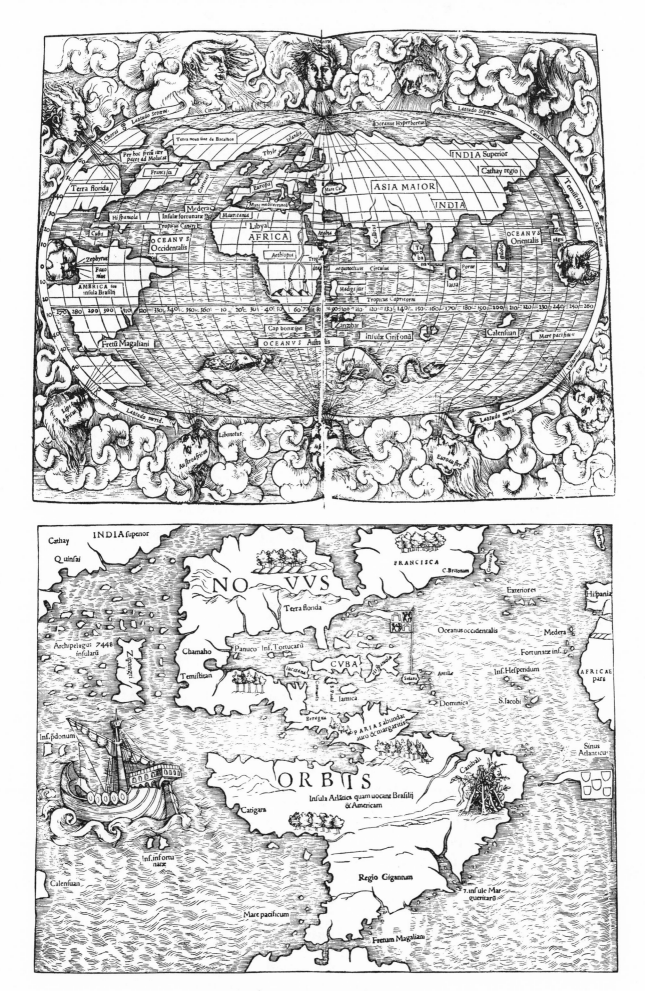

Munster's world and American maps.

But Munster's and his readers' interest in America was limited at best. In the edition of 1550, the last one he supervised personally, his tome of 1128 pages confines discussion of "The New Islands" to pages 764 to 773. He explains Columbus found the Canaries, Madeira, Santa Cruz Island with cannibals (he was a bit off the mark there) Hispaniola and Cuba and Vespucci traveled to the American "Island" and Paria. He throws in a little information about the Pinzons and that's about all. And, although his work teems with detailed European maps and city views his single American map includes only a few place names and random rivers. He fills in the rest with casually placed mountains and trees and for sensation includes some cannibals. For Munster America was just another island somewhere near Asia.

Eight years after the appearance of Munster's American map the prominent Italian cartographer, Giacomo Gastaldi, re-introduced the China connection. Working from information derived from Cabrillo's reconnaissance of the Pacific coast he traces it up to meet Asia at about forty-five degrees North and about 130 degrees off his prime meridian, the present site of Portland Oregon. These two maps in varying formats became competitive prototypes through the 1550's and '60's. In 1556 Ramusio refused to say more than he knew on a map prepared for his *Della Navigationi et Vaggi.* . . This, only the second printed map to separately depict America, now sixty-three years after discovery, leaves everything Ramusio is not sure of blank.

THE AMERICAN HORIZON: A BRIEF DIGRESSION

We cannot rush past Ramusio without making further note of his contribution to the progress of discovery.

Henry Harrisse in *Bibliotheca Americana Vetustissima* lists 476 notices of America between 1493 and 1550. At first glance this would seem a respectable number, but Harrisse assigns each edition of a work a separate number and they range from complete books to pamphlets and broadsheets or notices of America that made their way into works discussing other subjects. To this should be added the fact that about twenty percent of his list is confined to reprints or paraphrased information from two authors, Columbus and Vespucci. During this entire period only two separate works dealing with any part of North America saw print, Cabeza de Vaca's *Relation* of 1542 and Cartier's *Brief Recit.* . . of three years later. Tales of Mexico and Peru doubtless excited wonder and greed but given the large percentage of translations from the Spanish and brevity of most accounts information on America was still very thin.

Till Ramusio the most ambitious efforts to describe the world through voyagers' accounts were Munster and *Mundus Novus Regionum.* . . or to give its more complete title in English: *New Globe of the Regions and Islands Unknown to the Ancients.* . . *Some Other Treatises Containing Similar Things.* . . This is a bold Renaissance announcement that, not just America, but everything is to be seen in a new way betraying an outburst of curiosity about the size and nature of Earth. This folio is to the *Nuremberg Chronicle* what a fresco by Michelangelo

Ramusio's map of
the hemisphere.

is to a Byzantine mosaic. And the spirit of the work certainly makes it interesting. This is easily perceived by another look at Munster's map embellished by
Hans Holbein the younger. It displays a variegated world with a ship sailing the
South Atlantic to regions unimaginable forty years before. The orb is being
turned on its axis by a pair of mischievous angels (anticipating Copernicus'
publication by ten years) while the surround includes a cornucopia of miraculous new sights Europeans had barely thought about much less envisioned.

Mundus Novus was assembled by John Huttich, cannon of the Cathedral of
Strasbourg. A preface was contributed by Simon Grynaeus, personal friend of
Luther and inveterate talker. But like Munster Huttich offers little new to the
Americanist. He gives about forty pages to the first three voyages of Columbus,
Vincente Pinzon, Vespucci's four voyages and an extract from Martyr's forth
decade. Most of the remaining 560 pages are devoted to eastern voyages includ-
ing extracts from Polo and Ludovico di Varthema who published his travels to
the Orient in 1510. For Huttich *This* was the new world.

It fell to Giamatista Ramusio, secretary to the dreaded Venetian council of "The Ten", to go Huttich one better and open a new era in the literary history of discovery. Instead of carelessly copying previously published works complete with errors, to which most copyists managed to add a few of their own, Ramusio sought out and judiciously selected original narratives to complement already printed material and enriched them with notices which betray the hand of a scholar of great critical acumen.

The first edition of *Raccolta Delle Navigationi et Viaggi. . .* appeared as an anonymous folio in Venice (1550). A second edition in two volumes bearing his name came out shortly after. Being among the first to recognize the importance of the new hemisphere Ramusio got out a third volume largely devoted to America in 1556. He intended a forth but the project was interrupted by his death. All three folios are thick. The third is rivaled only by Martyr for New World news but is more inclusive. Martyr was limited to news coming into Spain till his death in 1526. Publishing later and deriving material from a variety of sources Ramusio produced, for the first time, a cohesive account of America.

Although he extracted material from previous works, Vespucci, Martyr, Cortez, etc., the *Raccolta* teems with fresh information. From Sebastian Cabot he received documents relating to his father's discovery. He describes the Coronado expedition as well as Verrazano's recognizance (making their debut in print fifty nine, sixteen and thirty-three years after the respective events). There is a "Discourse of a grand Captain of the French Sea," possibly Jean Parmentier who visited North America between Verrazano and Cartier. From Cartier he received information about Canada including enough material to provide tentative illustrations. He gathered information from his friend and one time business partner Oviedo including a letter written a month after Francisco de Orellanda's voyage down the Amazon to give Europe its first inkling of the Brazilian interior. He adds information about Mexico and much more.

The 1556 volume contains twenty-one woodcuts, some of plants provided by Oviedo, a view of Mexico City and a plan of Hochelaga which corresponds closely to Cartier's description.

Returning to the subject of maps we find Ramusio giving, in addition to his map of the hemisphere, a verbal map of the discoveries complete with descriptions of what was discovered. Another point is even more interesting. For most of the century cartographic interest in America was confined to getting it placed on the world map and then largely for purposes of figuring out how to get past it. Regional maps were almost non-existent even in manuscript. Martyr deserves credit for the first, a 1513 map of the Caribbean. Cortez also appended a small Caribbean map to his plan of Mexico City. Bordone managed to get in a map of Hispaniola. It seemingly took Ramusio to realize just how tactile America was. He provides a map of Hispaniola, another of Brazil and one of eastern Canada, the latter two embellished with images of what he could determine about Amerind life.

BACK TO THE PRINTED MAP

In 1561 Girolamo Ruscelli seconded Ramusio's motion when he suggested only a tentative connection between America and Asia but they were voices crying in the wilderness. Map makers hate to confess ignorance. When in doubt they cover confusion with a scroll.

Following Gastaldi the Italians who had already provided most of the pilots for maritime hopefuls began to contribute most of the maps. Many of their cartographers were referred to as the Lafreri School because their work was gathered into "binder's atlases" in which a customer could select maps he wanted and have them bound as a single book put out by Lafreri in Rome.

It fell to the Italians to deal with the Olaus Magnus - Iguana or Augustinian problem. Although hemispheric maps were as old as Waldseemuller's 1507 cartouche inset they were not popular. The idea of two worlds, one possibly cut off from the other was simply too fantastic and heretical to touch. Such maps that

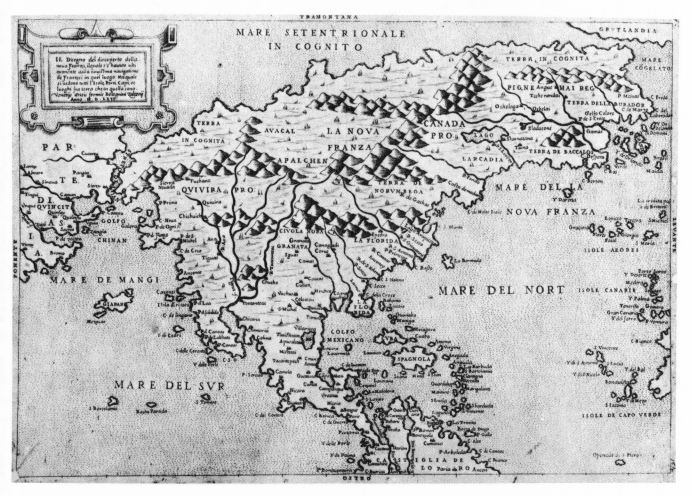

Bolognino Zaterini's map of North America (Venice, 1566).

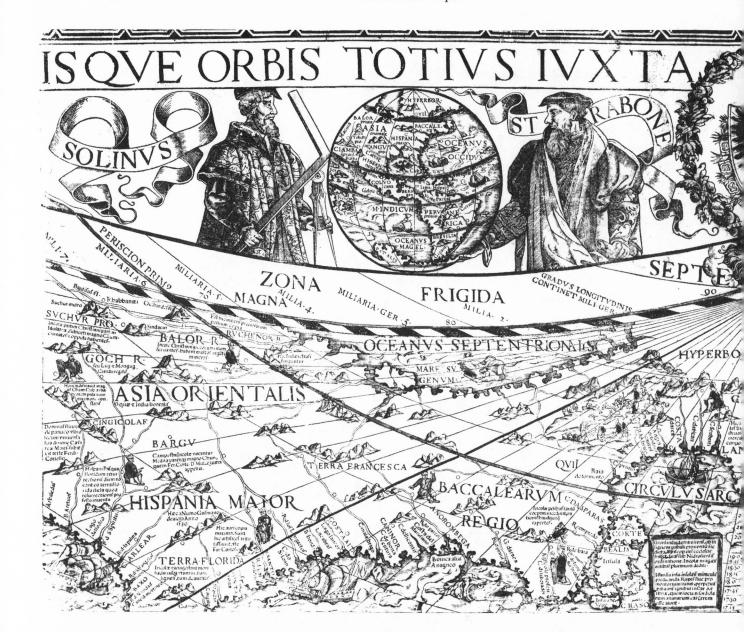

appeared as hemispheres usually beggared the issue by dividing the sphere in the middle of a continent (Waldseemuller, Fine and Mercator in 1538, for instance) or indicating a clear connection between America and Asia, either across the Pacific or over the pole. Maps like everything else had to retain an orthodox spiritual quality and stress the idea of one world which was "the house of all."

The Italians recognized the inadequacy of planispheres and oval projections. While continuing to produce oval maps (introduced by Bordone in 1528) they also realized America needed its own hemisphere. Providing hemispheric maps they gave the forth part of the world space to unravel and grow and finally enter consciousness as more than Verrazano's or Frisius' annoying sandbar.

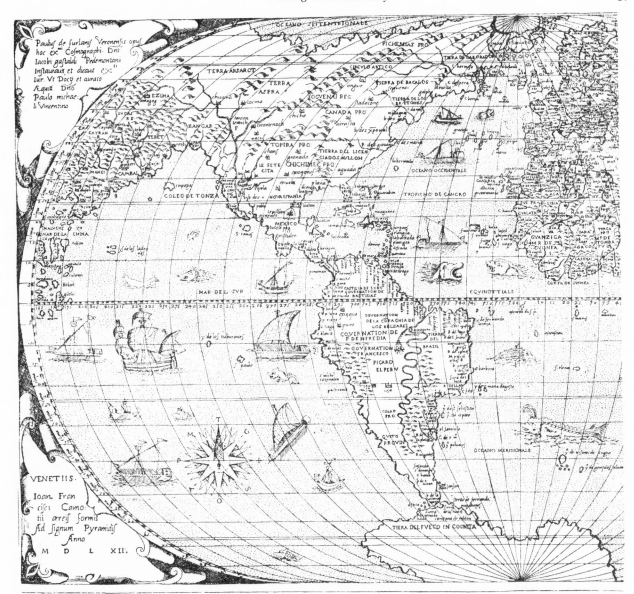

PAGE 66: Northwest portion of Caspar Vopell's large world map of 1545 (now extinct) as re-engraved by Giovanni Andrea Vavassore. Vopell notes on the map that he secured an audience with Charles V to gather information he received from his explorers. He asked Charles if the Western lands extended to China or were seperated by a rumored strait. The emperor categorically stated that the Spanish discoveries extended to China and pointed out that this placed them in the Spanish sphere.
ABOVE: Western portion of Gastaldi's world map of 1562. PAGES 68 - '9: Ortelius' world map.

A few seperate maps of America appeared during the 1550's and '60's, usually in conjunction with a corresponding map of the Eastern Hemisphere. One seperate map, perhaps the first to confine itself to North America, was drawn by Bolognino Zaltieri (Venice 1566.) Zaltieri seperates the hemispheres by the "Strait of Anian." Now the Northwest Passage had a name to make it official.

In 1569 Gerard Mercator produced a large world map using his newly created projection which is still used today. In many ways Mercator's projection is less satisfactory than the hemispheric because he presents longitude as broad as latitude no matter how far up or down the map. The result makes Greenland

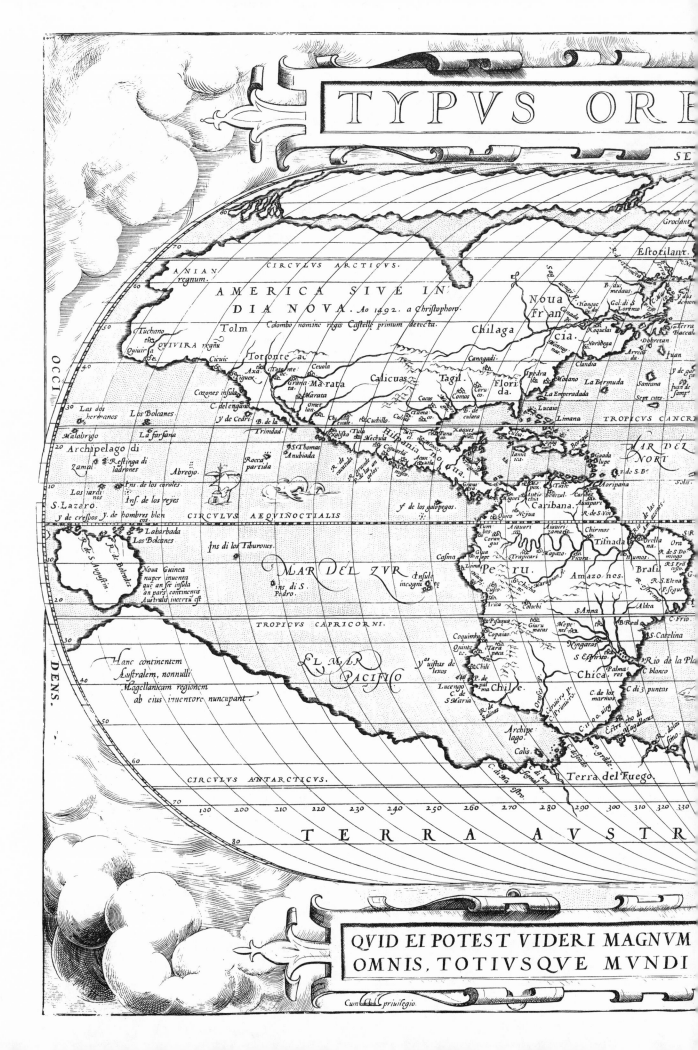

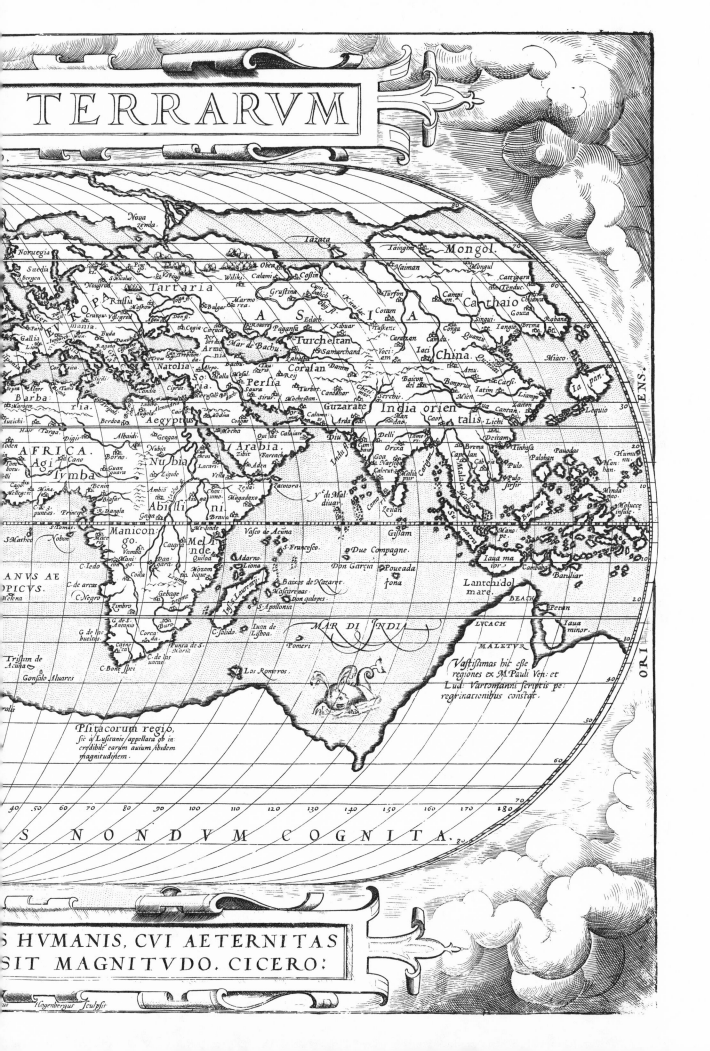

look as big as South America but this approach made it possible to see a single world with locations placed as accurately as possible. Using current information he produced the most modern map of his day.

When Mercator's friend and colleague, Abraham Ortelius,' atlas rolled off the presses of Christopher Plantin in 1570 he included an obligatory American map with its own hemisphere. Ortelius' work was the first true atlas, a uniform work of fifty-three maps (expanded over years to 163). He made the best effort to date to depict America, complete with place names, largely scattered along the coast. He describes important rivers rather than randomly placing them. (Although in the case of the St. Lawrence he makes too much of a good thing, following Mercator by extending it into Nebraska.) He tries a few place names in the interior and prophetically turns the West coast toward Asia calling the new space Anian and Quivera. And, though he had no guarantee the strait existed, separates the continents. Reluctant to give up the idea that the world was largely earth, he drew enormous arctic and antarctic continents on his world map, allowing mankind to roam the earth at will.

Ortelius' atlas enjoyed enormous success. It saw three reprints the first year and over forty editions in seven languages until 1612. Although Ortelius could not displace Munster's *Cosmography* which refused to go out of print his vision of America was the commonest modern image for forty some years.

Ortelius was followed into the atlas business by Mercator who included slightly improved world and American maps. Shortly after they were joined by the Jode family. (An interesting feature of the Jode Atlas is a sperate map of the Kingdom of Anian, attractively engraved and embellished with Chinese junks sailing off the coast and enough detail to convince the viewer it was actually there.)

While all this was going on England was becoming adventurous but her geography was a mix of naivete and wishful thinking.

For sixty years after discovery English presses remained silent on the subject of America. Even ptolemys and world maps which excited speculation elsewhere were notably absent. But the nation of shopkeepers was still interested in trade so in 1553 aging Sebastian Cabot, an inveterate promoter of voyages and himself, was in England talking up a voyage to China by a Northeast passage. Ships were duly fitted out and sailed before a cheering crowd.

The voyage failed to find China but discovered Russia instead. Apparently news of the enterprise stirred enough public interest to induce somebody to get out a broadsheet or pamphlet on geography. The publication came into the hands of Richard Eden, a Cambridge man with twelve children. Eden found this now lost effort unworthy so because of the, "Good affection I have ever borne the science of cosmograhy. . .and much more by the good will which of duty I bear my country and countrymen, which have of late to their great praise. . . attempted with new voyages to search the seas and new founde lands [when] there chanced of late to come into my hands a sheet of printed paper. . .entitled of the new found lands I thought it worthy of my travail. . .(as one not otherwise able to further their enterprise), to translate this book."

The book turned out to be short portions freely translated out of Munster's cosmography issued as: *A Treatise of the New India with Other Found Lands, as well, Eastwade as Westward. . .*

In a garrulous preface Eden takes pains explaining the earth is round and people can stand on either side. He finds that although ancients erred on points like habitability of the tropics and ignorance of America there is nothing new under the sun because marvels he describes were all known to Solomon. But beyond announcing there were new lands Eden does not have much to say.

A second, more elaborate, book came from his pen in 1555: *The Decades of the New World. . .* and as one might guess from the title it begins with a loose translation of Martyr's first three decades, taking American history to 1521. But the work grew under Eden's hand into a large shapeless compendium of overseas knowledge. To Martyr he adds an account of Magellan, the papal bull of 1493 (a prudent political move with Catholics Philip and Mary on the throne), subsequent disputes between Spain and Portugal and New World descriptions from Oviedo and Gomora. And, nearly six decades after the event, Englishmen read of their own American discovery by John Cabot. More followed: several descriptions of Russia, two accounts of English voyages to Africa and for good measure a treatise on metals and remarks by Frisius on measuring longitude.

Eden's work was as far from being complete as it was coherent but it was a notable achievement none the less for it was the first step in breaking England out of insulation. He made a further contribution to English geographic science by translating Medina's *Arte de Navegar* (Valladolid, 1545) into *Arte of Navigation* in 1561. But Eden's first step was only a step and it took another fifteen years for the English to get back into the business of discovery.

The result of that 1553 voyage to Russia was the formation of a trading company which made good profits but most of the products returned to England came from further East. The logical thing would be cut out the middleman. As early as 1566 Humphrey Gilbert signed a petition for a Northwest passage venture, while he poured over geographical classics to prepare his *Discourse of a Discoverie for a new Passage to Cataia* which finally appeared in 1576 with illustrations from ancient and modern sources to prove a route navigable as the English Channel. Who would look for it? Martin Frobisher did and in the process brought America to English attention in the same way it entered Spanish and French consciousness. A roadblock on the way to Cathay.

Frobisher sailed the year Gilbert's book appeared. The English, having no significant geographical works of their own, left Frobisher to rely largely on foreign material. What he carried is interesting as an example of what was available. It consisted of "a great carte of navigation," Mercator's "great map universal in print," and three smaller maps. This would not be much help for while Mercator was authoritative he was as speculative as everyone else on polar cartography. He had Thevet's cosmography and an English translation *Les Singularities de la France Antarctique. . .* which deals primarily with Brazil. He

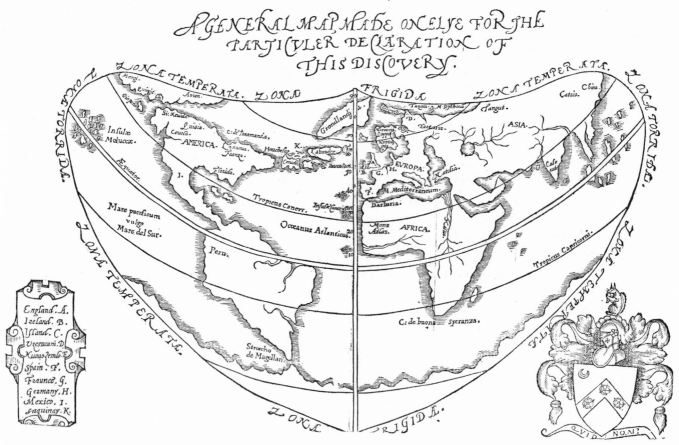

Map included in Sir Humphery Gilbert's DISCOURSE OF A DISCOVERIE FOR A NEW PASSAGE TO CATAIA

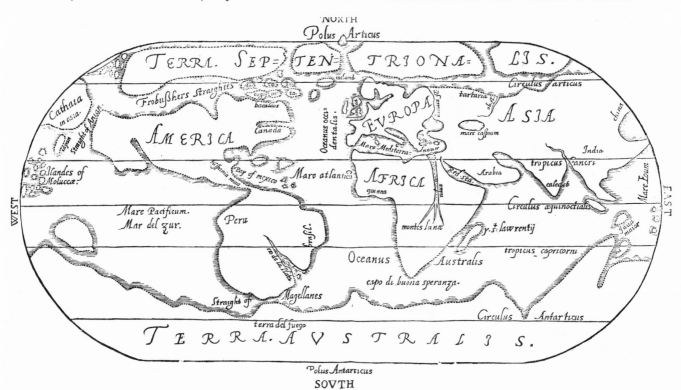

World map from George Best's TRUE DISCOURSE OF THE LATE VOYAGE...

had "a cosmographical glass," an early work on mathematical geography and astronomy and a *Castle of Knowledge*, an astronomy text of the same earlier period. They chose Medina's *Arte de Navegar* in preference to Eden's translation or the more recent (1574) *Regiment of the Sea* by William Bourne. The fleet was also equipped with some speculative manuscript maps by magician, philosopher, geographer and royal councillor, John Dee and William Borroughs. For good measure they added the still credited tales of Sir John Mandeville and a copy of the fictitious Zeno narrative. They did not have Gilbert's discourse because it was not in print when they sailed. In sum a naive library but what else was there?

Frobisher's three voyages culminated in a cul de sac on Baffin Island which still bears the name Frobisher Bay but for five years it was believed he had discovered gold and that was more interesting. The result was a flurry of books about the great discoverer and America in general. As Richard Willis said in 1577 when he published an expanded version of Eden's *Decades*. . . there had been a time when the art of grammar was esteemed, or when it had been honorable to be a poet. That time was past. Once logic and astrology wearied the heads of young scholars. That time was also past. Not long since, "happy was he that had any skil in Greke language." But that was all changed. Now "all Christians Jewes, Moores, Infidels and Barbares be this day in love with Geographie."

But for all that fascination with geography the English had little immediate effect on the printed map. If anything they pushed it backwards. A couple of the Frobisher related books contained simple world maps drawn for the sole purpose of displaying the nonexistent strait. Hakluyt was a walking cartographic anachronism. His *Divers Voyages touching the discovery of America* published in 1582 contained two maps. The first was Thorne's map of 1527 which he found in manuscript and published for the first time. The second was a North American map by Michael Lok freely copied from Munster. The same book contained the Zeno voyage which should have been discredited on the simple strength of Frobisher's experience. Even more silly was an interview he had with one David Ingram who the English slave trader Sir John Hawkins had been forced to leave behind when a Spanish fleet ambushed him at Vera Cruz. Ingram claimed to have escaped the Spanish and strolled overland from Mexico to Cape Breton and enjoyed a lively career telling tavern tales about it when he got home. Among other things he said a Breton told him Verrazano's sea could be viewed from Montreal. Hakluyt included this yarn in the first edition of his *Principal Navigations*. . . but finally became incredulous enough to omit it from the second. During a stint in Paris he got out a Latin edition of Martyr's entire eight decades which contained a modern map of the Western Hemisphere but one wonders how much he contributed to production or inclusion of the map because at the same time he wrote in a dedication to Laudonniere's *Florida*. . . "I am fully persuaded. . . that the land on the back part of Virginia extendeth nothing so far as is put down on maps of those parts." In other words Hakluyt is still wishfully thinking (in 1587) that an American colony could be a good

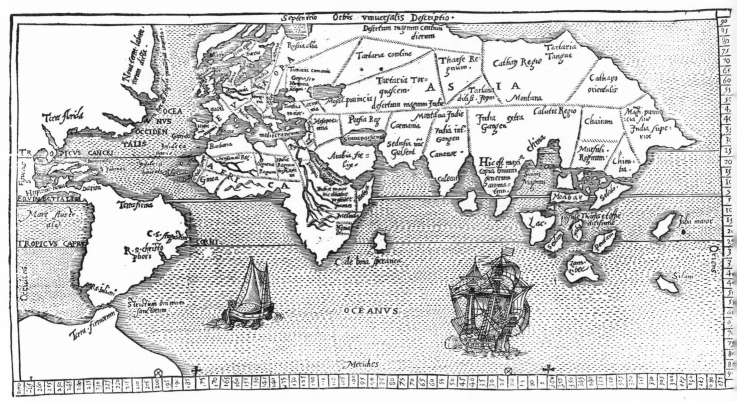

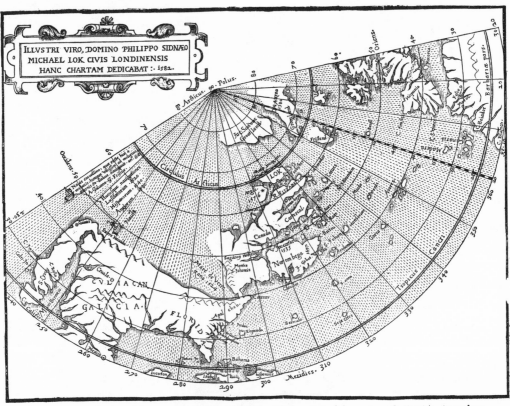

ABOVE: Thorne's world map of 1527. BELOW: Michael Lok's map of North America.
PAGE 75: The Western Hemisphere from Hakluyt's Paris edition of Martyr.
PAGES 76 - 77: The Wright Molyneaux world map.

jumping off place for a short voyage to China.

At century's end Hakluyt finally redeemed his cartographic crudity with the second edition of *Principal Navigations*. . . The first copies to come from the printer included a crude copy of Ortelius' world of 1570, only thirty years out of date. When the Wright-Molyneaux map of ca. 1600 became available he substituted it. This large map, saying no more than its cartographer knew, was the best and most intelligent map to appear for a long time. It was drawn on Mercator's projection, albeit with old fashioned rubb lines. We now find a Western Hemisphere Greenland and Drake's discoveries as far as San Francisco without any etching above either. There are no speculative antarctic or arctic lands or guarantees of a northern passage. Verrazano's sea is now extinct, replaced by a vague inland sea in the approximate area of the Great Lakes.

It fell to Theodore de Bry, no cartographer, explorer or even writer - but an engraver and publisher - to reintroduce regional maps of America in the 1590's. The first volume of his *Grands Voyages* reproduced John White's detailed map of Virginia with incredible fineness. His second volume did the same for Florida. There followed good maps of the Caribbean and South America along with one of the hemisphere. Ortelius, reluctantly concluding there was more out there than dead space contributed a single sheet of his expanding atlas to four separate maps, Florida, Mexico, Peru and the Caribbean. Realizing the importance of the Pacific he included a map of that sea complete with a picture of the *Victoria* which had sailed it seventy some years before.

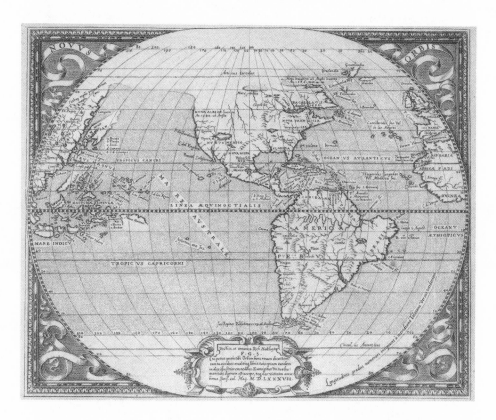

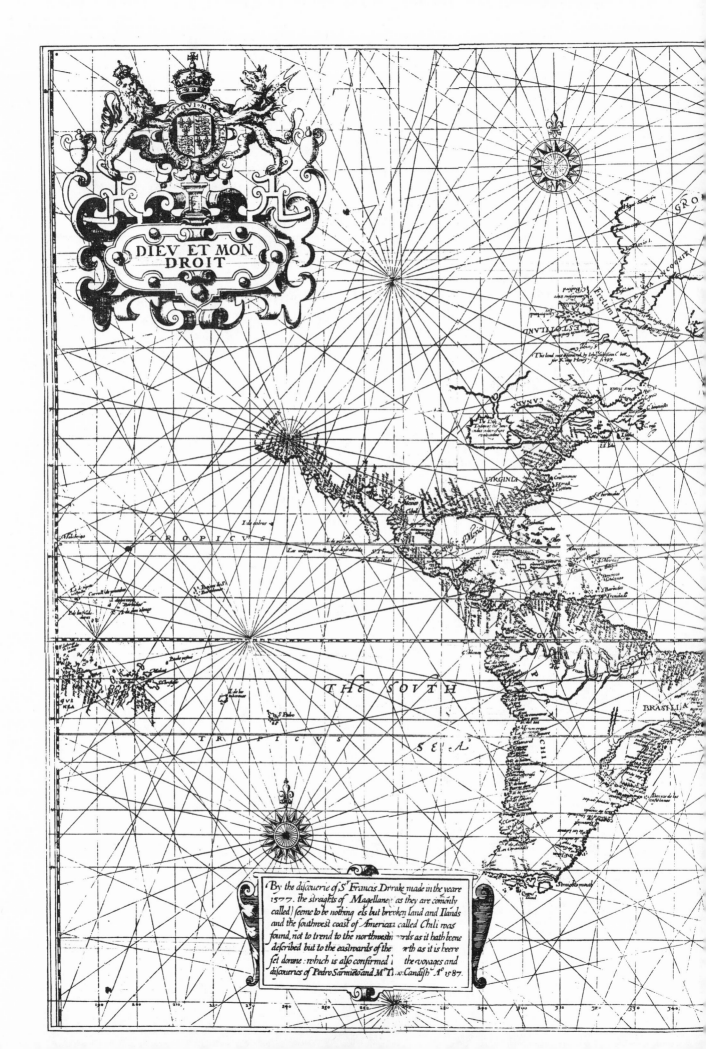

DIEV ET MON DROIT

GRO

FRETUM TRIUM

ESTOTILAND

The land was discovered by John Sebastian Cabot,
for K. Inge Henry 7. 1497.

CANADA

VIRGINIA

TROPICVS

THE SOVTH SEA

TROPICVS

BRASILIA

CHILI

Straights mouth

By the discouerie of Sr Francis Drake made in the yeare
1577. the straights of Magellane, as they are comonly
called) seeme to be nothing els but broken land and Ilands
and the southwest coast of America called Chili was
found, not to trend to the northwestwards as it hath beene
described but to the eastwards of the north as it is heere
set donne: which is also confirmed by the voyages and
discoueries of Pedro Sarmiento and Mr Tho: Candish A° 1587.

It appeareth by the discouerie of Francis Gaulle
a Spaniard, in yeare 1584: that the sea betweene the west part of America and the east of Asia
(which hath bene ordinarily set out as a straight
and named in most maps the streight of Anian) is
aboue 1200 leagues wide at the latitude of 38 degr.
And that the distance betweene cape Mendocino and
cape California which many maps and seacharts
make to be 1200. or 1300 leagues is scarce so much as 600

EUROPA

NORWAY

Mare Caspium

SAMERCAND
BOGHAR

MAGORES

CHINA

IEZ TARTARI

Fagiam

NOVA

C. EMBU

CANCRI

CAPRICORNI

C. bona speranza

thou hast here, gentle reader, a true hydrographical description of so much of the world as hath
bene hitherto discouered, and is come to our knowledge: which we haue in such sort performed, y
places herein set downe, haue the same positions and distances that they haue in the globe, being ther-
in placed in same longitudes and latitudes which they haue in this chart, which by the ordinarie sea
chart can in no wise be performed. The way to finde the position or course from any place to
another herein described, differeth nothing from that which is vsed in the ordinarie sea cha-
But tofinde the distance: if both places haue the same latitude, see how many degrees of
meridian taken at that latitude are conteyned betweene the two places, for so many score
leagues is the distance. If they differ in latitude, see how many degrees of the meridian
taken about the midst of that difference are conteyned betweene them and so many score
leagues is the distance.

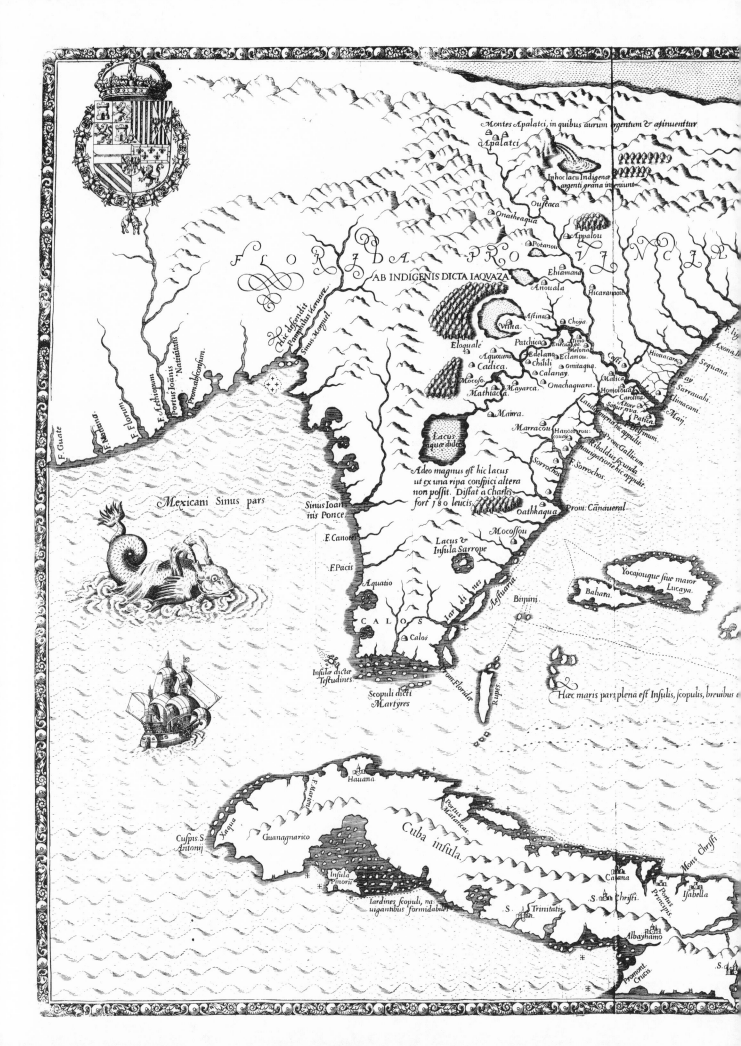

Montes Apalatci, in quibus aurum argentum & astinuentur

Apalatci

In hoc lacu Indigenæ argenti grana inueniunt

Oustaca

FLORIDA PROVINCIA
AB INDIGENIS DICTA IAQVAZA

Onatheaqua

Appalou

Potanou

Ehiamana

Anouala

Hicaramou

Vslita

Astina

Choya

Eloquale

Patchica

Vsima

Enecaqua pa

Melona

Aquouena

Cadica

Edelano

Eclanou

Chilili

Omitaqua

Mayarca

Onachaquara

Calanay

Hiouacara

Sequana

Mocoso

Mathiaca

Maira

Malica

Homoloua

Carolina

More

Satur.nua.

Patica

Sarrauahi

Climacani

Maij

Marracou

Hanocorou cou^y

Laudonnieris hic appulit

Prom. Gallicum

Ribaldus secunda nauigatione hic appulit

F. Sorrochos.

Prom: Cānaueral

Sorrochos

Lacus quæ dulcis

Adeo magnus est hic lacus ut ex una ripa conspici altera non possit. Distat a Charles fort 180 leucis.

Oathkaqua

Mexicani Sinus pars

Hic descendit Pamphilus Neruaez

Sinus Moquel

Sinus Ioannis Ponce

Sinus Ioannis Ponce

Mocossou

F. Guate

F. Medina

F. Florum

Portus Ioanis Natiuitatis

Prom abisconsum

F. Canore

F. Pacis

Aquatio

Lacus & Insula Sarrope

Icari di nes

Æstuaria

Bimini

Yocaiouque siue maior Lucaya.

Bahara.

F. Aethiopum

CALOS

Calos

Insulæ dictæ Testudines.

Prom Florida

Rupes.

Hæc maris pars plena est Insulis, scopulis, breuibus

Scopuli dicti Martyres

Hauana

F. Marien

Portus Matancas

Cuba insula.

Cuspis. S. Antonj

Xagua

Guanagnarico

Casana

Mons Christi

Insula Pinorū

Iardines scopuli, nauigantibus formidabiles

S. Christi

Portus Principis.

Isabella

S. Trinitatis.

Albayhamo

Promont. Crucis.

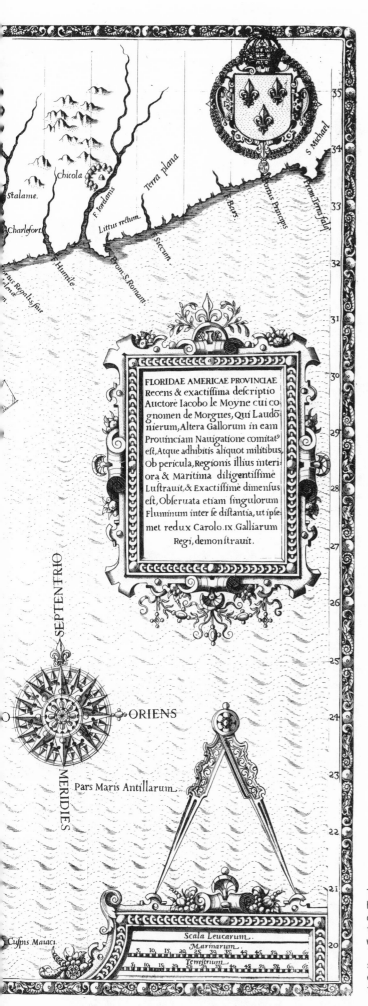

ORIENS

Pars Maris Antillarum.

Cufpis Maiaci.

FLORIDAE AMERICAE PROVINCIAE
Recens & exactiffima defcriptio
Auctore Iacobo le Moyne cui co-
gnomen de Morgues, Qui Laudô-
nierum, Altera Gallorum in eam
Prouinciam Nauigatione comitat°
eft, Atque adhibitis aliquot militibus,
Ob pericula, Regionis illius interi-
ora & Maritima diligentiffimè
Luftrauit, & Exactiffimè dimenfus
eft, Obferuata etiam fingulorum
Fluminum inter fe diftantia, utipfe-
met redux Carolo. ix Galliarum
Regi, demonftrauit.

Scala Leucarum.
Marinarum.
5   10   15   20   25   30   35   40   45   50   55
Terreftrium.
5   10   15   20   25   30   35   40   45   50   55   60   65

Theodore de Bry's map of Florida based on information
he received from le Moyne who he acknowledges in the
cartouche. This and his earlier map of Virginia were
the most accurate painstaking regional maps to appear
within a century of Columbus. Apparently he had been
listening to Hakluyt, however for Verrazano's sea
seems to be lurkring in the North. He subsequently
corrected this fault on a hemispheric map he derrived
from Peter Plancius.

In Louvain, in 1597, Cornelli Wytfliet started to get a grip on the problem. Ptolemy's world was not enough. That year he published *Descriptoins Potlemaicae Augmentum. . .* He divided the new hemisphere into eighteen portions including mythical Anian and Quivera and the supposed antarctic continent. In the process he contributed considerable information to the history of discovery.

Wytfliet's maps were small and they did not introduce much new information but he recognized the importance of separating an enormous space into convenient locales. His work was both inexpensive and popular going into seven editions through 1611. The title, "Augmenting Ptolemy" and his division of the New World into spaces resembling European maps set a precedent for 17th. Century cartographers. From then on increasingly detailed maps of America and its specific regions began to appear.

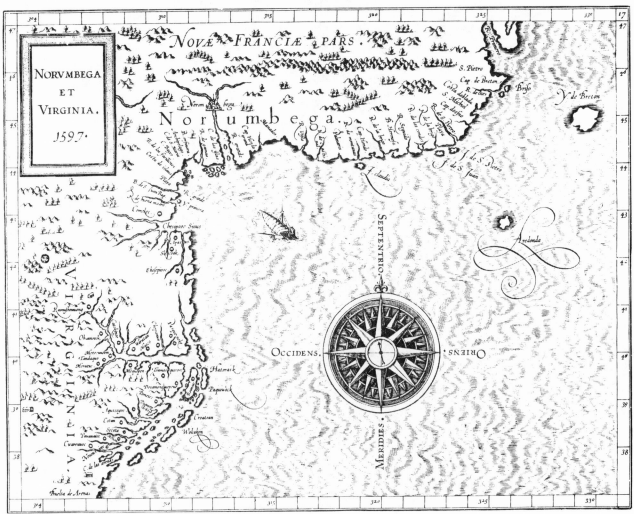

Cornelli Wytfliet's map of Virginia and Norumbrega.

Nature in or of the New World

UNTILL Vespucci the Greek *Oikoumene*, Latin, *Orbis Terrarum*, "Island of Earth," was considered the natural dwelling place of man. Everything of the Island of Earth or World, including man, was God's creation composed of four elements: earth, air, fire and water. Mela could postulate an antipodal *Orbis Alterius* but there was no reason to assign it any of the properties of the *Orbis Terrarum* and Christian philosophers, notably Augustine, insisted that if such a place existed it could not be populated.

Now imagine a traveller unprepared by *National Geographic*, travel brochures or color television visiting virgin tropics for the first time. Imagine falling onto a planet covered with rain forrest, filled with colorful birds and exotic animals where the climate stays balmy year round and gold is for the taking. It is hardly surprising first descriptions of America compare it with Elysium. Or another world.

Columbus was impressed, lauding the fertility and beauty of the land but welded as he was to a tripartite Earth compared new sights to what he knew or thought he knew from back home. If anything he was surprised at not finding ridiculous creatures out of Pliny's bestiary. But Columbus was an explorer, not a naturalist and though he does not minimize the quality of his discoveries or amazement, as when he thought the Orinoco flowed from the Mountain of Purgatory, he had already seen bizarre lands coasting Africa and refused to dwell on American nature to the extent of separating it from the Old World.

For that we can turn to Dr. Nicolo Scillacio who, though he never left Europe, insisted "I have not dared to alter anything beyond what I have heard or learned" when he penned *De Insulis Meridiani Atque Maris Nuper Inventis* in Pavia late in 1594 or early '95. This first independent account of Columbus is the most amusing.

"When Aurora, resplendent with her bright trappings ushered in the next morning they sailed with a gentle breeze for the Canaries," he says before going on to describe an amazing Caribbean. He admires Columbus for forbidding robbery and extortion of the natives but regrets he was unable to prevent them from trading gold for trinkets. As for his descriptions of islands what he says for one is good for all even though he does not know exactly where they are. "I would not be wrong in calling this island 'Felix'" he claims, "whether it be in Arabia or India." He identifies the Antilles with Ethiopia, Arabia, India and the Kingdom of Sheba imagining Columbus circumnavigated Africa sailing West.

He lauds the fertility of Hispaniola then attributes to it all the products of Asia, cinnamon, ginger, silk, etc., also rhubarb, "a useful remedy for all maladies."

The Indians "have easy going ways; all things held in common with no suspicion, no shameful, 'this is mine, this is your's.'" This sentence alone makes Scillacio the first published author to equate the newly discovered people with the Golden Age Noble Savage, an unprecedented marvel that glowed down through centuries.

"They live to an advanced age" and the women are modest, a touch lascivious, but do not let the Spaniards go too far. "They are sensuous of gesture, a little wanton in their gait; they play with us, and flirt rather boldly [this is modest?] so long as nothing improper occurs, for they get annoyed if you take the game too far." On the other hand every Spaniard grabbed himself five girls, "for the purpose of offspring I imagine." This brings him to a question that would soon bother Vespucci. If there is no private property why fight? Scillacio has the answer: The "uncontrolled lust for wives of the Indians was the cause of war and the incentive to hate."

Our author in addition to being a vicarious lecher was also apparently an incorrigible glutton. He dwells on delicious products of the islands and gourmet cannibals with the cruel habit of fattening up captured children, after castrating them like capons, before a feast.

A NEW WORLD

Vespucci was the first New World visitor, perhaps on the simple strength of entering a previously assumed impossible place, to appreciate and describe what he saw, but not without wonder. In his last letter to Medici he says:

> This land is very delightful, and covered with an infinite number of green trees and very big ones which never lose their foliage, and through the year yield the sweetest aromatic perfumes and produce an infinite variety of fruit, grateful to the taste and healthful for the body. And the fields produce herbs and flowers and many sweet and good roots, all of which are so marvelous that I fancied myself to be near the terrestrial paradise. And what can I say of the quantity of birds and their plumage and colors and songs, and of such variety and beauty? I wish not to enlarge on this, for I doubt it would be credible. How shall I enumerate the infinite variety of wild animals, lions, panthers, cats (not like those of Spain but of the antipodes), such as wolves, stags and monkeys of every sort, and many very big? And so many more animals we saw that I believed it would have been hard for them to have entered Noah's ark, [a tint of heresy here] such as wild pig, kid, deer, hare and rabbit.[1]

Vespucci, usually praised or damned for his navigational achievements, may have been read differently in his day. Sailing into a cut off region was hard to accept but his description of it was probably even more interesting. Doubts about the size of the Ark were chancy. Schoolmen-zoologists had already identified a finite collection of animals that might fit on the *Queen Elizabeth II* but Vespucci, in his original letters and the printed versions, faced other heretical problems as significant to the idea of a New World as antipodal discoveries. Nudity, first mentioned by Columbus, was a problem. According to the Bible Adam and Eve after the expulsion from the Garden covered their shame but nobody in Brazil wore clothes. Women took no particular care during pregnancy and were up and about as soon as giving birth. Heresy! *Genesis* specifically states women would suffer during childbirth, furthermore life would be short and full of toil but Vespucci (as well as Scillacio) finds a land so abundant labor is not necessary. More importantly both find the natives long lived. Vespucci discovered as many as four generations alive. Although Brazilians did not know how to count he asked one old codger to place a pebble on the ground for each full moon he observed and came up with a figure of 132 years.

There is no reason to attribute mastery of Amerindian languages to Vespucci or his understanding of his informant's accounting, but his information found ink and combined with the Mela geographical concept suggested a *very* different place.

THE EIGHT DECADES

While Columbus and Vespucci were probing the seas the first American history book was being written by a gosspiby monk in Spain, Peter Martyr d' Anghiera, who history remembers simply as Peter Martyr. And, since no early American history can be written without him, he best be introduced here. He was born in the 1440's in Arona, Italy. We know nothing of his early life or education but his writing demonstrates grounding in the classics. He was in Rome in 1478 where his mentor was Pomponius Laetus whose neo-paganism kept him a hair's breath from heresy. He left that city in 1487 for the Court of Spain where, save for a year long mission to Egypt on behalf of Ferdinand in 1501 - '02, he remained until his death in 1526. He served as liaison between their Catholic Majesties and the Roman curia, Isabella's chaplain and possibly tutor to her children.

The folio which appeared in 1530 entitled: *De Orbo Novo, Peter Martyis ab Angleria, Meriolanensis Proptrotarri...* consisted of eight "decades" of ten letters each Martyr had written to friends in Rome recanting news flowing from navigators. Already bitten by the exciting news rippling through the continent he wrote on May 17, 1493: "A few days after one Christopher Columbus, a Ligurian, returned from the western antipodes having with only three ships, penetrated to that province which he believed to be legendary; he brought substantial proofs in the shape of many precious things and particularly gold which is a natural product of those regions."

While Martyr initially accepted the discovery of the "Indies" at face value he failed to lose interest when Columbus came back in frustration and others were reading Vespucci like a cheap novel. For the rest of his life he watched the panorama unfold with realization of its importance.

Martyr is an unbiased observer content to report what he hears without need to justify, rationalize or prove. He is delighted to be part of an age that so greatly enlarged Christendom. He has a feel for the tasteful and eloquent despite some of the subject matter, describing an immense New World in all its variegated richness. For Martyr the new space is both a confirmation of classical legend and a promise of everything his age denied. He is glad to be in semi-barbarous Spain where news of discovery arrives regularly and abundantly. He can tremble at the idea of fearsome savages, admire multicolored parrots and handle gold nuggets, weighing as much as twenty ounces, drool at the sight of a pearl of more than forty ounces and keep in his house for a few days, and measure with awe, the enormous femur, desiccated with age, of a Mexican giant.

He questions Columbus, the Pinzons, Enciso, Oviedo, Sebastian Cabot and Colmenares and goes to the council of the Indies to hear boastful accounts of discoverers. He organizes veterans of the Indies to discuss theories of New World geography; he listens to reports of the miraculous phosphorescence of the firefly and shows the cardinal of Aragon the rotting corpse of a marsupial insisting he admire it from every angle. He derives equal pleasure from news he receives and his visitors' and correspondents' awe until even Pomponius Laetus, who years before discouraged him from leaving sophisticated Rome for uncultured Spain is tongue-tied. A sense of excitement and the conviction of a new era with a powerful impulse given to human progress is everywhere in his writing. Instance the beginning of the eighth book of his fifth decade: "Our ocean is more prolific than the Albanian sow, to which tradition assigns thirty pigs to a litter; but more liberal than a generous prince. Does it not each year disclose new lands, new nations and vast wealth?"

Although he never saw them Martyr's decades are peppered with salubrious descriptions of the Antilles. At one point he contrasts them with drafty palaces in Rome hinting the Pope might consider moving there.

As *Decades* and years roll on and Martyr is faced with barbarity, both Spanish and Amerind, but his fascination never ceases. His final decade speaks of "Those islands in the ocean brilliant as pearls and hidden since the beginning of the world from mankind." He then describes Jamaica as: "That remote and hidden part of the world where the Creator of everything placed the first man, after forming him from the slime of the earth, is called by sages of mosaic law and the New Testament the Terrestrial Paradise, because during the entire year there exists no difference between day and night; summer does not burn nor is winter severe; the air is salubrious, the springs clear, the rivers limpid. With all these blessings our beneficent mother nature has adorned my spouse."

Martyr, who we will hear more from later, may have laid down his pen for the last time regretting only that he left his spouse a widow and one gets a feeling he feared that without his record she might follow him into the grave.

GETTING ON WITH IT

In 1519 while Martyr was dashing off gushing epistles to friends in Rome a seventy-six leaf folio came off the press. The author was Martin Fernandez Enciso and the title: *Suma de Geographia*. Aside from Columbus' original letter it was the first book about America in Spanish. *The Sum of Geography* claims to describe the whole world but the title page promises particular attention to the Indies. It goes on to provide descriptions which made it a traveling companion of American voyagers for a generation.

Enciso came to America and practiced law with enough success to accumulate some wealth. Around 1510 he became the partner of the same slave stealing Alonso de Ojeda Vespucci sailed with. Together they founded Santa Maria del Darien on the Gulf of Uraba. For all its holy sounding name Santa Maria must have been the Dodge City of its day, hosting such illustrious rascals as Balboa, de Soto, Diego de Almagro, Pizarro, and conquistador-historians, Bernal Diaz del Castilio and Oviedo.

Even before discoveries in Mexico and Peru Enciso anticipates the wealth of the Indies and is pragmatic about exploitation. He describes abundant supplies of pearls and relates Indian tales of vast quantities of gold which, unfortunately he had not seen himself. (The Indians had already developed the ingenious trick of telling the Christians gold was abundant "a little further on" conveniently beyond their borders.) His fascination with exotic flora and fauna is less than others but the pragmatist describes what it edible and useful, potatoes, pineapples, maize, cotton and edible animals.

He hears of strange creatures, Amazons, Phoenixes and the Heyna that is female one year and male the next. Its eyes contain a stone that if placed under the tongue confers prophetic powers. He mentions the island of Meroe, below the equator, where there are monsters, men with heads like dogs and some without heads at all but is skeptical, remarking that little faith should be attached to those who venture beyond India. On one hand Enciso finds himself in the fabled Orient and draws descriptions from it but on the other he has not seen such marvels so prefers to rely on observation.

Pigafetta also hears of prodigies. There is an island inhabited solely by women (Martyr also mentions such islands but assumes they are convents of sorts). There are amazons who kill all men they encounter and are impregnated solely by wind. He mentions Brazilian longevity along with other familiar prodigies but prudently points out most were stories told to him and only a few marvels were based on personal observation.

Pigafetta's great contribution to the American bestiary was the Patagonian Giant, a subject which provided speculation for centuries. Vespucci also mentioned an encounter with giants but may not have been taken too seriously and the episode has been attributed to a delusion brought on by the malaria which finally killed him. Pigafetta's account stuck. He records: "One day we suddenly saw a man of the stature of a giant, standing naked on the water's edge, dancing, singing, and throwing dust on his head... He was so big that we only came up to his waist." The giant was soon joined by companions including giantesses loaded down like beasts of burden. The giantesses were shorter and fatter than their menfolk, with "teats half a yard long" and we can easily believe Pigafetta when he writes he found them rather ugly.

Magellan wanted to take a couple of the sturdiest specimens back to Spain to breed, but this turned out to be no simple matter. Two giants were eventually captured by a trick. They were loaded down with mirrors, knives and trinkets, and then offered a pair of splendid iron manacles, which they eyed greedily but their hands were full so the Spanish offered to place the manacles on their wrists to make them easier to carry. The unwary giants readily agreed and a moment later they were firmly chained. The Patagonians realizing they were tricked howled and snorted like bulls. The giantesses were luckier and managed to escape and one of their pursuers was killed with a poison arrow.

One of the prisoners on board the *San Antonio* (which deserted and returned to Spain under Esteban Gomez) died of heatstroke in the Atlantic. The other died of scurvy in the Pacific after kissing the cross and receiving baptism.

But he did not die in vain. Pigafetta struck up a friendship with the captured giant and got him to explain principals of native medicine and tenets of their religion which Pigafetta calls Devil worship. During long days at sea he got the giant to teach him the Patagonian language managing to accumulate a small vocabulary.

NEW SPAIN, A BRIEF NOTE

It was not until Cortez entered Mexico that Europeans found themselves in American territory that looked in anyway familiar. For the first time they experienced changing seasons, complete with snow covered mountains that resembled those at home. There were broad plains laid out for cultivation and neatly ordered cities and towns.

Cortez account of all this is contained in five letters which appeared between 1520 and 1526. Taken together they are the longest work penned by an American visitor so far. Although they enjoyed wide circulation (eighteen editions between 1520 and 1534) Cortez was not writing for the public but with an eye to justifying his actions and expenditures to Charles V and convince the latter he made a good bargain. Soldier and diplomat to the core Cortez (save for his interest in abundant minerals) does not have much of an eye for particularities of the land. He repeatedly compares cities and houses to those in Spain and his concern for terrain is largely confined to praising its fertility and suitability for European crops. He concludes: "Because of what I saw and

ABOVE LEFT: Title cut from an Antwerp, 1523, account of Cortez. ABOVE RIGHT: Title cut from an anonymous account of discovery of the Yucatan (1520). LOWER LEFT: Illustration from Cortez' first letter (Augsburg, 1522). A cactus from Ramusio.

The castellated cities in the three Cortez accounts demonstrate the problem Europeans had envisioning America. The Antwerp title cut is the most interesting. In addition to making Temistitan a European city the artist had seen pictures of Brazilians so he dresses Mexicans in their garb. About the only thing endemic to Mexico in the picture is the parrot. Ramusio was more fortunate having New World correspondents to provide sketches. He succeed in depicting several types of cactus.

understood regarding the similarity that all this land has to Spain, both in its fertility and its size and cold winters which it has, and many other things that made it similar thereto, it seemed to me that it was most suitable to give the same land the name New Spain of the Ocean Sea."

But the American experience was just beginning and there was still an immense amount of newness to account for.

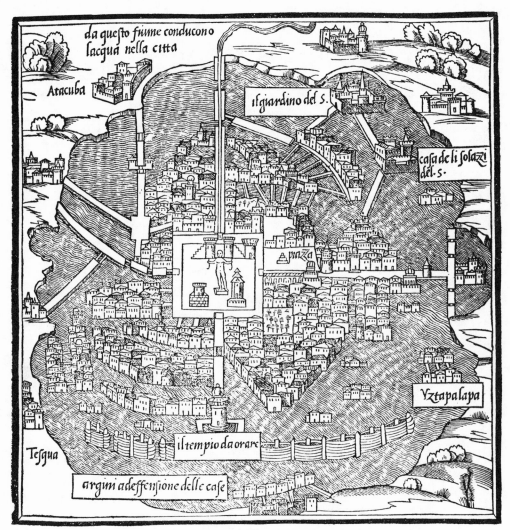

La gran citta di Temiſtitan.

Bordone's illustration of Temistitan from his ISOLARIO of 1528, based on Cortez' rendering. (See page 144.)

A CATALOGUE

Gonzalo Fernandes de Oviedo, like Martyr and las Casas, is one of those writers who became part of history, in Oviedo's case perhaps on the simple strength of longevity (b. 1478, d. 1557). He came to the New World in 1514 and spent much of the remainder of his life here in government positions.

In 1523 he returned to Spain, the forth crossing of an ocean he would traverse eight more times in the course of a turbulent career. As was his usual wont it was to grumble; this time about Pedrarias Davila, governor of Castile de Oro, who had made himself unpopular by, among other things, executing Balboa. In his audience with the emperor Oviedo may have mentioned his *Sumario de la Natural Historia de las Indias*, part of which he had completed but left in manuscript in Santo Domingo. Charles evidently expressed interest for Oviedo was granted leave to prepare a new history for the emperor to read during idle moments. The result was the first book devoted exclusively to the physical nature of America, *The Natural History of the West Indies*, which appeared in Toledo in 1526. Although short, Oviedo's work was the most objective account of nature in the Caribbean to date.

Often Oviedo conveys the impression he knows he is describing a plant or animal for the first time. He goes about his business in the most scientific manner available making him the best field naturalist America has seen so far. Two decades after Vespucci his amazement still bursts out in passages like: "Of all the things I have seen," he wrote of a bird with brilliant plumage, "this is the one which has most left me without hope of being able to describe in words." Of a strange tree he writes: "It needs to be painted by the hand of a Berruguete or some other excellent painter like him or by Leonardo da Vinci. . . famous painters I knew in Italy." To this he had the opportunity of introducing new American words to the language: canoe, hurricane maize and hammock among other descriptions of new animals and people.

Oviedo apparently had limited formal schooling but was self educated by, among other things, the above mentioned stint in Italy. This allowed him to observe directly and present data, usually without expressing opinions, a 180 degree turnabout from schoolmen with all the answers but none of the questions. His eyewitness descriptions saw wide circulation enabling home bound historians and armchair philosophers to embellish books with his information.

To begin at the end Oviedo concludes the *Natural History* with the remark:

> Two very notable things can be concluded regarding your Majesty's West Indies. [This is the first time I have seen *West* Indies in print, but from the rest of the paragraph one gathers Oviedo believed what the maps told him. He was in the westernmost Indies of antiquity rather than being separated from them by a third of the world.] One is the shortness of the route of the South Sea for commerce with the Spice Islands, and the innumerable riches of the provinces and dominions there. . . The other is to consider the great treasure that has entered Castile because of these Indies and continues to come in every day, and it is hoped this will continue, gold pearls and other things not known or enjoyed by other nations but only by your own subjects.[2]

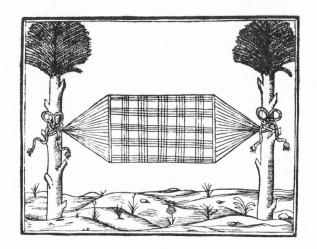

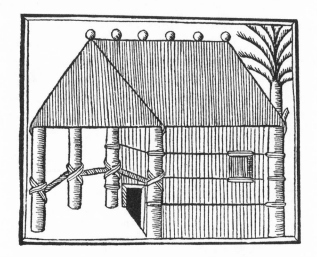

Woodcuts from Oviedo's HISTORIA of 1547.
At the top Indians are planting sweet
potatoes. Beneath are a hammock and an
Indian house. At bottom he tries to
draw an iguana and a canoe.

Oviedo starts with an account of Hispaniola's fecundity regretting it has not been more cultivated because adventurers continue to leave for new lands. This brings him to natural products of the Antilles and Tierra Firme. He explains food and manner of eating on the Main are much as they are in the islands although there are many more species of fruits and flesh.

All works describing the new land lump natives into the natural history pot and although we are trying to separate the two we can let a few of Oviedo's descriptions slip in here. The Indians along the Main he says: "eat human flesh; they are filthy, cruel and they are also sodomites. They shoot arrows poisoned with an herb so poisonous that it is miraculous if a man wounded by such an arrow does not die. Usually the wounded man dies in delirium, chewing his own flesh and biting the earth."

He describes Indian customs and superstitions with occasional amusement. For instance: "Since. . . they have no alphabet. . . I should say just how frightened they are of ours. . . when some Christian sends a message by an Indian to some other person. . . the Indians are astonished to see that at the other place the letter means what the Christian who sent it wants it to mean. Consequently the Indians carry messages with much respect and care for they believe that the letters will be able to tell what the messenger did along the way."

Occasionally, fascinated with their apparent stupidity, he looses his scientific bent explaining: "Their skulls are four times thicker than those of Christians. And so when one wages war with them and comes to hand to hand fighting, one must be very careful not to hit them on the head with the sword, because I have seen many swords broken in this fashion. In addition to being thick their skulls are very strong."

From Indians he passes to flora and fauna, making his remark about regretting the absence of Italian painters to record such marvels. He does his best to rectify the defect but drawing was not his metier. His original sketches (surviving in the Huntington Library) for the blocks reproduced here are cruder than the printed versions.

Oviedo catalogues lions, tigers, alligators, armadillos and a host of other creatures with the eye of a discoverer. His description of a sloth reminds me of my own fascination the first time I saw one:

> The sloth is the stupidest animal that can be found in the world, and is so awkward and slow in movement that it would require a whole day to go fifty paces. The first Christians to see this animal remember that in Spain we are accustomed to call a Negro "John White" - the saying to be taken in reverse. . . they give it a reverse name, calling it "swift" because it is very slow. . . Often these animals are captured in trees. . . hanging upside down with long claws. . . Sometimes the Christians. . . take them home and keep them. Even then the sloth will not move faster even if they are threatened or prodded. If one comes to a tree, it will climb to the top branches and remain there eight or ten or twenty days. No one can find out what this animal eats. I had one in my home and from my observation I have come to believe that this animal lives on air. I have never seen such an ugly animal or one that is more useless.[3]

mamei.   *guaiaua.*   *guanauana.*   *platano.*

TOP LEFT: A big tree with three roots. TOP
RIGHT: An Indian woman carrying a platinin
leaf; both from Ramusio who got his drawings
from Oviedo. CENTER: New World trees from
Benzoni's history. LEFT: A parrot from
Thevet's SINGULARITEZ...

Birds of all sorts, insects and vegetables, enormous trees (one of such girth sixteen men joining hands can barely embrace its trunk) all come under his scrutiny. He describes gold mines and the possibility of a strait between the North and South Seas.

If Peter Martyr saw the New World as a rediscovery of a classical age Oviedo saw it as completing the science of the Old by giving it back something it had lost. Oviedo rediscovers among Amerinds everything he knew about the earliest epochs of the world as if barbarian Scythians, Thracians, Germans and Tartars had not changed but gotten frozen in time and America. In this period of geographical uncertainty the linkage of twenty centuries and one hundred degrees of longitude produced very curious results.

In the course of Oviedo's comparisons he enters into a sort of dialogue with Pliny. At the beginning of his larger work, *The General and Natural History* of 1535 - 1557 he says that he is not, like Pliny, extracting "from two million volumes read, but from two million labors and deprivations and dangers in the twenty-two years I have been observing and experiencing these things in person." Our naturalist claims he does not need the ancient author to describe things he sees every day then finds Pliny describing Indian canoes and maize. Indian burial rites are compared with those of the ancient Persians and their witch doctors become ancient soothsayers. Indian tatoos remind him (along with Theodore de Bry at century's end) of the barbaric Britons and the promiscuity of native women can only be compared with that of the Thracians. And, in describing enormous West Indian turtles, Oviedo says, "should anyone doubt what I have said. . . let him consult Pliny." In other words monsters and customs of old confirm the verisimilitude of the new while Oviedo's observations reaffirm ancient authority.

The *Natural History* appeared in 1526 with five crude woodcuts. Both text and prints (for all their crudity) are the first deliberate attempt to describe nature in the New World and probably represent Oviedo at his most influential. After him descriptions of American flora and fauna, often illustrated, began appearing in accounts of the hemisphere, Gomora and Ramusio for instance. New World products began to show up in generalized herbals and Acosta mentions King Philip, at a cost of more than 60,000 ducats, commissioning Dr. Francisco Hernandez to have paintings made of all plants in the Indies and the number came of over 1,200.

Although our primary interest in swordsman-historian Cieza will be ethnolology this astute observer, writing at mid-century, is too interesting to ignore here. Pedro Cieza de Leon came to America "at so tender an age I had barely rounded out thirteen years." Seven years later he began keeping a journal because "there came over me a great desire to relate the admirable things that have existed and much of what I have written I have seen with my own eyes." This journal eventually ran to some 8,000 sheets of foolscap much of which traveled in his saddle bags even into battle. After seventeen years in the Indies he returned to Spain in 1550 to prepare his manuscripts for publication but only the *Parte Primera de la Cronica del Peru* (1553) came off the press during his lifetime.

One quality of American nature which was driving schoolmen into frenzies of distraction was not only the habitability but the fecundity of the Torrid Zone or worse the fact that you could actually freeze to death in Peru which lies right on it. Cieza accepts this calmly easily understanding that parts of the equatorial zone are cold because of altitude but he still finds it remarkable to live in a region where climates differ so widely. He offers no explanation simply saying, "This I state because of what I have seen, nor I understand more than I have said."

Cieza covered more territory than Oviedo (notably in Peru) and exceeds him in clarity of vision. He discusses the relative fertility of various regions and their suitability for different crops. Native crops are mentioned including Cocoa and Cocaine from which fortunes were already being made. He gives the first good descriptions of lamas, pumas, tapirs, etc. and snakes the size of logs "that despite their size and ferocious appearance even if one sits on them they do no harm." He says some Indians in Cuzco told him a story, "I shall set down here, because they assured me it was true." According to the Indians an old witch told the Inca she could enchant these monsters which had previously been venomous. The Inca gave her permission to cast her spells. "Saying certain words she changed them from the fierce wild creatures they were to the harmless, inoffensive things they now are. This may be one of their fictions or fables; but the fact remains that these snakes, for all they are so large, do no harm."

Since he is writing about the Golden Kingdom he has plenty to say on the subject making some interesting moral judgements in the process:

> In view of the great wealth we have seen in these regions,
> we can well believe what the Incas were said to posses is true.
> I am of the opinion...there is no kingdom in the world so rich
> in precious ores...And as gold is washed from the rivers...and
> silver is found in the mountains it all went to a single Inca,
> he could hold and possess so much wealth it amazed me that
> the whole city of Cuzco and its temples were not of solid gold.
> For what impoverishes princes and keeps them stripped of
> money is war as we have a patent example in what the Emper-
> or expended for this purpose from the year he was crowned
> until now. Possessing more silver and gold than any king of
> Spain from Don Rodrigo to himself, none of them were as
> hard up as His Majesty, [Charles V, and Cieza speaks true]
> and if he had no wars and remained in Spain, all Spain would
> be as full of treasure as Peru in the days of its Incas.[4]

Now Cieza lets specie poor Europe have it with both barrels:

> Accumulating such a fortune, and with the heir being
> obliged to leave the possessions of his predecessor untouched...
> not only in a single place but in many, especially the capitals
> of provinces, where there were many gold and silversmiths
> engaged in the manufacture of these objects. In their palaces
> and lodgings there were bars of these metals, and their clothes
> were covered with ornaments of silver, and emeralds and tur-
> quoise, and other precious stones of great value. And for their
> wives there was even greater luxury in their adornment and...
> their litters were all encrusted with silver and gold and
> jewels. Aside from this, they had a vast quantity of ingots of
> gold and unwrought silver...and still more of these treasures...
> Even their drums and chairs and musical instruments were of
> this metal. And to glorify their state, as if all this I have
> described were not enough, it was a law that none of the gold
> or silver brought into Cuzco could be removed, under penalty
> of death...With this law, and so much coming in and none
> going out, there was such an amount that if, when the
> Spaniards entered, they had behaved differently and had not
> so quickly displayed their cruelty by putting Atahualpa to
> death, I do not know how many ships would be needed to car-
> ry back to Spain the vast treasures lost in the bowels of the
> earth, where they will remain, for those who buried them are
> now dead.[5]

Cieza's descriptions of the very real prodigies of Peru were enough to
astound the 16th. Century reader just as they fascinate the 20th. Century visitor
but being a tall tail affectionado I don't want to leave him with a single
fantastic yarn. Speaking of Brazil he says:

> They say that in most of these places (although I have not seen
> them) there are large monkeys that live in the trees, and that, at
> the instigation of the Devil, who is always seeking ways to make
> men commit more and greater sins, these people cohabit with
> them; and they say that some of them bring forth monsters whose
> heads and private parts are like those of men; and the hands and
> feet are like those of monkeys. They are, it is said, small of size
> and monstrously shaped and covered with hair. In a word, they
> would seem to resemble (if it is true that they exist) their father
> the Devil.

Cieza's usual incredulity at such nonsense may have slipped a bit there but
intercourse with the Devil was not confined to America. During this period of
witchcraft delusion European women were tortured into admitting to it every
day. And he redeems himself a little with some amusing moralizing: "I do not
affirm this, but at the same time I know that many men of understanding and
reason, who know there is God in Heaven, and Hell, have left their wives and
befouled themselves with mules, bitches, mares and other animals which it
grieves me to state, so this may be true."[6]

Now a point, so brilliantly discussed by Antonello Gerbi, needs to be made, first in relation to American nature and latter in reference to the Indians. Oviedo's dialogue with Pliny kept American prodigies in a European framework. But for many everything was just too new and too fabulous. At the end of the century Juan de Cardenas wrote in his *Problemas y secretos maravillosos de las Indias*: "In the Indies everything is portentous, everything is surprising, everything is distinct and on a larger scale than that of the Old World." A half century later this awestruck rapture comes through the Castellan prose of Antonio de Leon Pinelo who devoted the forth book of *Paraiso en el Muevo Mundo* (1656) to the "strange," animals, trees spices minerals, including gold, with "its strange abundance in the Indies," and to the richness in gold, silver, and pearls, a "strange and portentous" product of the Indies.[7]

Most writers, as if they were struggling to overcome their own heretical doubts insisted America was not "New" but only newly found but there were some exceptions. Several writers (Gomora for instance) commented on Peruvian or Canadian legends of floods speculating on whether or not it was the universal deluge. John Donne referred to America as "That unripe side of Earth" that produced men naked like Adam before he ate the Apple and Samuel Daniel's referred to the "yet unformed Occident" in his *Musophilos; containing a General Defense of Learning* (1599). In the next century Francis Bacon in his *New Atlantis* and *Of Vicissitudes of Things* speculated Atlantis had not been destroyed by earthquake but a flood which also engulfed America and in the former essay made the curious remark "So as marvel you not at the thin population of America, nor at the rudeness and ignorance of the people; for you must account your inhabitants of America as a young people, a thousand years younger than the rest of the world because a thousand years passed between the universal flood and their particular inundation." In 1650 Thomas Thorowgood included an obtuse chapter on "Whether America be a New World or Part of the old" in his *Jews in America* but concluded there was only one world, the one mentioned in *Genesis* and "The whole world is the one house of all."

One writer cashing in on all this newness was Dr. Nicholas Monardes whose two volume *Historia Medicinal. . .* appeared at Seville in 1569 and was expanded to three in 1574. He reported sufficient trial of American plants, animals, medical stones and other natural pharmacopoeia that at last a whole array of medicines were available to heal Europe of its manifold diseases. Monardes saw translation into several languages including English. This last was done by John Frampton in 1577 and bore the title: *Joyfull Newes out of the Newe Founde World*. According to Frampton the work treats "of the singular and rare vertues of certaine Herbes, Trees, Oyles, Plantes, Stones and Drugges of the Weste Indias" which yield "wonderful cures of sundrie great diseases that otherwise thean by these remedies thei were incurable."

Amine and copall, a gum called tacamahaca, another known as caranna, the oil of the fig tree of hell, bitumen, liquid amber, balsam, guaiacan, the China root, "sarcaparaillia," the bloodstone, pepper, mechoacan, tobacco, and other

GOSSIPIVM.

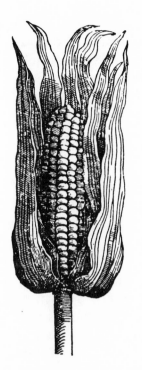

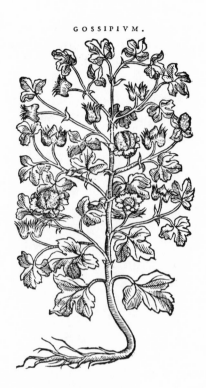

𝕰ſtas ſuertes de yeruas como mas princi-
pales, y en Eſpaña no conoctdas, entre mucbas otras de quien le baze men,
cion eneſta biſtoria ſe ponen aqui:po:que el lectoz ſepa y conoxca la manera
de cada vna dellas: y po:que en ſus lugares ꝓpꝛios do fuera razon ponc
llas, no ſe pudieron poncr.

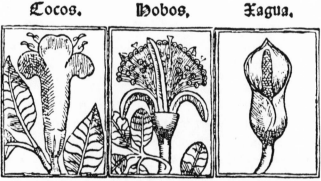

TOP, LEFT TO RIGHT: The oldest printed picture
of an ear of maize from Ramusio. The cotton
plant from P. A. Mattheoli's COMPENDIUM DE
PLANTIS... (Venice, 1571). Stalks of American
corn from Rembrant Dodoens' FRUMENTORUM LEG-
UMINUM... (Antwerp, 1566).

BENEATH: New World plants and a buffalo from
Gomora.

New World discoveries will obviously end the all the ills flesh is heir to. Take for example sassafras, which "comforteth the Liver and Stomacke and doth disopilate," is good for headaches, "griefes of the breast" and of the stomach, casts out "gravell and stones," provokes urine, "taketh awaie mervelouslie" toothaches, is excellent for gout and "evill of the Joyntes. . . maketh a man go to stoole," and "dooeth great profite" in the evil of women. In short it is:"for all manner of disease, without making exception of any, And beying sicke of any manner of evill which commeth into them [the Spaniards], sharpe, or large, hot, or colde, greevous or otherwise, they doe cure all with one manner of fashion and they heale all with one manner of water, without makyth any difference, and the best is that all be healed, and of this they have so much trust, that they feare not the evilles which are present nor have any care of them that be to come, and so they have it for a universal remedy. . . "[8]

Monardes also recognizes various diseases originating in America but he, or Frampton for him, assures the reader these are also curable by these new drugs.

It is not my intent to discuss the real effect of New World herbs and spices on disease. Monardes relied heavily on the doctrine of correspondences (the association of a particular star with a particular stone with a particular part of the body, etc. which is most obvious today in astrology), so one wonders just how effective his cures could be. But for all his medievalism Monardes' work provided a powerful impulse to experimentation. Acosta mentions him and in the process acknowledges the effectiveness of certain Indian medical practices. He predicts America will yield important pharmaceutical products which will "be of no less efficiency than the drugs that come from the East."

ENGLAND AND FRANCE

Through translation Spanish experience became the Americana the 16th. Century, for the simple reason that for most of the period they were the only ones on the scene. This obviously presented a rather lopsided view of the hemisphere, for what was true of part was presumably true of all. And, as far as American natural history was concerned, the most mentioned product was gold.

Cartier was the first to make the mistake. When he sailed from Saint Malo in 1534 he carried a commission to "make a voyage from this kingdom to 'Terres Neufves' to discover certain islands and countries where there is said to be found a vast quantity of gold and other rich things." Less than a month later he was in Labrador of which he said "I am inclined to regard this land as the one God gave to Cain." Entering the St. Lawrence he became more enthusiastic. Ramusio, the first to print an account of this voyage, says he found Spruce trees tall enough to mast a ship of three hundred tons, a temperate climate and rich soil, "fairest you could see anywhere." There were beautiful flowers and waters teeming with Salmon.

It was here the Fur Trade started, introducing the most important natural treasure of early North America. Cartier encountered a party of Indians who brought them strips of broiled seal. The French responded with gifts of hatchets, knives, paternoster beads *et al*. This started a brisk trade in pelts and whatever else the French wanted. Men and women came freely to the sailors trading furs they wore to retire trinket laden but mother naked.

On his second voyage Cartier visited Hochelaga and (naturally) asked if there was gold nearby. Indians responded by touching his silver whistle chain and a sailor's gold handled dagger, pointing Northwest and crying "Saguenay! Saguenay!" Having sailed or rowed almost a thousand miles from open sea Cartier had come far enough for one voyage but when as he sailed back to Quebec he thought he was on to something.

From this expedition we pick up bits of North American natural history. Cartier's *Brief Recit. . .* printed ten years later contains the first mention of tobacco and clay pipes in North America. According to the Indians "it keeps them warm and in good health, and never go abroad without it." Frenchmen tried a few drags but found the smoke too hot to bear, "like powdered pepper." I wonder whether some early references to tobacco were in fact marijuana but it is probably a moot point. As anyone who tried to quit smoking knows the stuff grows on you and by 1600 so much was flowing into Europe James I found it necessary to write his famous *Counterblaste*, the first anti-smoking campaign.

Another interesting pharmacy item was introduced while the French fleet lay frozen under the rock of Quebec. The *Brief Recit* says scurvy broke out, first among the Hurons, then the French. Cartier, suspicious of his native hosts at Stadcona (Quebec) put up a brave front. Although he had 110 men "not ten were well enough to help the others, a thing pitiful to see." Cartier kept his healthy men making noise behind his palisades as if scores were carousing and brawling. Then "God in His holy grace took pity on us and sent us knowledge of a remedy," after Cartier vowed to make a pilgrimage to Rocomadour and staged a service of intercession to Our Lady.

Domagaya, son of Donnaconna, chief of the Indians settled around Quebec, told Cartier the disease could be healed with juice concocted from a species of the common arborvitae. He sent two women with Cartier to gather branches and "showed us how grind the bark and boil it in water then drink the potion every other day and apply the residue as a poultice to swollen and infected legs." Within a few days everyone who drank the magic potion was cured, even some who had suffered syphilis for years claimed they were cured of that! Cartier remarked that all the doctors of Louvain and Montpellier with all the drugs of Alexandria "could not have done as much in a year as this tree did in a week."

But the subject on Cartier's mind was gold and although his *Brief Recit. . .* dwells on the abundance of the country he had not yet found it. Failing to realize myth making was part of Amerind culture and that aborigines tend to be yes men, considering "yes you are going in the right direction" more polite than telling someone he has made a mistake Cartier asked Donnaconna about Saguenay. And Donnaconna told him all about it. He had been there himself and seen immense quantities of gold, rubies and other valuable things. The people were white as Frenchmen and went about clothed in woolens. The captain even swallowed a yarn about a race of uniped pygmies and another people with no anus, hence subsisted on liquids they could void as urine.

Donnaconna paid heavily for his fun. Cartier decided to kidnap him so he could tell King Francis convincingly about the wonders of Saguenay. During a ceremonial cross raising several well rehearsed sailors seized the chief, his two sons and two leading subjects and sailed off to France with them.

All the Hurons Cartier carried to France died within a relatively short time but Donnaconna did enjoy four years of glorious life as publicity agent for the golden Kingdom of Saguenay. While Francis fretted about all that lucre flowing into Seville Donnaconna was regaling him with stories of the wonderful kingdom, just North of his own. Noting the king's interest in spices he added clove, nutmeg and pepper to the products of this chilly region besides repeating stories of unipeds and anus-less people and adding a few more prodigies which the king loved to repeat to his friends. For instance Saguenay grew oranges and pomegranates and nourished a race with wings instead of arms and flew from tree to tree like bats. To one skeptic the king testily replied that Donnaconna's stories never varied and, under pain of death for blasphemy, had sworn to their truth before a notary.

The result was a new project. This time it would be a permanent colony, hopefully in downtown Saguenay. According to the official and rather hypocritical statement the colony would be for the purpose of: "Establish[ing] the Christian faith in a savage land far from France... even though [the king] knew full well no gold or silver mines were to be found there, nor any other gains save the conquest of souls for God to deliver them from the tyranny of the infernal Demon, to whom they sacrifice even their children."

This was in 1538 after Francis had been listening to Donnaconna for over two years. I could needlessly add Hurons did not practice human sacrifice but the piety of it all is so beautiful, and given the current vagueness about America human sacrifice in Canada was credible enough. What was true for one part was true for all.

1541 saw Cartier camped at the mouth of the Ottawa River which Donnaconna said led to Saguenay. There he set his men about collecting quartz (diamonds) and iron pyrites (gold). After another miserable winter he raised camp in June of 1542 and sailed back to France with eleven barrels of "gold," a basket of "precious stones such as rubies and diamonds" and seven barrels of "silver" all of which Paris assayers promptly pronounced worthless. Cartier was through and disgusted but Saguenay, stayed on the map for the next century as a will of the wisp Peru. Finally it was reduced to an insignificant river.

While Cartier was gathering rocks in Canada de Soto was wandering around the gulf states also looking for a new Peru. His contribution to the myth of North American gold can be confined to a single phrase. The Indians, always wishing Soto on their enemies, told him gold "was just a little further on." This did not stop the Gentleman of Elvas in his relation of de Soto's fiasco from including a curious poem on the title page of his book by "Fernando da Silveira, Senhor da Serdas, great poet and very illustrious, respecting the Material of this Book and in praise of the author."

> He who would see the New World,
> The Golden Pole, the second,*
> Achievements great, and wars,
> And such things attempted
> As alarm gives pleasure,
> Stike terror and lend delight;
> Where nothing fabulous is told,
> All worthy of being esteemed,
> Read, considered, used.

> *We inhabit the Northern Artic Pole, and that people inhabit the Southern Antarctic Pole. Golden Pole is used because that region is rich.

Although I have never seen a poem with an asterisk in it before I will reserve judgement on Silveira's poetry but his geography stinks.

The English were the next to be bitten by the goldbug. For the first three quarters of the century after having made two attempts to sail past it to Cathay they totally forgot about it. Then in 1576 in the course of a third attempt to force a passage everything changed. Martin Frobisher having sailed about three quarters up the bay that bears his name was confident he had finally found the strait but his crew, reduced to thirteen men and boys, was exhausted so he turned for home. Before doing so however he put men ashore to gather tokens of possession. One of these happened to be a piece of iron pyrites, another was an Eskimo.

October, 1576 saw Frobisher sailing up the Thames to dock at London where his sailors were "joyfully received with the great admiration of the people, bringing with them their strange man and his bote, which was such a wonder unto the whole city and the rest of the realm that heard of yt."

Frobisher after announcing he had "discovered the passage to the South Sea" submitted his "peace of blacke stone" to assayers who pronounced it worthless. However an Italian alchemist(?) named Angelo insisted it was gold ore and after three trials produced a speck of gold dust. To skeptical Michael Lok, inquiring how he found gold after others had found none Angelo replied, "nature needs a little coaxing." A German mineralogist named Schultz seconded Angelo's opinion. Whatever happened, salting by Angelo himself, bribery, who knows? The English were about to experience what the French had four decades earlier. News quickly spread Frobisher had discovered a mine.

Optimism about gold and the likelihood that Frobisher's "strait" would lead to China ran high. The result was a royally chartered Company of Cathay with

Frobisher appointed "High Admiral of all seas and waters, countries, lands and isles as well of Cathay as of all other places of new discovery" - quite a position.

In May 1577 Frobisher returned to Canada where he loaded 200 tons of worthless rock into three ships which he duly returned to London and turned over to German assayers hired by the company. Although the assayers seemed to be taking their time confidence remained undimmed. Dionysius Settle by way of explaining the "ore" contained gold said he could find no hurtful creeping beasts around Baffin Island "except some spiders (which as many affirme, are signes of great store of gold)." And as usual the natives made "signes of certaine people" living somewhere else "that wear bright plates of gold in their foreheads, and other places of their bodies."

The following spring Frobisher sailed again, this time with a fleet of fifteen ships to spend the summer filling his hulls with a walloping 1350 tons of gold. Remembering how those Paris assayers thirty-five years before had unhesitatingly shown up Cartier's worthless gold and diamonds one wonders whether those German assayers were corrupt or just plain stupid. They fiddled around for five years trying to turn pyrites into gold. Finally the company went broke and Camden says in his *Annals*: "when neither gold silver nor any other metall could be drawne [from the rocks] we saw them throwne away to repayve the highways." Frobisher, also broke, went back to his old trade - piracy.

But for a while Frobisher's apparent success sparked a blaze of interest in America. Dionysius Settle, a crew member on the second voyage, rushed into print as soon as he got home with *A True Report of the Last Voyage into the West and Northwest Regions. . .* That started the presses rolling. His little work of twenty-four leaves went through two printings in 1577. The same year Richard Willis got out his expanded edition of Eden's *Decades* (the place where he said "all Christians Jewes, Turkes, Moores, Infidels and Barbares be this day in love with Geographie"). George Best wrote an eyewitness account of all three voyages: *A True Discourse of the Late Voyages of Discovery. . .* in 1578. Thomas Ellis, also part of the third expedition, produced *A True Report of the Third and Last Voyage into Meta Incognita. . .* that same year.

Frobisher became a sort of 16th. Century pop star. Stay at home writers had a field day extolling him in prose and verse. But Frobisher could have been a flash in the pan, effective as Cabot and Rut, had not his "gold" and "passage" opened publishers' doors to others. Now the English tide of discovery flowed on a sea of ink. Two authors who rode on Frobisher's coattails were the above

George Best's narwhal from his TRUE DISCOURSE...

Eskimos hunting sea birds, probably after a drawing by John White, from a Nurenberg edition of Settle (1580).

mentioned John Frampton and Thomas Nicholas. Neither had any academic pretensions; they learned Spanish for the practical reason they had lived in Spain (and incidentally both had been imprisoned by the Inquisition) and knew the wealth of the Indies. Till Frobisher Britain had exactly one book on America penned by an Englishman who had been there, *A True Declaration of the Troublesome Voyage. . . To the Parties of Guynea and the West Indies* by John Hawkins.

During the period of Frobisher euphoria Nicholas found a new career. In 1577, when the passage to China looked like a reality he got out a little octavo of six leaves entitled: *The Strange and marvelous Newes late come from the Kingdom of Chyna.* A more important work came the next year, a loose translation of Gomora bearing the title: *The Pleasant History of the Conquest of the Weast India, Now called New Spayne, achieved by the worthy Prince Hernando Cortes, Marques of the Valley of Huaxacac, most delectable to reade: Translated out of the Spanish tongue by T.N.* In his dedication Nicholas makes no bones about Frobisher's "success" encouraging him to undertake the project. He says it was previously believed New World treasure was confined to southern regions but:

> it is novve approued by the venterous trauellour and vvorthy
> captaine Martin Frobisher...that the same golden mettall
> dothe also lie incorporate in the bovvelles of the Norvveast
> parties, enuironned vvith admirable Tovvers, Pillers and
> Pynacles, of Rockes, Stone, and Ise, possessed of a people
> bothe straunge, & rare in shape, attire and luying, yea suche
> a Countrey and people, as all Europe had forsaken and made

no account of, except our moste gratious Queene and hir subjectes, vvhome vudoubtedly God hath appoynted, not onely to be supreme Princess ouer them, but also to be a meane that the name of Christ may be knovven vunto this Heathenish and Sauage generation. 9

Nicholas now sets out to give the English some account of what they can expect. He nowhere mentions Gomora but says he got the story from an "ancient gentleman" he met on the road from Toledo to Old Castile. It must have been a long trip because the small format octavo runs to 405 pages plus dedication and index. A goodly part of those pages are given over to the subject on everybody's mind. Thus by page twelve Nicholas is providing a three page inventory of the treasure Grijalva accumulated on the Yucatan with a half page list of the junk he traded for it. Later come several more pages inventorying gifts Montezuma presented to Cortez and fulsome descriptions of the wealth of Templistan. Nicholas cavalierly shortens Gomora's original, taking little interest in natural phenomenon or things that happened to Cortez if they occurred remote from the capital. Of course the battles are too dramatic to ignore as are gristly descriptions of Aztec religion so there is plenty of room for spine tingling gore. Interestingly Nicholas, who had no reason to love the Spanish, does not wallow in anti-Spanish polemic and by selecting Gomora - Cortez' votary - for translation locks himself into admiration for Cortez. But Gomora's well written *Conquista. . .* was a natural choice. Unlike Martyr and Cortez himself Gomora had an opportunity to organize a cohesive exciting story instead of reporting events as they happened.

The second part of the thinges that
☞ Of a certayne kinde of Barley.

THE

Pleafant Hiftorie of the
Conqueft of the VVeaft India,
now called new Spayne,

Atchieued by the vvorthy Prince
Hernande Cortes Marques of the valley of
*Huaxacac,*moft delectable to Reade :
Tranflated out of the Spa-
niſhe tongue, by T . N.
Anno.1 5 7 8.

¶ Imprinted at London by
Henry Bynneman.

LEFT: A stalk of barely
from Frampton's JOYFULL
NEWES...

RIGHT: Nicholas' title
page.

Having given Englishmen their first opportunity to read about Mexico fifty-five years after the conquest Nicholas went on, in 1581, to give them their first view of Peru. That year saw publication of a quarto titled: *The strange and delectable History of the Discouerie and Conquest of the Prouinces of Peru. . . And of the notable things which were found: and also the bloudie Ciuill Warres which there happened. . . Written in foure bookes by Augustine Sarate. . . And also of the riche Mines of Potosi. Translated out of the Spanish by T. Nicholas.* That Nicholas saw fit to append a description of Potosi to his translation of Zarate gives a pretty good idea of what the book was all about. More treasure.

Frobisher's "gold" and Nicholas' sugar plum visions of specie brought out the goldbugs. Given the paucity of information about North America as late as the Frobisher period it is not amazing how confidently colonial propaganda depicted the wealth of the continent. Humphrey Gilbert was so certain he would discover gold in Newfoundland he promised to ask no man for a penny to finance an expedition and Sir George Peckham's *True Report. . .* lists as probable products of the same land gold, silver, crystal, copper, lead, tin, turquoise, rubies, pearls, marble and jasper. Wow! Hakluyt's *Divers Voyages. . .* of 1582 contained a list only marginally less impressive.

Of course reports of treasure were obligatory to lure settlers into the American wilderness so even after the initial euphoria faded Harriot's *Brief and True Report* on Raleigh's ill fated Virginia colony tells of a man who gathered 5,000 pearls from Indians, "which for their likeness and uniformity in roundnesse, orientnesse, and pidenesse of excellent colors, with equality in greatness, were very faire and rare: and had therefore beene presented to her Majesty," but "through the extremity of a storme," they were lost "in coming away from the countrey." And, although such gold as was found in Florida was washed ashore from wrecks Laudonniere's report of the pathetic French colony there, appearing about the same time as Harriot's *Virginia* reported "a good quantitie of gold and silver" among the savages.

Every subject covered by Hakluyt's *Principal Navigations*, be it history, geography, ethnology, name it, runs the gamut from pragmatic, prosaic and factual to fantastic, legendary and fabled. On the fantastic side we hear that David Ingram, during his walk across the continent had run into kings carried around on sumptuous chairs of silver or crystal garnished with "divers sorts of precious stones" and a "great abundance of pearl, for in every cottage be found pearl: in some a quart, in some a bottle, in some a peck." Everybody wore bracelets of gold and silver as thick as a man's finger and the women wear breast plates of gold as well. He saw lumps of gold big as a man's fist and loads of crystal. He describes an abundance of flora and fauna (some fantastic) all useful marketable commodities. The North American cannibals were not a problem - you could instantly recognize them because they had teeth like dogs.

Another of Hakluyt's contributors Henry Hawks, a trader who had visited Mexico, provides abundant accounts of wealth and a paradisiacal climate that permitted the Indians to live to a ripe old age. He had met many over a hundred himself. Harriot and John Hawkins tend to be more pragmatic praising a healthy climate, rich soil, and carefully and thoughtfully describing flora and fauna, though Hawkins adds a unicorn to his list of American animals and suspects there might also be elephants and rhinoceroses. Harriot makes some note of American pharmacologia and marvelous cures and lauds the quality of the soil. In Virginia they managed to get two hundred bushels of corn, beans or peas per acre while in England "forty bushels yielded out of such an acre is thought to be much."

After Frobisher English works on America tended to be subsidized by members of the Colonial party, as evidenced by dedications to its various worthies, Raleigh, Gilbert, etc. Presumably public interest in the place was not great enough to make such works profitable otherwise. As a result the bountiful, real or not, was emphasized and negatives ignored. Hakluyt provides a good example of this. In 1583 Antonio Espejo led an expedition North from Mexico and found silver about thirty-eight degrees North. An account of the expedition was printed in Madrid in 1586. Hakluyt, as soon as he came upon the book dispatched a copy to Raleigh and set about translating and getting it through the press, first in French as *Histoire des terres nouvellement descouvertes. . . par Antoine Espio.* (Paris, 1586), then in English as *New Mexico, otherwise the voyage of Anthony Espio* (London 1587). That the silver was in Colorado was unimportant. Thirty-eight degrees North was thirty-eight degrees North and for Hakluyt's garbled geography it could have just as easily be in Virginia.

More interesting is Raleigh who got taken in by his own propaganda. Ever since the discovery of gold in tombs on the coast of Columbia early in the century rumors about fantastic kingdoms in the interior floated around the Main until they finally crescendoed into print in Gomora's Peruvian history. Raleigh, who had lost a bundle on his Virginia venture, bought the story hook line and sinker and set out in 1595 to recoup his fortune in Guiana. The result was his *Discovery of Guiana* of that year. He did not find any gold but found a "kind of white stone (wherein gold engendered). . . in divers hills and rocks and every part of Guiana, wherein we traveled. . . al the rocks, mountains, al stones in ye plaines, woods & by the rivers side ware in effect through shinning and seem marvelous rich." and were probably "El madre del oro." Why he did not pick up any is unclear but this fails to keep the usually scholarly and skeptical Raleigh from repeating some tall tales. He paraphrases Gomora to the effect that in the "Inga" of Guiana's house:

> All the vessels. . . table and kitchen were of gold and silver, and the meanest of silver. . . He had in his wardrobe hollow statues of gold which seemed giants, and [golden replicas] of birds, trees, and herbes. . . and of all the fishes that the sea or waters of his kingdome breedeth. . . Finally, there was nothing in his countrey, say whereof he had not the counterfait in gold: Yea and they say the Ingas had a garden of pleasure in an yland neere Puna where they went to recreat themselves, when they would take the aire of the Sea, which had all kinde of garden hearbs, flowers and trees of golde and silver, an invention, and magnificence till then never seen.

Raleigh struggled up the Orinoco towards the mythical "Inga's" equally mythical golden capital of Manoa, but legendary places tend to be hard to find so Raleigh never reached it. In the course of his trek however he learned from Antonio de Berrio, a Spaniard who had made several expeditions into the country, of another Spaniard who had visited it, then been led away blindfolded and later christened the city El Dorado. There:

> when the emperour carowseth with his captaines, tributaries, and governours, the manner is thus: All that pledge him are first stripped naked, and are anointed all over with a kind of white balsamum... certeine servants of the emperor, having prepared golde made into fine powder, blow it through hollow canes upon their naked bodies, until they be all shining from the foot to the head: and in this sort they sit drinking by twenties, and hundreds...

Raleigh simply could no understand why, while Spanish fleets were shipping gold home by the bushel, Englishmen had yet to find a single nugget. Undeterred he prepared *Discovery of Guiana* as propaganda for future expeditions predicting "whatsoever prince shall possesse it, that Prince shall be Lord of more golde, and a more beautiful Empire, and of more Cities and people, than either the King of Spaine, or the great Turke":

> The commonest souldier shall here fight for golde, and pay himselfe in steede of pence, with plates of half a foote broad, whereas he breaketh his bones in other warres for provant and penury. Those commanders and chieftaines that shoot at honour and abundance, shall finde there more rich and beautiful cities, more temples adorned with golden images, more sepulchers filled with treasure, than either Cortez found in Mexico or Pizarro in Peru... Guiana is a countrey that hath yet her maydenhead, never sackt, turned, nor wrought... the graves have not bene opened for golde, the mines not broken with sledges, nor their Images puld downe out of their temples.

If Raleigh's description does not sound like Guiana as we know it neither does his description of the natives which include Amazons and Ewaiponomas, a race with "eyes in their shoulders and their mouths in the middle of their breasts." But Raleigh assures us, "Had such a nation been described by Mandeville, it would have been taken for a fable" but since the Indies have been discovered "wee find his relations true of such thinges as heeretofore were held incredible."[10]

Still sounds pretty incredible.

GETTING THINGS IN PERSPECTIVE

Stardate 2295: We have just entered a new sector of the Romulain Galaxy. Our sensors detect an unusual presence which we are unable to identify. We will beam down a search party to determine if there intelligent beings on this planet. - Captain James Kirk, log of the Starship Enterprise.

For "trekies" these lines are familiar enough, as are subsequent events. The party beams down and discovers something previous experience has given them no means of comprehending or initially dealing with. Good science fiction. So was 16th. Century America. And if we have been running into a lot of Captain Kirks we need a Mr. Spock to explain the reason and logic of everything to poor Jim Kirk - after he gets it figured out himself.

Till 1500 nothing about the American experience was uncomfortable to biblical or ancient authority, the two stables of latter middle age and Renaissance thought. During the following century this *weltanschauung* was badly shattered. The torrid zone was not only crossable into the antipodes, but habitable and fertile. Skin color in America did not change with latitude as Ptolemy would have us believe. Esdras' theory that the Earth was mostly land did not look so good anymore. Even more serious the gospel had not been preached to the four corners of the Earth and nobody was even sure if Indians were the posterity of Noah or Adam. A lot needed explaining and this Father Joseph Acosta set out to do in his *Natural and Moral History of the Indies*. Since Acosta examined every feature of American nature and pre-Columbian history he could find we will meet him frequently in the following pages.

He was born in Medina del Campo in Old Castile. At thirteen he entered the Society of Jesus where he devoted most of his time to the study of classical and Biblical authorities. So much so one gets the idea he never heard of anybody much after Augustine or Aquinas - he uses the words "ancients" and "philosophers" interchangeably. Among the pagans he quotes Aristotle regularly, and occasionally Plato. He is familiar with the ptolemaic theory of the universe. Of Copernicus who published fifty years before him he has heard not a word. Still he was a man of great learning and speculative mind when he set out for the New World in 1570. He spent the next fifteen years in Peru where he served largely in academic functions, working on translations of religious tracts for the Indians, studying Indian customs in order to root out superstition and advising priests and government officials. During that time he traveled over most of the country. He spent 1586 in Mexico and returned home with the treasure fleet of 1587.

Back in Spain Acosta published a series of scholarly works including the *Historia Natural y Moral de las Indias* which first appeared in its completed form as a quarto in Seville in 1590. It was followed by a Barcelona quarto the next year. Madrid editions came out in 1608 and 1610. An Italian version appeared in 1596 at Venice. The work was translated into Dutch by the great traveller and travel writer Huygen van Linschoten in 1598 and followed by another printing in 1624. A French translation appeared in Paris in 1597 and again in 1600. The British picked up on him with a London edition of 1604 and de Bry included a compilation as part of his *Grands Voyages* in 1601 and was still printing it in 1624.

The popularity of Acosta, particularly in Protestant countries and France is unusual for he is an occasional Spanish apologist. Why? His references to the wealth of the Indies must have made lip smacking reading (for pirates at least). For instance he says the treasure fleet he sailed with had a very precious cargo: twelve chests of gold, each weighing 100 pounds, 11,000,000 ounces (?) of silver, a couple of hundred pound chests of emeralds, assorted herbs and spices, Brazilwood and nearly 100,000 hides from Santo Domingo. When they unloaded in Seville Acosta tells us in an un-monkish manner it was a wonderful thing to behold the river and the arsenal piled with so much merchandise. The remark is an amusing juxta position to Cieza. The soldier taunted the Emperor on having lost so much gold in America through barbarity, then wasting the rest on European wars. The priest beholding enough treasure to feed Spain for a year and accomplish miracles in America just thought it was a wonderful thing. Of course Acosta does not tell us how worldly he was and he was doubtlessly gratified that most of the loot would be spent stamping out Protestants.

Acosta's popularity might be attributable to his descriptions of Amerind religion, the most fulsome and gruesome to appear so far. They doubtless kept people up nights looking for the goblin under the bed. Maybe Northern Europe was just getting interested in America and Acosta was the most *au courant*. But a forth reason is suggested by the translation I am using. English editions of Spanish authors tend to be short, poorly translated abridgements which often as not were published as propaganda, but the English Acosta of 1604 is a carefully translated long work which faithfully follows the original. This suggests his book was eagerly perused by schoolmen interested not only in his explanation of America but the new cosmic picture. It would be safe enough to say Acosta's American experience not only influenced but reflects the world view of his day.

For modern Peruvian anthropologists Acosta is rivaled only by Cieza as a 16th. Century source, but once he gets away from pre-Columbian custom he, on first reading at least, sounds like an archaic pedant, like a textbook author who hasn't heard the latest theories. While others used ancient accounts to describe the new Acosta repeatedly seeks out ancient sources to render description orthodox. Oviedo's dialogue with Pliny is not for him. If he cannot find ancient or Biblical authority for something it should not be there. He exacerbates this tendency to explain rather than observe by seeing the hand of God in absolutely everything. Reading between the lines, however, we often find a rational man trying to rebut an assortment of wild ideas floating around his times. He becomes interesting for the very ideas he finds it necessary to address.

As noted above the American discovery was more than geographic, scientific or ethnological. It was cosmic and for this we can turn to Acosta for he will accept nothing short of the big picture. Thus he starts with the heavens, acknowledging "the greatest part (yea the most famous among the philosophers) have well known that the Heaven was round." He cites contrary opinions of about a half dozen church fathers but concludes: "seeing all their study hath been to know, preach and serve the Creator of all things. . . and having well employed their studies in causes of greater weight, is a small matter in them not have known all the particularities concerning the creatures."

Father Joseph goes on to prove the Earth is round by describing Magellan's voyage and cites the movements of the moon and stars to explain that Heaven being the most perfect body also has the most perfect figure "which without doubt is round." and turns on the axis of the North and South Pole. He needs to explain that although some doubt the Moon borrows its light from the Sun it is easily observable during eclipses when Earth is directly between the two. Similarly night is the result of the world blocking the Sun's rays from entering the other hemisphere of Heaven. He devotes enough space to this that, Copernicus notwithstanding, one gathers this was pretty deep stuff for 1590.

For Acosta stars do not move but Heaven rotates carrying them with it in fixed positions. He can tell because there are lighter and darker portions of Heaven. The lighter ones are the Milky Way and the darker parts are those with few stars which are very thin, too transparent to receive light, and these sections rotate in conjunction.

By chapter three of the first book we get down to Earth and Acosta is ready to explain "how Holy Scripture teacheth us that the Earth is in the middest of the world." Here he runs into trouble with the church fathers again and even scripture, notably *Job* IX which says God placed the Earth upon the waters but the Bible also refers to the roundness of Earth in many places and Acosta goes on to list them. He describes the land and sea as an integrated globe with projecting peninsulas and bays, embracing and uniting the disparate elements. He also boldly suggests experience would seem to indicate the sea is not bottomless but in fact has land under it.

Finally he gets around to a short description of the southern sky. But he is prepared to "let others speak of them with greater curiosity and let that which we have said suffice for this time." (This is not the only time Acosta turns away from observation in the interest of philosophy, but if the point has not been made by now it will become excruciatingly obvious that we are still in the age of schoolmen and "natural history" meant something very different to Acosta than it does to us.) But he knows what he is at: "It is no small labor to have unfolded this doubt. . . that there is a Heaven in these parts of the Indies, which doth cover them as in Europe. . ." he says. In other words he has spent all this time assuring his stay at home readers that if they visit the Southern Hemisphere they will remain under God's protection. He speaks of homesick Spaniards wanting to return to Spain but Father Joseph feels no need to go home, "being as near unto Heaven in Peru, as in Spain: As Saint Jerome saith well. . . 'the gates of Heaven are as near unto Britain as Jerusalem.'"

With the second book the *Natural History* becomes a little more natural, but first he has to absolve "the ancients" of the error of believing the burning zone uninhabitable. In this connection he says on his voyage to Peru he approached the equator with trepidation and curiosity but when he crossed it he was so cold he had to go out in the sun to warm up, at which point he "laughed at Aristotle." Explanation requires several turgid passages wallowing in comparisons of Ptolemy's North Africa with the Andes. Having done that he explains the Sun wobbles back and forth between the tropics effecting changes in season. The tropics of course are least effected but in Chile, lying in approximately the same southern latitude as Spain in the North the "disposition of the seasons is like that in Europe," but of course it is winter in Chile when it is summer in Europe. And, "This realm of Chile approacheth nearer the temperature of Europe than any other part of the Indies, as well in the fruits of the Earth as in the bodies and spirits of men." (Acosta here is right about at least some of the above but we see him striving for balance which comes through not only in his writing but other works of the period. It was one of the reasons outsized antarctic continents stayed on the map - to keep approximately equal amounts of land in both hemispheres. It is probably also the reason Mercator drew a map of the Arctic dividing it into four islands, one for each continent.) Acosta, elsewhere expresses this need for balance. Discussing the probably of a Northwest passage he concludes since there is one in the South logically there should be one in the North: "agreeing with the order of wisdom of the Creator, and the goodly order of nature, that as there is a communication and passage between the two seas at the Pole Antarctic, so should in the like sort, be one at the Pole Arctic."

He adduces four reasons why different areas in the same latitude can have different climates. The first is the ocean which by its great depth cannot change temperature as fast as land. Second is the "situation of the land" to the ocean, a third is the "nature and property of sundry winds." This opens up a bestiary of winds which can best be imagined by looking at a period map with windheads drawn around it. Each has a special property, some are hot, others cold, barren or tempestuous; others rain fleas or frogs. Some are victorious others are vanquished. They can be sickly, heathy and so on. And the quality of wind effects the quality of life. Acosta challenges tradition by suggesting wind can change quality depending on the country it blows over, influencing temperature and precipitation. In all he devotes about eight chapters to air, finding American breezes in the tropics more felicitous, even to the point of suggesting the Terrestrial Paradise might be on the Equator, "but it would be too great a temerity to affirm this for certain." He contradicts his contemporary Herrera (who never visited America) who claimed the Old World was better suited to human life because it stretched further East and West than the New so it kept "more quality with regard to the cold of the North and the heat of the South" and uses it to explain Amerindian crudity.

To these first three qualities Acosta adds a forth, "hidden and less apparent, which is... the particular influence of the heavens." He notes the higher up you get the colder it gets and describes painful experiences with altitude sickness he suffered several times. Finally he is happily back in synch with ancient philosophy. Aristotle, he tells us, identified three spheres, an outer realm of fire, a middle region of air, the natural property of which is cold, thrusting back the heat of the fiery region. He admits he cannot understand how the lower region warms up again but he "will not contradict Aristotle, but in that which [he is] most certain" and his experience in the Andes confirmed Aristotle's opinion.

Acosta finally gets around to America specifically, or as specifically as he can given his tedious pedantry, explaining his first two books had been devoted to "that which concerns the habitation [habitability] of the Indies generally, it behooves us now to treat of the three elements; air, water and land, and their components which be metals, plants and beasts." He is not bothering with fire because it does not seem much different in America than anywhere else.

To describe water he draws a verbal map of America based on the proximity of the Atlantic to the South Sea. He is particularly interested in the area around Darien where the two oceans come close together. He says canal schemes had been put forward but opponents of the measure pointed out that such a project would be dangerous because one sea might be higher than the other and if a passage were cut one might rush into the other and drown the land. Beyond that he notes: "I believe there is no human power able to beat and break down those strong and impenetrable mountains, which god hath placed betwixt the two seas. . . And although it were possible to men, yet in my opinion they should fear punishment from Heaven in seeking to correct the works which the Creator in his great providence hath ordained and disposed in his framing of the universal world."

On the subject of tides he says some believe they are like water sloshing back and forth in a bowl, rising on one side and falling on the other but a pilot who had been trying to chase Drake back through the Straits of Magellan told him that was not so. Tides rose and fell in the Pacific concurrently with the Atlantic. This point Father Joseph is willing to leave as one of those wonders of nature that only angels can see because no man could run fast enough to get from one sea to the other in time to find out.

Water leads to fish and we get a brief ichthyology, an interesting account of a battle between a puma and an allegator and an equally interesting description of Indian whalers, "wherein appears the power and greatness of the Creator to give so base a nation as be the Indians, the industry and courage to encounter the most fierce and deformed beast in the world and not only fight with him, but also vanquish him."

Water runs through this section of the book in conjunction with the other elements, integrated with them in the classical manner. In the process Acosta clears up some millenniums old mysteries, like the annual inundation of the Nile which flowing from the torrid zone probably should not be a river at all. He describes the Amazon and Plata noting especially in the case of the later the annual flood. He has discovered melting snow in the torrid zone, a revolutionary idea!

Other mysteries are unsolvable. Peru has springs, quite close to each other which give off either hot or cold water. There is another which "casts forth hot water, and in running the water turns to rock." It is poisonous if you drink it because it will turn to stone within you. Saline springs are curious because salt was supposed to be confined to the sea and springs spouting pitch are also a matter for concern. However wedded to Biblical-classical authority he was Acosta looked, saw and wondered about a place very different from the tidy Mediterranean.

The third element, land is even more interesting. Acosta starts out with a new verbal map, this time topographical and if he describes like a tourist just back from Alaska or Hawaii who can blame him? The most interesting thing is seismic activity which while hardly unknown in Europe was rare. He begins his account of volcanos with an anecdote about a greedy priest who convinced himself a volcano that remained molten at bottom must contain "heaps of gold he did see burning, imagining it could be no other matter or substance which had burnt so many years and not consumed." When he tried to scoop it out with a kettle on a chain "the fire scorned him, for no sooner did his iron caldron approach near the fire, but suddenly they were broken in pieces." But the last time Acosta heard of him he was still obstinate, "seeking other inventions to draw it out the gold as he imagined."

Our author notes several theories of volcanos. Some argued they were simply consuming fuel and would eventually burn out. "Others say that it is Hell fire which issueth there, to serve as a warning, thereby to consider what is of the other life; but if Hell (as Divines hold) be in the center of the earth. . .we cannot judge that this fire is from the center; for that Hell fire (as St. Basil and other Saints teach) is very different from this which we see, that it is without light, and burneth without comparison much more than ours."

He speculates volcanos were like springs that tapped underground streams except volcanos drew "unto themselves hot exhalations and. . .convert them into fire and smoke." As evidence he points out volcanos are not constantly active nor are many springs during dry periods. He ascribes similar causes to earthquakes which he suspects are caused by gases or water building up pressure to split the land apart. But the nascent scientist cannot leave this subject without one of his moralizing diatribes so he contributes an anecdote about a village called Angoango: "were many Indians dwelt that were sorcerers and idolaters [which] fell suddenly to ruin, so as a great part thereof was raised up and carried away and many of the Indians smothered, and the earth was severed and so beaten down, and did run and slide upon the. . .space of a league and a half, as it had been. . .wax molten. . .and filled up a lake."

Sounds like Sodom and Gomorrah.

Having dealt with the three elements which might have special American properties Acosta begins his forth book describing their compounds like a medieval chemistry teacher. He starts at bottom with minerals which he explains grow in the bowels of the earth, "not that they have any inward vegetative life. . . . but they are engendered. . .by the virtue and force of the Sun and other planets, and in the continuance of time they increase and multiply after the manner of plants."

Of course we already know the American minerals that preoccupied Europe so we get a digression tracing the history of silver and gold (predictably) to ancient times. This brings him to the conclusion that to esteem silver and gold is to be civilized. He observes some Indians, notably barbarians in Florida, hold it of no repute. He exonerates the Aztecs and Incas of this shortcoming as they used it in their temples. But:

> It is true, their covetousness has not yet come to the height of ours, neither have they so much worshiped gold and silver, although they were idolaters, as some blind Christians, who have committed many great outrages for gold and silver. Yet it is a thing very worthy of consideration, that the wisdom of the Eternal Lord would enrich these parts of the world which are most remote, and which are peopled with men of less civility and government, planting there great store of mines, and in the greatest abundance that everywhere, thereby to invite men to search out these lands, to the end that by this occasion, they might plant religion, and the worship of the true God... Hereupon a wise man said, that what a father doth to marry his daughter well, is to give her a great portion in marriage; the like hath God done for this land...giving it great riches in mines, that by this means it might be more sought after.[11]

There follows a discussion of the wealth of various regions, the forms in which gold and silver are found, methods of mining and refining and so on. He updates Cieza's description of Potosi saying:

> The ground and soil of this mountain is dry, cold, and very unpleasant, yea, altogether barren which neither engenders nor brings forth any fruit, grass, nor grain; it is naturally uninhabitable...But the force of silver, which draws unto it the desire of all things, hath peopled this mountain more than any other place in all these kingdoms, making it so fruitful of all kinds of meats, as there wants nothing that can be desired, yea, in great abundance...every place abounds so with fruit, conserves, exquisite wines, silks, and all other delacates, as it is not inferior to any other part.[12]

We hear that as of 1585 a trillion pieces of silver (I am not sure what a "piece" means in this case. It was not a *Peso* and may have been as little as five cents. Still, a trillion is a trillion even if it is only nickels.) had gone to the custom house. In addition innumerable amounts had been skimmed or not left the country so did not appear in the customs books.

Now Acosta makes a point which would endear him to Protestant publishers, notably de Bry, who loved to engrave pictures of Spaniards lashing Black and Indian slaves to work in fields and mines. The Catholic classicist quotes the church father Boetius (d. ca. 525 A. D.) who complained of the invention of mines.

> Alas, who was the first,
> So curious and accurate,
> Who digged out of the mine,
> Mans' mind to undermine,
> Heavy weights of gold ore,
> Better concealed before:
> And pearls crept into ground,
> Pale for fear to be found:
> Galling gold, wringing rings,
> Perhaps, but precious things.

We learn there were mines in ancient Italy but since mining was dangerous the Romans left the job to Spaniards "to preserve [their own] people... The like doth Spain now with the Indies." Now Spaniards will not work their own mines "by reason of the inconveniences which happen daily, but they bring [bullion] from the Indies where they [Indians] dig it with much labor and peril." He gives a fulsome account of exactly what the labor and peril is and quotes Pliny: "We enter even into the bowels of the Earth, and go hunting after riches, even to the place of the damned."

None of this makes Acosta a las Casas. He seems almost indifferent to the plight of the Indians because he sees everything as part of God's plan. Besides, better a Christian slave than a soul burning in Hell.

From silver he passes to emeralds lamenting they are not as valuable as they used to be because so many had been discovered in America. He offers an anecdote to explain, unwittingly describing the effect all that Peruvian silver was having on the European economy. A Spaniard returning from the Indies presented an enormous emerald to a lapidary and asked its worth. The jeweler offered a handsome price. When the Spaniard offered a similar specimen the price was halved. Then the Spaniard showed him a bushel and the jeweler told him they were worth a ducat each.

The same thing happened with pearls which had also been discovered in quantity: "At first [they] were of so great estimations as not but royal persons were suffered to wear them; but at this day there is such abundance that the negresses themselves do wear chains thereof."

On page 228 (out of 295 in the first volume of the Hakluyt Society edition of this "natural history") Acosta finally gets around to plants. He begins with maize and various uses Indians made of it. He decides Pliny did not know about it which worries him but works it out explaining, "God hath imparted to every region what is needful." He describes rice, potatoes, edible roots and various fruits like the pineapple noting in passing that somebody had gone to condeserable "paine and care" to bring one back to Spain for presentation to Charles V but the Holy Roman Emperor was afraid to taste it.

The big cash crops, however were cacao and "coca" and Acosta devotes a chapter to them. He mentions Indians use beans of the former for money and prepare it into a beverage called chocolate "where of they make great account in that country, foolishly, and without reason for it is loathsome." (Apparently Father Joseph lacked a sweet tooth.) But he acknowledges its popularity noting there was such an extensive trade Drake on a costal raid burnt 100,000 cases in one town. On coca he has more to say, making him perhaps the first author to discuss the merits of non-European opiates the voyagers were discovering. He says the annual trade in coca leaves in Potosi alone amounted to 500,000 dollars. The problem he finds is:

> The Indians endure much labor and pain to entertain it, and often many die, for they go from the Sierra and cold places to till and gather them in the valleys. And therefor there hath been great question and diversity of opinions among learned men, whether it were more expedient to pull up these trees, or let them grow, but in the end they remained...[the Indians] say it gives them great courage and is very pleasing to them. Many grave men hold this as a superstition and mere imagination; for my part and to speak the truth, I persuade not myself that it is an imagination; but contrariwise, I think it works and gives force and courage to the Indians; for we see the effects which cannot be attributed to imagination...I have tasted [it and] all these things were not inconvenient, were not the hazard of the traffic thereof, wherein so many men are occupied.[13]

"It were not possible to reckon all the fruits and trees at the Indies," Acosta says, "For... I remember not many and there are many more whereof I have no knowledge; and in my opinion it were troublesome to speak of all those I now remember," but he lists a few and suggests some could profitably be cultivated in Spain before marveling at God's creation. The Indians are great flower lovers and he describes a few, among them passion flowers and "the flower they call the Sun, hath the figure of the Sun and turns according to [its] motion." He does not dwell too long on medical herbs either, referring readers to Monardes.

Animals are more interesting. He divides them into three groups, those common to the Old World and New, those introduced by Europeans and those exclusive to the New. To determine which are which he uses the ingenious device of seeing if the Indians had a name for an animal in their own language. If they did not they simply adopted the Spanish name thereby demonstrating an imported breed.

Acosta is not overly worried at the presence of previously unknown species because he realizes that even in the Old World different types of animals were indigenous to different areas. But like Vespucci ninety years before he is encountering a whole new menagerie and may have been fretting about just how large the Ark was. He wonders "whether these beasts differ in kind. . . from all others or if this difference be accidental, which might grow from divers accidents, as we see in the linages of men, some are white, others black, some giants, others dwarfs." And 350 years before Darwin he gives the scientist an accolade: "Whosoever would by this discourse, showing only these accidental differences, preserve the propagation of beasts at the Indies, and reduce them to those of Europe, he shall undertake a charge that will hardly discharge his honor. For if we shall judge the kinds of beasts by their properties, those of the Indies are so diverse, as to call an egg a chestnut, to seek to reduce them to the kinds of Europe."

One animal he finds particularly interesting is the monkey:

> It were long to report the fooleries, travesties, and plesant sports they make when they are taught which seem not to come from brute beasts, but from manlike understanding. I saw one in Carthagena. . . so taught as the things he did seemed incredible. They sent him to a tavern for wine, putting the pot in one hand and the money in the other, and they could not possibly get the money out of his hand before he had his pot full of wine. If any children met him in the street and threw any stones at him he would set his pot down. . . and cast stones at the children till he had assured his way, then he would carry home his pot. And which is more, although he [drank]. . . yet would never touch it until leave was given him. . . I do not think there is any beast in the world which approacheth so near the conversation of a man as this monkey doth.[14]

If Acosta had stopped writing with the "natural" part of his history the work would not find a great deal of space on Americana bookshelves. On the plus side his fascination with flora and fauna must have stimulated speculation on the diversity of nature, but so had Oviedo, Monardes, Cieza, Vespucci and many others, all of whom were more modern than he was. The first half of the book is devoted to an exposition of archaic natural laws and the second redundantly harks back to the same points with chapter headings like "For what reason the ancients held the burning zone was not inhabitable" or "How Scripture teaches us. . ." (Fill in the blank.) Much of the *Natural History* reads like Acosta is trying to absolve America from the heresy of existing and being inhabited. But Acosta was writing against a vision of a place that made an ideal stage set for *The Tempest*. His is the most extensive effort so far to understand the New World. The search for authority, a world view we can live with, is no less in our day than it was in his and he did the best he could even if he had to constantly break out Pliny and the Bible to do it.

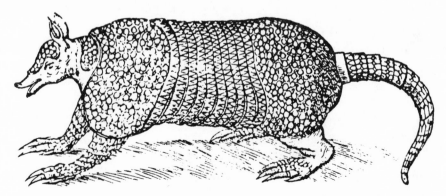

An armadilio after Monardes.

Indian Origins &

Theological Problems

ANCIENT writers had no difficulty accepting variety in people. Direct observation made it obvious. Obvious to the point they could even believe in chimerical creatures described by Pliny. If some of them lived in Mela's *Orbis Alterius* or were cut of from humanity by the torrid zone it was not a problem for Aristotle, Plato or Ptolemy and if they were a different species entirely it still was not a problem. Christians also had eyes enough to realize people differ. They accepted Pliny's bestiary and even added a fantastic creature or two of their own. But for Christians, differences notwithstanding, there could only be one race of men. According to the Bible Earth was inhabited by a single family, descended from Adam. After the expulsion Cain slew Able for which he was exiled to the Land of Nod. When Cain's posterity multiplied, their wickedness increasing as their numbers mounted, God's patience became exhausted. A flood was sent to destroy the evil doers and their works. When the waters receded the only souls left on this soggy planet were Noah, his wife, his three sons and their wives. In this demographic emergency "God blessed Noah and his sons bidding them, 'be fruitful and multiply and replenish the Earth'"

According to Moses nations descended from number one son, Japheth, were the Cimmerians, Magog's heard, the Medes, Ionians, Tubal, Meshek, Tiras and others. From Ham sprung Ethiopians, Put and Canaan. Shem produced Elamites, Assyrians, Apachshad, Libyans and Aram.

This brings us to the eleventh chapter of *Genesis* when man became presumptuous enough to build a tower reaching to heaven. Once again the Almighty was displeased. He made up his mind to "make a babble of their tongues on the spot so that they could not understand one another's speech." Forthwith men and their languages were scattered "all over the wide Earth." And this was the sum total of medieval ethnology and anthropology.

Long after the destruction of the Tower of Babble Jesus came along and his apostles spread the Gospel to the ends of the Earth. Now the possibility of beings cut off by sea or a fiery equatorial zone became heretical. How could they be descended from Adam and Noah and how was the Gospel have preached there? These insurmountable problems obliged Augustine to deny the existence of antipodal lands and even on the assumption, which for him had not been proved, Earth was actually a sphere insist they were not populated. His tremendous authority, combined with that of Isidore and Bede settled the question for a thousand years.

As long as America was identified with Asia orthodoxy was not seriously breached. If Portuguese could cross the Equator so could anybody else. It was Ptolemy's mistake and we already heard Acosta excusing church fathers for not bothering to check up when they had weightier matters on their minds.

The Asia connection found theological expression almost immediately. An anonymous painting of the adoration of the Magi of about 1505 for the Cathedral of Viseu, Portugal shows one of the wise men from the East as coppery colored, wearing feathers and carrying a Timpinamba spear. More important was evangelism. That Brazilian who came to adore baby Jesus did not carry the Gospel back with him. Now St. Thomas came to the rescue. In 1514 a German newsletter reported Indians met by Portuguese in Brazil eagerly pointed out Thomas' footprints in the hinterland. For his doubts Thomas made the greatest amends by traveling further than any other apostle and his footsteps were miraculously preserved.

Later Martyr wrote to the Pope, "Crosses have been found amongst [the Mayans] and when they were asked. . . the meaning of that emblem, some of them answered that a very beautiful man had once lived amongst them, who had left them this symbol as a remembrance of him; others said that a man more radiant than the sun had died upon that cross."

Further inquiries about the cross were rewarded by an old Indian who remembered a *pintura* with a figure attached crucifix-like on two columns. The face of the sufferer indicated agony, hence he was "reproaching God." The codex was held in great reverence; when exhibited for purposes of instruction it was never unfolded by hand but with a special wand kept for the purpose. The document was lost, for the person entrusted with it buried it to keep it from Spaniards and it rotted underground but they learned the cross was styled, "the true tree of this world." Further discoveries of crosses in Palenque and images on surviving *pinturas* served to keep the apostle theory alive.

Of course the Indians, probably including the one whose painting rotted, were giving missionaries *ex posto facto* answers, giving yes or no like someone before a medieval inquisitor. Eager to please they usually answered "yes !"

According to Lewis Hanke at least one 16th. Century writer identified the Mexican god/culture giver Quetzalcoatl, as Thomas Aquinas but Peru was much better and more dangerous. There lived a tripartite god, complete with monasteries, convents and priests to serve him, Tici-Viracola. At the beginning of the 17th. Century the half Indian historian Vega explained Peruvian religion with its similarities to Christianity was based on logic rather than (necessarily orthodox) revelation wrote: "I tell you then that our father the Sun must have another Lord more powerful than himself, who orders him to make this journey day by day without resting. If he [the sun] were the supreme Lord he would occasionally go aside from his course or rest for his pleasure."

Cieza wrote about Tici-Viracola with ambivalent respect. Although he used the word Devil to describe their other divinities he does not apply it to Tici-Viracola. The Peruvians told him he was a large white man, father of the Sun and performer of miracles who taught them "to love one another and use charity towards all." After him came a similar man, Viracola, who healed the sick and restored sight. Coming to the Sea he spread his cloak, "moved over the waves and never again appeared." Cieza went to see a statue of this wonderful man because, "The Spaniards claim and insist that it might have been some apostle. I even heard many of them say that it had a rosary in its hands which is nonsense, unless I am blind, for though I looked at it carefully I saw nothing of the sort." (Acosta visited the statue several years later and he could not find a rosary either.) But Cieza only committed himself to: "I am of the opinion that if he were one of the apostles, his teachings, with God's aid, would have had an effect on these peoples who are simple and devoid of malice, and there should be some evidence of it." Cieza was seconded by the greatest jurist of his day, Pereira Slozano, who found the idea St. Thomas visited America widespread enough to require a denial in his *Politica Indiana* (Madrid, 1548).

If the Gospel had not been spread to the four corners of the Earth then what? Emperor Maximilian became curious enough to ask an opinion from the philosopher Juan de Heindenburg who replied in his *Curiositas Regia* of 1521 that in the hereafter "Those infidels who had lived innocent lives would suffer no positive punishment whatsoever, though they would be excluded from supernatural felicity and divine vision." In other words, Limbo.

TRUE MEN?

Meanwhile there was the Pomponius Mela problem. As antipodal discovery, exotic flora and fauna and odd native customs increasingly separated America from the Old World this heresy began to make more sense. Physician-magician-scientist, Paracelsus came out and said it in 1520, writing he could not believe people found "in out of the way islands" were "the posterity of Adam and Eve." He doubted if they had souls and proposed a theory of polygenesis to account for them.

Strong enough words for a maverick like Paracelsus but worse yet when they were seconded by clergy. A Scottish theologian, John Major, (ca. 1510) and various Dominican friars denied Indians all traditional attributes of humanity. One of those Dominicans, Father Gregorio (1512) called them speaking animals.

The apparent irrationality of the Indians, from the European point of view, resulted in experimental communes in Cuba and Hispaniola where Spanish officials endeavored to determine if Indians could "live like Christian laborers in Castile." This early social experiment failed to settle the issue. Finally it became necessary for a papal bull of 1537 to declare the Indians "true men." but this did not stop another Dominican, Domingo de Betanzos, from insisting the Indians were brute beasts incapable of learning mysteries of the Faith. Although he recanted on his deathbed in 1549 his views gained wide currency in the meantime. A few years later (1557) Nicholas Durand de Villegigon, who had depicted Indians sympathetically enough in colonial propaganda wrote to John

Calvin that the Brazilians were "a fierce and savage people, far removed from us in learning and doing. So much so that it has occurred to me to wonder if we have fallen among beasts in the form of humans."

Paracelsus' heresy of a separate creation ran as an undercurrent through the century and beyond. Acosta was forced to deal with it. Recognizing enormous differences in people and nature he wondered briefly if America was a separate creation but with his usual logic(?) found it contrary to Scripture. The world was created in six days, the Bible says. God would not have had time to take out another day to create America. (Acosta however worried about absence of references to America in the Bible but concluded it was there is spirit because God certainly knew about it.)

The depth of disagreement over the nature of the Indians is suggested by moving remarks by Cieza and Father Sahagun. The former cited one reason for writing his Peruvian histories was since, "We and these Indians all have our origin in our common parents, it is just that the world should know how so great a multitude. . . were brought into the lap of the Church." Father Sahagun in the prologue to his *History of Things of New Spain* is "very certain that these people are our brothers, proceeding like us from the stock of Adam. They are our fellow creatures, whom we are obliged to love as ourselves."

It required the wisdom of a las Casas to understand the problem. Writing in his *Apologetic History* he says, "From this failure [to understand Amerindian life and psychology] has sprung an error that is no means insignificant, and whose pernicious character will be realized on the day of the Last Judgement - the tendency to regard [the Indians] as beasts." But Sahagun, Casas and most of Cieza did not see publication for centuries.

There was the other heretical possibility that Americans were descended from Adam but not Noah. This brings us back to floods. Henry Hanks writing for Hakluyt's *Principal Navigations* said the Indians themselves did not know if they came to America before the flood or after. Lescarbot commented on Canadian legends of a flood and Gomora and Acosta picked up on similar Peruvian legends but the later concluded it was some local deluge.

SO WHO WHERE THEY?

If the Indians were true men they had to come from somewhere and this introduced another ticklish problem. Who were they? When asked where they came from the Indians invariably responded they had always been here, much to the annoyance of the Spanish. As Acosta after collecting an assortment of fables none of which shed any light on which of Noah's sons they sprung from put it: "they believe confidently, that they were created at their first beginning at this New World, where they now dwell. But we have freed them of this error by our faith which teacheth us that all men came from the first man." He dismisses Indian legends of creation with the remark, "It is no matter of any great importance to know what the Indians themselves report of their beginnings, being more like unto dreams than true histories. . . But what availeth it to speak more seeing that all is full of lies and vanity, and far from reason?"

We get an idea of who the Indians might have been by taking another look at the map. As late as 1562 Gastaldi has America lying East of Alexander's Gate. This was a legendary wall based on Alexander's achievements in extending civilization (which came to be understood as Chiristendom) enclosing notorious louts presided over by Gog and Magog. Medieval legend identified them with various barbaric tribes, Tartars, Goths, Scythians, etc. and one biblical nation, the ten lost tribes of Israel. All these groups were put forward as possible Indian ancestors.

The problem of Indian ancestry grew in direct proportion to the map. Columbus, for instance, had no cause to speculate. He was confident about where he was and consequently who he was talking to. By Oviedo's time it was becoming an issue. Although Oviedo does not speculate on origins specifically he assumes the Indians picked up their nasty habits from Tartars. His previously noted interest in Olaus Magus' map, since it absolved America of being in anyway cutoff from the rest of the World, made the problem academic. Later the question of land bridges or passable straits became an issue. In 1578 Urban Chauveton, adding notes to Benzoni's history, conjectured such passages. He based his suggestion on proximity and although he probably never saw an Indian or Tartar similarities between them. He further assumed portions of America lying West and South had been peopled by Asians coming from the East while the North had been entered by the same people coming across Greenland. It only remained to determine which particular Asians they were. Everybody had an opinion but the commonest, which held the floor for centuries, maintained the Indians were the lost tribes of Israel.

It is not hard to imagine how this belief originated. If the Bible was the commonest source of ethnography the Jews were the commonest nation discussed so there was plenty of opportunity for comparison. Furthermore they had been missing since Shalmadeser IV "carried Israel away into Assyria" (*Second Kings* XVII, 6:23). An entire nation missing for that long had to be around someplace. Since nobody had found them yet America seemed a reasonable location.

There was another reason for the theory's popularity. The presence of so many people to whom God had apparently denied an opportunity for salvation was displeasing to theologians who were dissatisfied with Heindenburg's Limbo. If the Indians were Jews they were saved under the Old Covenant, at least until they heard the Gospel. This wiped out the Doubting Thomas problem and made the Spanish the new apostles.

The originator of this notion is unknown but it seems to have been introduced early. Torquemanda attributes authorship to Casas on the grounds that he found it along with extracts from that excellent man's will.

The Americans, this writer claims, are the greatest nation in the world and well they should be considering the size of their continent. So much being granted he invites attention to the prophet Hosea and asks is it not written "The

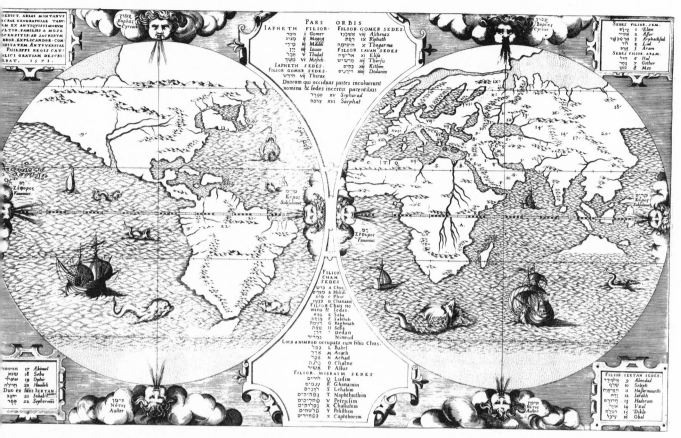

Arias Montanus' world map of 1571, from BIBLA SACARA... (Antwerp, 1571 - '73). Each number represents a family of Jews.

number of the children of Israel shall be as the sand of the Sea?" This alone should be conclusive but if any difficulty should be felt it is removed by considering American languages which are nothing but a slew of Hebrew dialects. The very names of the islands are taken from the holy tongue. Consider the word Cuba. Is that not excellent Hebrew? Some imaginary cavalier may object "Cuba" means "helmet." Of course, Saul arrayed David with a brass helmet when he went out to slay Philistines. The West Indian islands received their names from the various chieftains who discovered them as written in the Forty-eighth Psalm, *Vocaverunt nominia sua terris suis.* The Jewish chieftain who first reached Cuba was named Helmet after the magnificent David-like headdress he wore. As a remarkable confirmation of this logic we are reminded Cuba has been renamed Ferdinanda, after the King of Spain, surely a great chief.

From Cuba our author passes to Haiti: the true name of which he says is Caitin-tateacuth. He supposes this is also derived from a Jewish chief. In any event it is pure Hebrew, although we are not enlightened as to its meaning. He identifies various other regions as taking names from the Hebrew along with articles and titles, for instance cacique, carib and canoe. He further cites similarities between Hebrew and Amerind customs.

Gomora found a strong resemblance between Indians and Jews, noting, "They are all very like Jews in appearance and voice, for they have large noses and speak through their throat. . ." Another of the many writers who noticed similarities was Diego de Landa, zealous bishop of the Yucatan, who in the 1560's was recalled to Spain for exceeding his authority. While there he wrote his (not published till much later) *Relacion de la Cosas de Yucatan* in which he made this curious remark: "Some of the old people of the Yucatan say that they have heard from their ancestors that this land was occupied by a race of people, who came from the East and whom God had delivered opening twelve paths through the sea. If this were true, it necessarily follows that all the inhabitants of the Indies are descended from the Jews; since having passed the Straits of Magellan, they must have extended over more than two thousand leagues of land which Spain now governs."

In any event the full theory was in print by 1569 when it was included in a tract published in Venice urging conversion of the Jews: J. F. Lumnius' *De extremo Dei iudicoet Indorum vocatione.* Two years later Arias Montanus prepared a world map giving locations of dispersed Jews. He places one group in California and others in Peru (Ophir) and Brazil.

Acosta found the problem of Indian origins difficult admitting "Truly I have often times considered thereof myself, as many others have done, but never could find anything to satisfy me," but he got to work on the problem in his natural history, summarizing opinions put forward so far. He thinks Seneca made his famous prophecy on the strength of a Carthagenian voyage mentioned by Pliny. He expects Atlantis is a fable but says it is accepted by many learned men and it certainly would clear up a lot of questions. Atlantis was supposed to be bigger than Asia and Africa together, therefore it would occupy the entire Atlantic allowing easy passage from the Old World. Sinking it stirred up enough waves to render the ocean unnavigable until his own time, leaving America stranded on the other side.

His experience leads him to reject the opinion Peru was Ophir for while Peru abounds in gold it does not exist in such quantities as Solomon took from Ophir nor does it have the precious stones and exotic wood that graced his temple. But he is not too sure on the point because he contradicts it several times in his forth book.

He says, "It is not likely there was another Noah's Ark. . . and much less any Angel to carry the first man to this New World, holding him by the hair of his head. . . for we entreat not of the mighty power of God, but only of that which is comfortable unto reason." (Sometimes it is easy to forget just how reasonable Father Joseph is given the ideas he has to confront. About the time he wrote Theodore de Bry published an illustration showing humanity being carried to America by just such an angel. Although it is allegorical the inference is the idea had been suggested.)

He weights various possibilities: Obviously the Indians had arrived by land or sea and either intentionally or by accident. He admires the maritime skill of the Carthagenians and Solomon but since they did not have the compass a determined voyage from the Old World to the New was out of the question. Of course a ship could have steered off course or been blown by a storm. Here old Pliny comes to his aid, hardly for the first time. He described "remainders of Spanish ships that perished" on the shores of the Red Sea and another case where "Indians sailing from India, for their traffic, were cast upon Germany by force of tempest." Finding these yarns credible enough he adds, "they report a ship of Carthage, which was driven out of the Mediterranean Sea by a North wind, to view this New World." He adds his own experience of having crossed from the Canaries in a mere fifteen days and complains it would have been faster if the mariners had set more sail.

Acosta, however, believes the Indians came by land. The reason is another one of those difficulties which he says "trouble me much." How did the animals get here? Domestic animals might have been introduced by ships but he wonders why there are so many "wolves, tigers, and other ravenous beasts, which breed no profit to man." He cites Augustine's doubts such animals were even carried on the Ark and the possibility they had survived the deluge by swimming but finds it contrary to scripture (*Genesis* VII). Nor is it likely "according to the order of Nature, nor comfortable to the order of government established by God, that perfect creatures as lions, tigers and wolves, should be engendered of the earth as. . . rats, frogs, bees and other imperfect creatures are commonly engendered."

They could have been shipwrecked on their way to zoos ordained by noblemen but the variety seems too large. This brings him to his speculative geography which is more prudent and tentative than the cartographers'. He reminds the reader that much of America remains to be discovered, it might spread toward Europe or Asia as it moves North and in the South nobody knows what lies below the Straits of Magellan. Acosta thinks it most likely the first inhabitants came to the Indies from Asian, European or Antarctic land bridges or easily passable straits, "changing by little and little their lands and habitations. Some peopling the lands they found, and others seeking for new, in time they came to inhabit and people the Indies, with so many nations, peoples and tongues as we see."

He notes the lost tribes theory listing similarities various other authors had adduced and pointing out as many dissimilarities. Father Joseph explains that if they were Jews, "they have forgotten their lineage, their law, their ceremonies, their messiahs; and finally, their Judaism." He reinforces this argument by citing *Esdras* - Acosta will take on the holy fathers but not scripture. And poor old Esdras who probably had no interest in geography and only understood ethnology in terms of Jews versus Gentiles runs through the century from Columbus to Ortelius (who could not help drawing in monsterous mythical continents to fill up seven eighths of the world) to Acosta who uses him against the Jewish Indian theory. Acosta explains that according to the ancient prophet "the ten tribes went from the multitude of the heathen, to keep their faith and ceremonies, and we see the Indians given to all the idolatries in the world."

THE DEVIL MADE THEM DO IT

The idolatries Acosta just mentioned introduce a new actor to the American stage. The Devil.

Although most books on America discuss Indian religion, usually in gristly terms, works that saw print tend not to delve deeply, but rather use accounts (mostly of human sacrifice) for sensation or as rationalization for conquest. Sahagun, Casas, Landa among other friars and some native Americans wrote detailed descriptions of native rites and beliefs all of which were censored into manuscript for centuries. Why all this silence? One would think Indian myths would be interesting reading, even if they were taken as nonsense. There are several possibilities. One was the Devil.

Against the sanctity of the evangelizing crusade lay something darker and more ominous. America was discovered right in the middle of that frenzied period usually referred to as the Witchcraft Delusion (1400 - 1700). Perhaps as many as 200,000 "witches" were burnt at the stake during those years. Christians saw their world in the grip of demons with human allies everywhere. Any threat to the stability of society could be labeled as part of the never ending offensive waged by Satan against the Kingdom of God on Earth.

On the sound principal of "know your enemy" directories of leading figures in Satan's kingdom were prepared. Reginald Scot in his *Discoverie of Witchcraft* (1584) gave dozens of mini biographies of such characters. Others listed even more, but all agreed such personages existed and could be summoned and controlled by magicians. There were rational rebuttals but many demonologies were authored by eminent jurists like Jean Bodin so they carried enormous authority.

The point is that during the 16th. Century when someone mentions the Devil he is not referring to some vague being but a very tactile creature with horns and tail. When they say Devil they mean THE DEVIL. This was a time when a copy of *Malleus Maleficarum* (Hammer of Witches) lay open on every jurists' desk. And if the Devil lurked around corners in Europe he roamed America at will, ready to greet visitors on arrival.

That witchcraft was practiced in Europe is indisputable. Around 1680 the Paris police chief, Nicholas de la Reynie, turned up Abbe Guibourg who performed black masses involving human sacrifice on a wholesale basis. Jean Bodin claimed Catherine de Medici ordered one in 1574. This introduces an interesting point. Prior to the Medici Mass there is no evidence of human sacrifice in sabats or sorcery (save for the story of Gilles de Rais, bodyguard of Joan of Arc and model for Blackbeard, who was executed for murder and heresy in 1440 perhaps on trumped up charges or his proclivity for sadism). The medieval sabat was more innocent, understood to some extent at least, as an offer to the Devil who God with his almighty power could supervise at leisure to perform what his supplicants saw fit. The human sacrifice angle suggests an idea traveling from

West to East. Another example of this transference is the gruesome Aztec practice of priests flaying sacrificial victims and running around town attired in their skin (described by Acosta among others). These "cloaks" also started appearing in European demonologies so maybe the censors had a point.

An interesting example of this censorship appears in the *Jesuit Relations* which they began printing in 1585 to describe their labors around the world. A report from Michoacan by Father Franisco Ramierez that year trotted out the St. Thomas story, saying the local population "apparently had some notion of the Flood." This was due to earlier preaching by local priests, who "led them so far into the things of our faith that they did not find much novelty in listening to us." This passage was specifically edited out of the printed volume.

There could be several reasons for this. First it introduces the idea of religion by natural reason instead of divine revelation. In the early 17th. Century Vega got this heresy into print in the passage cited above. A second possibility was it contributed to the hotly debated Doubting Thomas issue. If the Indians heard the Gospel they certainly had not understood it very well and their souls were in Hell. If not they were languishing in Limbo (never officially recognized by the Catholic Church). The third possibility, suggested by Acosta, was the Devil was doing God's handiwork for him by pre-instructing Indians to prepare them for Christianization by trying to imitate God in the New World.

This last suggestion, wild as it seems, was rational enough for the time. Sabats or Black Masses tended to counterfeit and/or reverse Christian mass, prayers were repeated backwards with Satin's name in place of God's; according to such demonologists whose works have reached our day menstrual blood or semen could be used in place of wine and aborted fetuses in place of the host.

It was bad enough for Christians to find competitive religions in the quagmires of heathenism but worse still to discover institutions which seemed to resemble Judeo-Christian customs: convents, monasteries, tripartite gods and even sacrifices and sacrificial blood. Echoing Acosta the early 17th. Century literary hack, Herrera, described the travels of the Aztecs through Mexico in a fashion resembling the wanderings of the Israelites in the wilderness, carrying with them a pseudo ark of the covenant: "When they halted, they made an altar like that in use in the Catholic Church. . . for never did the Devil hold such familiar concourse with men as he [Huizilopochtli, god of the Aztecs] and accordingly he thought proper in all things to copy the departure from Egypt and the pilgrimage performed by the children of Israel."

While other reasons for censorship can be adduced, for instance the possibility of rational beings who did not necessarily need foreign interference, the non appearance of Casas, Landa, Sahagun, *et al* in print may have been reluctance of inquisitors in charge of licensing books to promulgate Satan's liturgy. It took Acosta with his firm belief that "the Devil cannot hiss. . . whereas the Cross of Christ hath been planted" to bring extensive descriptions of Amerindian religion to print.

Even Acosta had problems with censorship. The 1596 Italian translator of *Histoira Natural y Moral des las Indias* warned "many things are missing. . . which are in the Spanish original, because this was the superior's decision." Among the cuts were Peruvian trinitarian beliefs. All of chapter thirty of book five disappeared where Father Joseph points out the advantages of learning Indian superstition.

Most 16th. and 17th. Century Americana when referring to Indian gods use the word "Devil." Early on Oviedo observed:

> The Indians depict the way the Devil appears, when he talks to them, in a variety of forms and colors. They also make those figures of gold and carved on wood, very frightfull and always ugly, and in as many different forms as our artists may paint him at the feet of Saint Michael the Archangel, Saint Bartholomew, or any other place they may paint the terrifying figure.
>
> When the Devil wishes to frighten the Indians he predicts a hurricane...It was a terrible thing to see and could not be looked upon without great fear. Without doubt this destruction appeared to the Indians the work of the Devil.
>
> In this regard every Christian should contemplate the fact that everywhere Holy Communion has been celebrated, these hurricanes and terrific storms have not occurred in large numbers, nor as destructive as they used to be.[1]

There is something very wrong with the above paragraph which anybody with a tract house in the Gulf states can easily identify. The weather has not changed much and if it has it was not in Oviedo's time when there were ruinous tropical storms. The modern historian Antonello Gerbi,[2] the best scholar on Oviedo to whom I am indebted for much information, makes light of his supersition. He uses a description of his visit to a volcano in Nicaragua to make the point. Oviedo provides a picturesque description of the erupting volcano doubting a single Christian "who recalling the existence of Hell, does not see this and repent of his sins." He learns from a cacique that a demon used to arise from this well.

Gerbi quotes Oviedo: "The Indians are endlessly talking of these and other foolishness," but he is forced to concede that Oviedo also claims "Although Pliny denies or doubts Hell, we Christians know and believe it exists." By way of demonstrating Oviedo's rationality Gerbi also points to overheard stories of miraculous apparitions among the clouds over Quinto after a sudden eclipse of the Sun: armies in battle, lions devouring one another, mysterious cries and drops of blood raining down causing people to die of fright. Oviedo calmly observes empty headed people can easily imagine such shadowy and evanescent shapes in the clouds, "if they fail to recognize that they are the natural effect of the wind." But, Oviedo hedges his bet, incongruously adding the odious crimes of Gonzalo Pizarro may have provoked "human and divine justice" into giving such signs of warning.

It would seem Oviedo well understood the superior power of God over the Devil and when he uses the word "foolishness" he is saying it is foolish to believe what the Devil taught. So, while explaining the native depopulation of Hispaniola from the million or so Columbus found to less than 500 in 1548 he recognizes the effects of Spanish abuse and disease but suggests God in his justice permitted the slaughter because of the Indians' heinous sins and implies God apparently forgot about the Indians for a long time and, coincidentally remembering them at the time of the conquest, noticed their wickedness was so great he "allowed their lives to be ended."

Although sophisticated Martyr frequently expresses joy that God has finally been introduced in America he, initially at least, does not seem too concerned about Hell fire. Even his realization that Aztecs and Toletecs practiced human sacrifice did not lure him into speculation. Explaining that Huizilopochtil was the greatest Aztec god to whom:

> victims are not sacrificed by cutting their throats, but by opening their breasts above the heart; and while these unfortunates are still living and realize their unhappy fate, their hearts are torn out and offered to the gods. The lips of the idols are smeared with the blood that flows from the heart, and the latter is burned, to appease, as they think, the anger of the divinity: at least the priests have taught the people this absurdity.
>
> I will be asked and with reason what is done with the members and flesh of these unhappy victims. O abominable and nauseous disgust! Just as the Jews under ancient law formerly ate the lambs they sacrificed, so do these natives devour the human flesh, leaving only the hands, feet and entrails untouched.

Martyr changes Cortez from swordsman to theologian when he orders the idols overthrown and the walls of the temples cleansed. When Montezuma protested Cortez rationally replied:

> Is it possible to imagine anything more monsterous and more absurd? Do you believe that these figures, made by the hands of your own servants, are gods? Are the works of your own hands superior to your dignity as men? O Montezuma! Is this thing made by the hands of your artisan, perhaps a vile slave, more honorable than your own majesty? What blindness or what mad credulity! Is it because of these senseless idols that you yearly sacrifice so many human victims? Do you then believe that these objects can neither see nor hear, can think? There is but one God, who has created the heavens and the earth, and it is him you should adore.[3]

By his final decade, however, Martyr is no longer so cavalier on the subject. He tells the story of a friar, Pedro de Cordova, "esteemed as a saint by all" who wanted to:

> discover the secrets of the [witchdoctors] and verify for himself whether they really prophesied under demonic influence and pronounced oracles...He learned that it was really true, for he witnessed the ceremonies...The demons struck the [witchdoctor] to the ground, like a kite seizing a rabbit. Much astonished the monk put on his stole, and taking holy water in his right hand...he grasped the crucifix in his left and spoke in the following terms: "If thou art a demon who dost overcome this man, in the name of this instrument of salvation, whose power thou knowest well (and he exhibited the crucifix) I adjure you not to leave this place without first answering what I shall ask you..."
>
> He asked him several questions, both in Latin and Spanish, and the man lying on the ground responded in neither Latin nor Spanish, but in his own tongue, and his answers always fitted the questions. Among other things the good monk asked him the following: "Now tell me, where do the souls of the natives of Chiribichi go when they leave their corporeal prison?" - "They taken by us to the eternal flames and fires that they may be punished with us for their crimes." These things took place in the presence of many of the natives who were present by the friar's orders...
>
> The good Pedro de Cordova turned to the [witchdoctor] still lying on the ground and cried, "Come out from that man's body thou filthy spirit!" Hardly had he pronounced these words than the [witchdoctor] suddenly sprang to his feet, but he had so far lost his senses that he remained a long time as if bewildered, and scarcely able to stand.[4]

The demonic theme recurs in frequent references to serpents in many early descriptions. As any Latin America visitor knows reptiles are common enough but they suggest a familiar creature from the Bible. Thus Father Sahagun provides an ample herpetology for Mexico including a snake with a head at both ends, capable of moving either direction it wanted. (Which head made the decision Sahagun does not explain.) Quetzacoatl, the feathered serpent, so revered in Mexico, only exacerbated the theme.

Gomora comes right out and says, "The principal god of the Mexicans was the Devil." He devotes an entire chapter to "How the Devil appeared to the Indians," explaining "The Devil did many times talk with the priests and with other rulers and particular persons, but not with all sorts of men." He continues "The wicked spirit appeared unto them in a thousand shapes and fashions and finally he was constant with them very often." He provides numerous examples of Montezuma going to a special chapel to talk with Satan.

Torquemenda writing much later remade Acosta's point (censored out of the Italian edition) it was "the wish of the Devil to substitute himself in the place of God." He did not dwell on it though, admitting he was afraid of the censor.

The North Americans were just as bad. The Gentleman of Elvas says in the Gulf states, "The Indians are worshipers of the Devil, and it is their custom to make sacrifices of the blood and bodies of their people, or any of those they come by; and they affirm too, that when he speaks, telling them that he is an atheist, and they must sacrifice to him." But the Gentleman of Elvas is ambivalent at least. He makes a couple of other references to Satin but his tone suggests the Prince of Darkness was not much worse than de Soto.

In *Principal Navigations* Hakluyt quotes David Ingram who on his stroll through America ran into the Devil on a few occasions and Henry Hawks: "They use divers times to talk with the Devil, to whom they do certain sacrifices and oblations; many times I have seen them taken with the same, and seen them most cruelly punished for that offense."

Tropical storms, volcanic activity and plague led to mutual recriminations. Disease broke out among Indians as soon as they encountered Whitemen. Indians blamed Europeans, which was probably true but they attributed the cause to witchcraft. While Indians blamed Spanish witchcraft for their troubles English were blaming the Indians. Francis Drake in his report of his 1577 - '80 voyage around the world says coasting along Brazil he watched Indians making fires, "a sacrifice (as we learned) to the devils, about which they use conjurations, make up heapes of sande and other ceremonies, that when any ship shall goe about to stay upon their coast. . . stormes and tempests may arise, to the casting away of ships and men." But by the time Drake wrote the Spanish had already sent out a commission to investigate.

In his notes to Benzoni's history Calvinist Urban Chauveton, who never visited America, gives a garbled account of savages based on what he read. On one hand they are depraved and brutal while on the other, eager to heap coals on Spanish heads, he makes them innocent, simple, peaceful and intelligent. But on one point he is positive. America before the conquest was the realm of Satan. The Spanish by their cruel acts made the name of Christ hateful to the Indians and strengthened Satan's hold over them. Such names Indians gave their deities they were mere pseudonymous for Satan who gradually stifled what natural reason Indians had, depriving them of their sense of right and wrong and seducing them into all sorts of wickedness. Like the Spanish who he so loathes Chauveton also picks up on the Devil counterfeiting Christian ceremonies theme.

Guillaumme Postel's *Merveilles du Monde* (Paris, 1553) has a different slant. He detects two heritages drawn from Noah, one "spiritual, masculine, ascendant, heavenly and immutable." The other, descended from the cursed Ham (from whom no European would acknowledge descent), moved West. The further West you got the closer to the infernal until in the New World people worshiped the Devil. This sounds different from Columbus', Vespucci's and Martyr's speculation on placement of terrestrial paradise but everyone is entitled to an opinion.

Newe zeittung. von dem lande. das die
Sponier funden haben ym 1521.iare genant Jucatan.

Newe zeittung vō Prußla/vō Kay: Ma: hofe 18 Martze. 1522.

Newe zceyt von des Turcken halben von Offen geschrieben.

Title page of an anonymous German newsletter reporting on Mexico.
It depicts human sacrifice and the Devil lecturing his disciples.

Even that great champion of Indians, Casas, to paraphrase a homily, could quote the Devil for his own purpose. Rationalizing various offensive customs, such as ceremonial drunkenness, he explains they not faults endemic to Indians but "a defect of all the heathen thanks to the industry of the Devil." Sahagun was even better, blaming Aztec sacrifices on the "most cruel hatred of our enemy Satan, who with the most malign cunning persuaded them to engage in such infernal acts." Sahagun also worried about the Aztec calendar, which provided dates for feasts and ceremonies and seemed to include prophecies, calling it "either an art of sorcery or a compact and fabrication of the Devil."

Visually this negative emphasis appears on the cover of an anonymous German newsletter of ca. 1522 reporting a voyage to Yucatan and the Turkish threat. It depicts two Toletec priests dismembering children while a third worships an idol. In the foreground acolytes are throwing the mutilated bodies down a flight of stairs while the Devil lectures his disciples in an upper corner. A woodcut in Lery's description of Brazil includes flying demons and an anonymous Portuguese painting of ca. 1540 - '50 shows Satin wearing feathers (by now universal symbol of Indians) presiding over torture of the damned. At century's end de Bry depicted Amerindian idols and the American Devil himself.

These are a few examples among scores and while there may have been some fine points of disagreement on this one issue Protestant and Catholic agreed. The Devil lived in America.

Other non European cultures were subject to similar scrutiny and accusation but America was different. The mighty fortress had been fighting a stalemated border war with infidels they knew or at least though they knew for a thousand years. Ability to penetrate was limited. America was penetratable and reducible. This is the pragmatic issue. The philosophical? America was just too different, a possibly cut off land where nudity, cannibalism, human sacrifice and sodomy (this last, a frequent charge laid against Amerinds, was no small matter - God destroyed an entire town in Palestine for this sin) flourished was too much. By mid-century Europe had discovered an entire hemisphere in league with the Devil in a plot to overthrow God.

Acosta again has the opportunity to examine the findings of a century in his moral history, i.e., "history of customs," and was able to compose the longest (about 100 pages in the Hakluyt Society edition) and most speculative account of American religion to see print so far and (save la Vega) for a long time after. He echoes Casas and Sahagun in blaming the Devil for the Indians' failure to lead proper lives. This brings him to begin the first book of the *Moral History* with a dissertation on the pride and malice of the Devil developed from assorted Old Testament authors in which he finds the Devil so proud, presumptuous and obstinate, "that always he seeks and strives to be honored as God." Fortunately "he had been rooted out of the best and most notable parts of the world, yet he hath retired himself into the most remote parts, and hath ruled in that other part of the world which, although it be much inferior in nobility, yet is of no less compass." He says the Devil conceived a mortal hatred of mankind and "he knows the greatest misery of man is to worship [Satan] for God."

Following the "know your enemy" principal Acosta examines Indian religion and customs providing a pantheon of Mexican and Peruvian deities, no small task for someone writing sixty-five years after zealous monks, who Cortez could not even control, wiped out every trace of Mexican civilization. So completely had they razed Mexico City that a book by Fray Diego Valdes, *Rhetorica Christiana* (Perugia, 1579), with illustrations supposed to have been drawn in Mexico City show almost no trace of Amerindian influence and Mexican and Peruvian artifacts had long since been melted down. Acosta grumbles about

Mayan "books of leaves of trees, folded and squared after their manner, in which the wise Indians contained the distributions of their times, the knowledge of the planets. . . But it seemed to some pedant [Landa] that all this was an enchantment and magic art. . . so they were committed to the fire. Which not only the Indians found to be ill done, but also curious Spaniards." Acosta who is hardly above an occasional witchcraft tale himself deplores the fact that this has been done elsewhere too noting it "proceeds of a foolish and ignorant zeal, who not knowing, nor seeking to know what concerned the Indians, say prejudicially they are all but witchcrafts." During his travels Father Joseph saw an assortment of ruins but as to their function he could only guess. He had to glean what he could from aged Indians and other priests but in sum he did a pretty good job.

Acosta gets away from the wandering apostle problem by finding with St. Paul (*Acts* XVII and XVIII) infidels have some knowledge God. This makes conversion easier, "but it is hard to root out of their minds that there is no other God." He finds the Peruvians believe the soul is eternal living in glory or pain after death "so there is little difficulty to persuade them of these articles. But they have not yet come to the knowledge that the bodies should rise with the souls," hence mummification.

Following Cieza and Gomora he describes the slaying of households of great men in both Mexico and Peru on the death of the master (sometimes as many as a thousand servants) to accompany their lord in his future life, "and those that were appointed do death held themselves happy." He finds it regrettable that even in his own time Indians occasionally dig their dead out of church yards and bury them somewhere else providing them with food and gold for their other worldly wanderings.

Acosta describes ritual human sacrifice in Mexico explaining the Aztecs would select a captive they thought worthy of the occasion, dress him in the costume of an idol and give him the idol's name. For a specific period, ranging from a few weeks to a year depending on the feast they revered him as the idol during which time: "he did eat, drink and be merry. When he went through the streets, the people came forth to worship him, and everyone brought him alms, with children and sick folks, that he might cure and bless them, suffering him to do all things at his pleasure, only he was accompanied with ten or twelve men least he should flee. . . The feast being come, and he grown fat they killed him, opened him, and ate him making a solemn sacrifice of him."

In his discussion of various Mexican festivals and religious services Acosta never ceases to repeat this description, occasionally changing one gory detail for another; removing the still beating heart, casting the corpse down the temple steps, flaying the victim, smearing blood on the temple walls and on and on *ad nauseam*.

Although Acosta is an acute observer he cannot escape the same superstition he was trying to eradicate. One of several examples occurs in his description of idols where he says, "I believe verily that the Devil in whose honor they make these idols, was pleased to cause himself worshiped in these deformities, and it truth it was found so, that the Devil spake and answered in many of these. . . idols." Although in his *Natural History* he said he would only confine himself to what was comfortable to reason other examples appear in a chapter devoted to "signs and portents" of destruction of Amerindian empires. He explains Montezuma had become "so puffed in his conceit, as he caused himself to be worshiped as a god, [so] the Almighty Lord, began to chastise him. . . suffering even the very devils he worshiped to. . . tell him of the ruin of his kingdom." Acosta reminds us that "We must understand that although the Devil be the father of lies, yet the King of Glories makes him often to confess the truth against his will."

He credits apparitions described by Indians beginning with a pronouncement from a statue of Quetzalcoatl to the effect that strangers would come to possess his kingdom. Various sorcerers brought Montezuma the same news. He because so troubled he sought to appease the anger of his gods by having a "huge stone" (Idol) transported to Templestan so he could make sacrifices to it. As his laborers strove to move the idol it spoke saying, "they labored in vain, and that they should not raise it, for the Lord of all things created would no more suffer these things to be done there. Montezuma, understanding this, commanded the sacrifice to be performed in that place, and they say the voice spoke again. . . [saying] 'that you may know this is so I will suffer myself to be transported a little, then you shall not move me.'" It was easily carried a short distance then it would not move again "till after many prayers it suffered itself to be transported to the city of Mexico, where suddenly it fell into the lake, where seeking for it they could not find it, but it was afterwards found in the same place from whence they had moved it." To this Acosta adds a gaggle of other apparitions including a pyramid of flame in the night sky that lasted for a year and "many voices as of women in pain, which said sometimes,'Oh my children, the time of your destruction is come.'"

He is fascinated with the Devil trying to imitate God and tends to agree with contemporary demonologists back home who imagined the Devil counterfeiting Christian ceremonies. But unlike the European inquisitors who had pretty well made up their mind what went on at a sabat and merely read out a list of questions requiring yes or no answers to tortured victims until they got a "yes" Acosta had a tactile body of information to work from. This leads him to descriptions of various temples, the priests and their offices, "the monastery of virgins the Devil hath invented for his service" and similar institutions for heathen monks. There were Peruvian flagellants doing penance before the Devil who "hath always desired to be served to the great hurt and spoil of man." He discusses the trinitarian god of Peru, Mexican unction and baptism and Mexican and Peruvian communions, confessions and marriage ceremonies. His fellow Jesuits told him about ceremonies in the Orient giving him an opportunity for comparison while at the same time recognizing an affinity with Christianity. Thus the *Moral History* becomes the first book on comparative religion.

But one of Acosta's purposes besides his avowed point that it was necessary to understand the Indians to eradicate idolatry is to remind the reader that God is able to force the Devil to do his handiwork. Anybody who remembers poor old Job knows the Devil never wins. By instructing the Indians in counterfeit Christianity he made conversion easier. A civil war in Peru simplified Spanish entry. Even better was Inca Yupanqui who informed his soldiers after a victorious battle he won because Viracocha sent him "certain bearded men. . . no man could see but himself." When Pizarro's small band of bearded troops overwhelmed Atahualpa's superior army the Indians began calling them Viracochas making it easier to "win souls unto Almighty God." He adds, however, "and in truth, if we had given them better example [which Acosta is sorry had not been the case] these Indians had well applied it in saying they were men sent from God." In addition to these examples Acosta points out that by conquering vast empires the Devil worshiping Aztecs and Incas reduced polyglot tribes to a single tongue making it easier for the missionaries who "had not the gift of many tongues as in old times." Lamentably the Devil had not seen fit to extend these empires into Florida and Brazil where less had been accomplished in fifty years than five in Mexico and Peru.

Having dwelt at such length on sacrifices of children, virgins, animals and captives Acosta concludes with compassion and kudos to his fellow missionaries: It was "the great awe the ministers of these idols kept. . . [abusing] the poor people. . . [who] inwardly wanted to be freed from so heavy a yoke." Ignoring the fact the Indians had no choice in the matter he finds the reason Christianity was so readily accepted in the remark of an Indian who said, "We found the religion that you preached had no cruelties in it. . . and [was] both just and good, we understood and believed that it was the true law."

American allegory of ca. 1579 - 1600. An inscription describes America as a female glutton who devours men, is rich in gold and mighty with the bow. She rears parrots and wears garlands of feathers.

-by Philipp Gale.

All Sorts of Indians

VESPUCCI was the first New World visitor to seriously look at the people he saw. In his 1501 letter to de Medici he refers to what he calls the "reasoning animals" (as opposed to his natural history descriptions). He says:

> We found all the earth inhabited by people completely nude, men as well as women, without bothering to cover their shame. They have bodies well proportioned white in color with black hair and little or no beard. I tried very hard to understand their life and customs because for twenty-seven days I ate and slept with them, and that which I learned... follows:
>
> They have no laws or faith and live according to nature. They do not recognize the immortality of the soul, they have among them no private property, because everything is held in common, they have no boundaries of kingdoms and provinces, and no king! They obey nobody, each a lord unto himself, no justice, no gratitude, which to them is unnecessary because it is not part of their code...[1]

Vespucci explains they have no heirs because they hold no private property. They sleep in hammocks, live in large communal houses which he finds remarkable in their construction because there are no metal tools. Men bore holes in their lips and cheeks in order to appear ferocious. They are promiscuous but jealous of their wives. They are bellicose which confuses Amerigo who "could find no reason... since they have no property or lords or kings or desire for plunder, or lust to rule, which seems to me the causes of war and disorder." They are cannibals who bury their own dead but eat the flesh of enemies slain in battle. Captives are enslaved or married into the tribe but sometimes also slain and eaten along with any offspring they may have had in the meantime. One Indian "confessed to me that he had eaten the flesh of more than two hundred bodies... and that's enough."

Amerigo's vivid descriptions, based on serious questioning and careful observation, were the best evaluation of the antipodes and its inhabitants to yet appear and for a long time after. He discovered and examined a new type of man but largely refused to paint him as one of the monsters associated with the mysterious Orient or antipodes. He did throw in the giant story incurred during his voyage with Ojedo and Brazilian longevity which we attempted to dismiss on previous pages. His heresies also mentioned above were the result of clear vision, for instance women effortlessly giving birth and the new one of people without much beard suggesting again a new world with different people.

When the printing press came into play the situation changed. His stories about long lived nude cannibals with multiple wives living in antipodes made good reading for the demand in his day as in our's was for spiced up narratives and competition was intense - Venice alone supported 268 printers, all vying for bookshelf space. With a little help from an editor he made a good seller.

Amerigo's original letters while hardly uninteresting simply were not lurid enough. They did not even come up to reprints of Mandeville's or Polo's descriptions of the fabulous Orient. Where were the unipeds, dog headed men or those with eyes beneath their shoulders? He had not seen tailed tribes or people who lived on air or even mention a sea serpent. The publishers of *Mundus Novus* and the *Four Voyages* did their best to rectify these defects. In his letters to de Medici Amerigo wrote that to dwell on nudity and some of the natives' uncouth habits "would be entering upon obscenity" and it was "better to keep silence" but in the printed letters sexual and scatological matters take over. Now we hear the Guarani are:

> A naked race... they go entirely nude, men as well as women, without covering any shameful part... They do not practice marriage: each man takes all the women he desires; and when he wishes to discard them, he repudiates them without discrieting himself or disgracing the woman; for the women are at as much liberty as the man. They are not very jealous [a clear contradiction of his letter to de Medici], and excessively libidinous and the women as much as the man; for I refrain out of decency from telling you of the art with which they gratify their immoderate lust... They are so lacking in affection and so cruel that if they become angry with their husbands, they immediately by artificial means destroy the embryo within the womb and bring about an abortion... The women are charming of person very well proportioned so that their bodies show no ill shaped part or limb. And although they go about completely nude they are fleshy women, and that part of their sexual organ which he who has never seen it may imagine, is invisible for their thighs conceal all that part for which nature provided no concealment... In short they are no more ashamed of displaying their sex organs than we are of showing the nose and mouth. Very rarely will you see low hanging paps on a woman, or a belly shrunken from too much childbearing or other wrinkles; for they all look as if they had never born a child. They made it obvious that they desired to copulate with us... The greatest mark of friendship which they show you is that they give you their wives and daughters and fathers or mothers feel highly honored when they bring you their daughter, even though she be a virgin, if you sleep with her. In this practice they express the fullest hospitality... They offered us their women in such a way that we could not refuse them... countless numbers of people came out of curiosity to see us. And the elders invited us to come futher inland to other villages, indicating their intention to do us great honor; wherefore we decided to go; and it would be out of the question for me to tell you the honor they did us.[2]

Must have been quite an orgy.

For about fifteen years after the initial appearance of *Mundus Novus* Vespucci's only competitor in the American literature market was Peter Martyr who if anything goes him one better in describing some very unusual people. Although Martyr takes in a wider range, eventually reaching as far as Montezuma's empire, his admiration and fascination continue to come through.

He is intrigued by the primitive innocence and happiness of the Indians of Hispaniola, naked, without weights and measures and the fatal curse of money. They live without false judges or books, content with nature without a care for the future. He sees the Indians in the mirror of humanism and the shining image reflects back like a poet's vision of an ideal society where nature is the only rule. America would be perfect if only it had Christianity. Of course he is aware the tribes wage war on each other but Martyr is not sure the golden age was altogether immune from that plague either.

According to Martyr three features characterize the blessed condition of the natives. The first two are wisdom and bravery, both qualities contradicted by Columbus with his talk of docile, malleable Indians. The third is generosity based on primitive communism. Martyr is so drawn to the idyllic and borne on a wave of classicism that he cannot fail to merge Amerinds with the Noble Savage of antiquity and so etch the vision into history. He compares a squaw who escaped with her companions from Columbus' ship to Clelia, a Roman virgin in Livy's Book II who, fleeing the Etruscan camp at the head of a band of female hostages, swam the Tiber under a shower of darts and got them all safely back to Rome. And as for their wisdom: he has an old cacique telling Columbus:

> 'It is reported to us that you have visited all these countries, formerly unknown to you, and have inspired the inhabitants with great fear. Now I tell and warn you, since you should know this, that the soul, when it quits the body, follows one of two courses; the first is dark and dreadful, and is reserved for the enemies and the tyrants of the human race; joyous and delectable is the second, which is reserved for those who during their lives have promoted the peace and tranquility of others. If, therefore, you are a mortal, and believe that each one will meet the fate he deserves, you will harm no one.'

> Thanks to his native interpreter, the Admiral understood this speech and many others of the same tenor, and was astonished to discover such sound judgement in a man who went naked. He answered: 'I have knowledge of what you have said concerning the two courses and the two destinies of our souls when they leave our bodies; but I had thought until now that these mysteries were unknown to you and to your countrymen, because you live in a state of nature.'[3]

In another place he has the son of a native cacique lecturing the Spanish on their greed and in the process expressing amazement at Christian lust for gold, mere unwrought pieces of earth.

As for communism Martyr picks up where Vespucci (who he never mentions) left off:

> It is proven that amongst them the land belongs to everybody, just as does the sun or the water. They know no difference between *meum* and *tuum*, that source of all evils. It requires so little to satisfy them, that in that vast region there is always more land to cultivate than is needed. It is indeed a golden age, neither ditches, nor hedges, nor walls to close their domains; they live in gardens open to all, without laws and without judges; their conduct is naturally equitable, and whoever injures his neighbor is considered a criminal and an outlaw.[4]

He reinforces the generosity theme with an amusing tale:

> A singular custom prevails in our islands of Hispaniola, Cuba, and Jamaica, where a marriageable woman who has granted her favors and prostituted herself to the greatest number is reputed to be the most generous and honorable of all. The following story, amongst others, is a singular proof. Several Spaniards, in company with islanders from Jamaica, crossed to Hispaniola having with them a very beautiful woman, who had until then kept her virginity and remained chaste. The Spaniards agreed among themselves to accuse her of meanness, and they were so skillful and persistent that they transformed that young girl into an enraged woman, who determined to accept the embraces of any one who wanted her. She, who had formerly resisted everyone, showed herself more than generous to all who solicited her favors. Through the archipelago there is no worse insult than to be called mean.[5]

When he discovers the Mexicans and their gristly religion (this after nearly three decades of writing) he sends the news back to the Pope with all the scandalized horror of an old lady who has just discovered the goblin she always knew lurked under her bed: "let not your holiness be overwhelmed with disgust!" But even as he describes their demonic religion with all its gore he cannot repress fascination with the quality of their artifacts, which seem to outweigh Mexican sacrilege. He marvels over the first booty sent back by Cortez. Martyr's salubrious descriptions of Mexican craftsmanship, at least one of which describes statues of birds and animals which at a short distance appear to be real confuse this writer. One can imagine his fascination with fans made of brilliant feathers and maybe plates or chalices but surviving Indian artifacts tend to be abstract and presumably unpleasing to the Renaissance eye. Me thinks Martyr protests too much.

He is equally enthusiastic about Mexican palaces describing several. One outside Mexico City will serve for all:

> a very remarkable building. . . The wood work is also very artistic and some of the beams of royal dimensions. The interior apartments. . . are hung with tapestries, beautiful beyond all praise. This royal residence likewise contains gardens filled with various trees, vegetables, fruits, and sweet scented flowers; not to mention vast ponds swarming with different species of fish and. . . every sort of aquatic bird. There is a marble flight of stairs leading down to the bottom of these ponds. Marvelous tales are told of the arbors bordered by hedges. . . These hedges are so disposed as to please in a thousand different ways, just as about the house of the more cultivated of our cardinals. . . everything pleases the eye.[6]

TWO VIEWS OF THE SAME THING - IN ENGLAND

The message of these two seminal writers reached England in a rather unusual way. The name "America" and the first description of it in English was published, not in England, but Antwerp by Jan van Doesborch sometime between 1510 and 1522. It bore the title: *Of the newe landes and of ye people founde by the messengers of the kynge of portyugale named Emanuel.* Doesborch's book is a hodge podge of Asian and African lands along with an abbreviated description of Brazil freely translated from the *Four Voyages* which is probably as remarkable for its archaic English as anything else. He starts right off with America where Vespucci (who he does not mention by name) "sawe meny wonders of beestes and fowles yat we haue neuer seen before." He picks up on Vespucci's remarks about the absence of kings and God, the common posession of goods and of course nudity. Then he gets a little carried away "And the men hath couersacyon with the wymen. . . who they fyrst mete is she his syster, his mother, his daughter or any other kyndred. And the wymen be very hoote and dysposed to lecherdnes. And they ete on[e] a nother. The man etethe his wyff his children. . . they lyue commonly, iii C [300] yere and more. . ."[7]

And they are always fighting among themselves and eating their enemies. Doesborch certainly described an unusual place but his little book was no best seller for it only survives in a few copies. The English just were not interested in America, except for one that is. Thomas More.

More had also been reading Vespucci (and Martyr) and also discovered a strange place. To describe it he invented a new island, *Utopia*. The first edition (1516) purports to be a story told to More by Raphael Hythodaeus who identifies himself as a sailor who traveled with Vespucci to some new world under the equator far removed from Europe. More professes not to know where this place is but according to Hythodaeus Utopia is a land very much like what Vespucci described, a land without religious doctrine or laws where people live according to nature, without a king or private property, a place where everybody is his

VTOPIAE INSVLAE FIGVRA

ABOVE: Woodcuts used by Doesborgh in a series of
broadsheets and his aglicized version of Vespucci.
BOTTOM RIGHT: One of serveral depictions of Utopia,
this one a Louvain. 1516 printing.

PAGE 143: This print:"The Battle oт Nudes in a Forrest" seems to recreate the Vespucci/More theme.
Master N.H. (active ca. 1518-'26) appended a poem which begins: "An island called Utopian/ which
lies not far from Morian,/ Where there occurred an awful slaughter..." The emphasis is still on
Europe but the American associations are obvious.

own master and there is no administration of justice which in that realm is unnecessary. An equally explicit reference to Vespucci appears in a 1557 London edition of *Utopia* speaking of his repute said, "these IIII voyages are now in print and abode in every manne's hands."

If Martyr saw America as more than geographical discovery it is even more so for the Englishman. It was virgin space where a new manner of life, conjured by dreams could start up. Utopia sprang as much from the author's mind as anything he could deduce from Martyr or Vespucci. It was an opportunity, and a longing that never quite came true. Hythodaeus had visited Martyr's ancient golden age in the here and now. Like Martyr More never visited the New World or understood Amerindian society except as an ideal.

Utopia was popular and influential though, describing a way of life which seemed unobtainable in the Old World. The Utopians live by reason. Flagellant Christian poverty is missing along with evangelism and rigid orthodoxy. Even priests are elected and spiritual life is a personal thing. The magistrates of Utopia do not cut windows into souls, like inquisitors, and a citizen is subject to banishment for trying to apostatize. Utopia thrives on absence of private property and the law of reason. More, unlike practically every other writer of his century, did not seek to tame the savage by importing the European system to America. Instead he saw it as an alternative.

This alternative offered something both very old and very new. Maps and pictures of Utopia appeared almost immediately. Nobody knows if More's contemporary, Albrecht Durer read *Utopia* but he saw and admired Mexican arti-

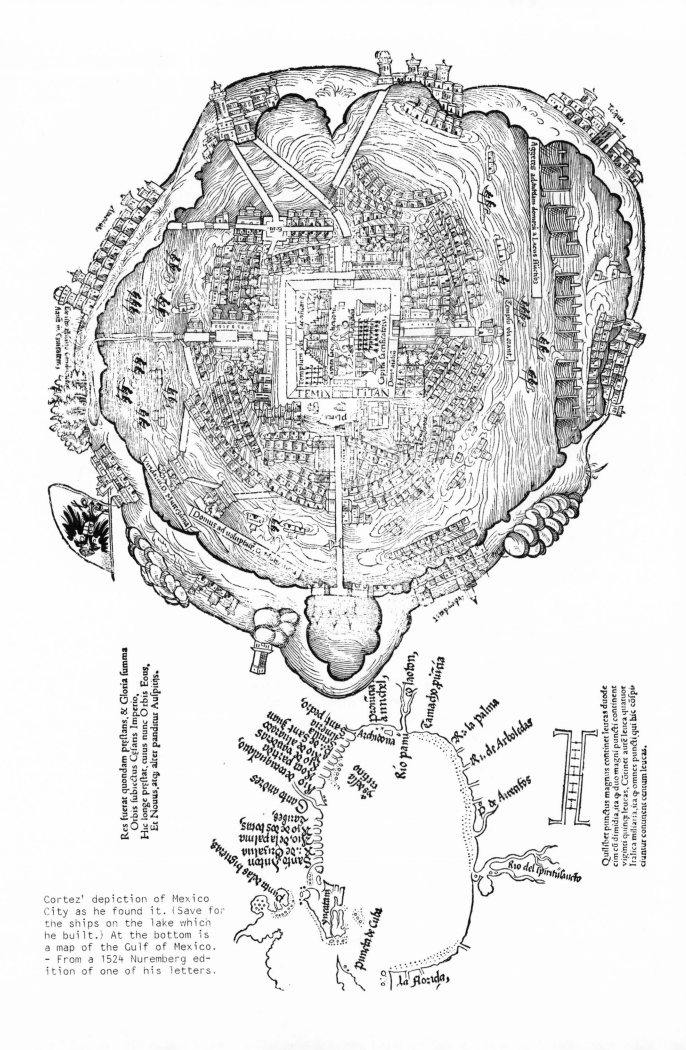

Cortez' depiction of Mexico
City as he found it. (Save for
the ships on the lake which
he built.) At the bottom is
a map of the Gulf of Mexico.
- From a 1524 Nuremberg edition of one of his letters.

facts and many have speculated Cortez' plan of Templastian inspired his picture of the ideal city.

More's American alternative glittered so bright that in the following century Campananella made one of the interlocutors in his *City of the Sun* "the helmsman of Columbus," and he almost certainly used Cortez' plan of Templastian as his civic model. But Scillaco had already suggested a land any part of which could be called "Felix" and Jehan Lambert's 1505 edition of Vespucci has an outburst of griffins in the margin, hinting of the marvels of the New World, surrounding a tree bearing a plaque emblazoned with the same word. For a few America already represented the longing for a better or different world that has been endemic to the human soul since the expulsion from the Garden. Meanwhile More had introduced a new word to the language.

SOME REDSKINS

Initial encounters, tended to support the noble or at least gracious savage theme. Verrazno was the first North American visitor to meet Redskins and write about them. Somewhere around Cape Fear he sent a boat ashore and consorted with natives who "came harde to the sea side, seeming to rejoice very much at the sight of us; and marveling greatly at our apparel, shape and whiteness, showed us by sundry signs where we might most commodiously come aland with our boat, offering us also of their victuals to eat." He says:

> They go naked except only that they cover their privy parts with certain skins of beasts like unto martens, which they fasten onto a narrow girdle made of grass, very artificially [artfully] wrought, hanged about with tails of divers other beasts, which round about their bodies hanging down to their knees. Some of them wear garlands of bird's feathers. The people are of color russet, and not much unlike the Saracens; their hair black, thick and not very long, which they tie together in a knot behind, and wear it like a tail. They are well featured in their limbs, of mean [average] stature, commonly somewhat bigger than we; broad breasted, strong arms, their legs and other parts of their bodies well fashioned, and they are disfigured in nothing, saving that they have somewhat broad visages, and yet not all of them, for we saw many of them well favored, having black and great eyes, with a cheerful and steady look, not strong of body, yet sharp witted, nimble and great runners, as far as we could learn by experience; and in those two last qualities they are like to them of the uttermost parts of China.[8]

Further along on his cruse, running short of water, he sent a boat shoreward to look for some but:

> by reason of great tides and continual waves that beat against the shore, being an open coast without succor, none of our men could possibly go ashore without losing our boat. We saw there many people, which came into the shore, making divers signs of friendship, and showing that they were content we should come a-land, and by trial we found them to be courteous and gentle, as Your Majesty shall understand by the success. To this intent we might send them some of our things, which the Indians commonly desire and esteem, as sheets of paper, glasses, bells and such trifles. We sent a young man... ashore, who swimming towards them, cast the things upon the shore. Seeking afterwards to return, he was thrust with such violence of the waves beaten upon the shore, that he was so bruised that he lay there almost dead, which the Indians perceiving, ran out to catch him, and drawing him out, they carried him a little way off from the sea.

The young man, fearing to be killed, "cried out piteously" but these Redskins had no sinister intention. They laid him down at the foot of a dune to dry in the sun and beheld him "with great admiration marveling at the whiteness of his flesh." They stripped him down and "made him warm at a great fire" which caused his shipmates to expect him to be roast and eaten.

"The young man, having recovered his strength, and having stayed a while with them, showed them by signs that he was desirous to return to the ship; and they with great love clapping him fast around and with many embracing accompanied him into the sea; and with more assurance, leaving him alone they went unto a high ground and stood there, beholding him, until he was entered into the boat. This young man observed, as we did also, that these are of color inclining to black, as the others were; and their flesh very shining, of mean stature, handsome visage, and delicate limbs, and of very little strength; but prompt of wit."[9]

When he reached Newport Verrazano again encountered the noble savage, this time the Wampanoag who he calls "the goodliest people and fairest of condition that we have found in this our voyage." It was not until he got to Maine that he encountered Indians "of such crudity and evil manners, so barbarous that despite all the signs we could make, we could never converse with them... [they used] all signs of discourtesy and destain as was possible for any brute creature to invent, such as exhibiting their bare behinds and laughing immoderately."

Cartier is a partial exception to the rule as far as initial encounters go. He formed a poor opinion of the Huron immediately and never entirely trusted them noting, "They are wonderful thieves, filching anything they can lay hold of." He also set a precedent by dubbing them savages - the word the French invariably used to describe Indians.

In his *Brief Recuit* describing his second expedition the captain introduced a few other interesting American features. Although this work is mostly a gazetteer of the St. Lawrence it devotes several pages to his savage hosts. He never

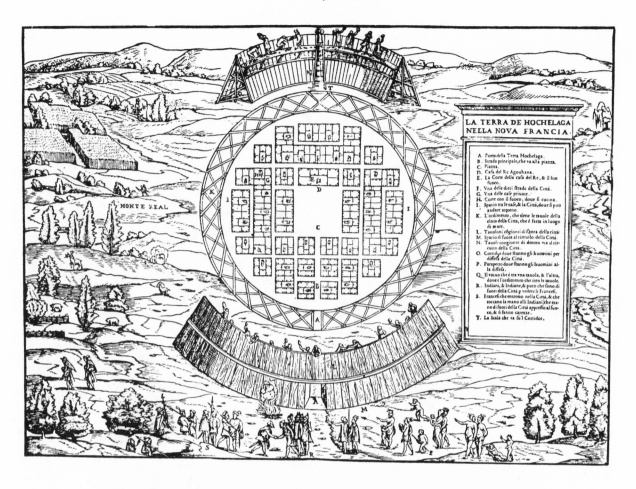

PAGE 147 top: Ramusio's plan of Hochelaga.
It closely follows Cartier's description,
save for the rendering of palaisades and
fighting platforms which should be ver-
tical tree truncks. BOTTOM: Canadian warfare from Thevet's COSMOGRAPHIE.

ABOVE LEFT: Buffalo hunt in Canada from
The COSMOGRAPHIE. LEFT: Indians hunting on
snowshoes from Thevet's SINGULARITEZ.

ABOVE: An Inuit squaw and her daughter
brought to Antwerp in 1566 and put on ex-
hibition. From a handbill advertising the
occasion.

PAGE 149: An Iroquois parade from SIN-
GULARITEZ.

fails to marvel at their going around almost naked even in the dead of winter. One custom rather shocked him. Young girls were placed in common brothels where the men of the community took their pleasure and no girl could leave until she hooked a husband but as the Hurons took multiple wives most probably did not stay too long. Those that did became community drudges. Shocked though he may have been he visited several of these establishments "and found these houses as full of girls as schoolrooms in France are of boys." He notes these *maisons de plaisir* also served as casinos where the men played a crude dice game, staking their all, even to jock straps and emerged mother naked.

A couple of other more pertinent issues may have seeped through Cartier's mind in the course of this second expedition. One was that these simple children of nature in fact had sophisticated military and trading alliances. Donnacona discouraged his going up river, seeking to keep the French to himself as a source of barter material and possible allies. Another issue was ceremonial carrying (depicted on Ramusio's picture of Hochelaga). The French assumed this was deference to European superiority but when one of them got dropped and subsequently punched his Indian bearer he got beat up. This cultural confusion peppers Cartier's narrative along with just about everything else written about the Indians until they were erased from North America.

A few points might be made here by way of digression. First of all initial encounters were generally friendly. Indians on first meeting the Whiteman were fascinated and assumed they had no reason to fear these new people with trinkets they handed out so freely. In some cases even slave catching was easy because the Indians, seeing strangers arriving out of the boundless sea on tall ships with billowing sails occasionally regarded them as gods. They wanted to go on the ships out of curiosity and some even were persuaded to return to the heaven these supernatural creatures came from. Of course there were exceptions. Characters like Ojeda could alienate his hosts within minutes of arrival and there were doubtless xenophobic cannibals who regarded any foreigner a delicacy. But generally first meetings were friendly as Cartier himself claims. The second point was that whether a report was prepared for the printing press or officialdom explorers were anxious to justify their activities. They usually stressed points about natives anxious to trade gold for trinkets, cordial receptions and willingness to receive the faith. Again Cartier's account of his first encounter is no exception. The third point is anachronism. Cartier's and Verrazano's first optimistic descriptions did not appear until Ramusio picked them up in 1556 and race relations deteriorated quickly. Cartier had long since become disgusted with Indians and there years later one of his pilots, Jean Fonteneau in his *Les Voyages Avantureuz* depicted the Newfoundlanders as porcine louts with "no more God than beasts." Time like geography created wildly different anticipations of what subsequent visitors would encounter. As late as 1580 Hakluyt translated these accounts out of Ramusio as if they were tomorrow's news.

BACK TO ELOQUENCE BRAVERY AND GENEROSITY

Another North American visitor picked up on Martyr's noble savage in a dramatic way when in 1557 when he published a book in Evora, Portugal with the (englished) title: *True relation of the vicissitudes that attended the Governor Don Hernando de Soto and some nobles of Portugal in the discovery of the Province of Florida now given by a Gentleman of Elvas.* Whoever the Gentleman of Elvas was he was not an unqualified admirer of Soto but he depicts a rather unusual Indian.

According to our anonymous author Soto's pattern when he approached a village to was an exchange of gifts then he would be welcomed with a florid speech like:

> POWERFUL LORD;
>
> Not without reason, now, I will ask that some light mishap befall me, in return for so great good fortune, and deem my lot a happy one; since I have come to what I most wished in life, to behold and have the opportunity in some way to serve you. Thus the tongue casts the shadow of the thought; but I nevertheless, am as unable to produce the perfect image of my feelings as to control the appearance of my contentment. By what circumstance has this your land, which I govern, deserved to be seen by one so superior and excellent that all on earth should obey and serve him as a prince? And those who here inhabit being so insignificant, how can they forget, in receiving this vast enjoyment, that, in the order of things,

will follow on it some great adversity? If we are held worthy
of being yours, we can never be other than favored, nor less
protected in whatever is reasonable a just; for they that fail
of deserving either, with the nature of men can only be
considered brutes. From the depth of my heart, and with the
respect due to such a chief, I make mine offer; and pray that,
in return for so much goodwill, you dispose of me, my country, and my vassals.[10]

Our author repeats orations like this with slight variation *ad nauseam* until
finally, becoming aware of his redundancy he confines himself to, "The speech
of this cacique - like those of other chiefs, and all messengers in their behalf
who came before the governor - no orator could more elegantly phase." (The
use of the word governor here and elsewhere is a partial explanation of the
arrogance of characters like de Soto and Pizarro. They had been appointed
governor of their respective realms back in Spain. They were duly constituted
authority. How well they filled their term of office is another matter.)

De Soto would usually answer that he was pleased with the gifts the cacique
had presented and would consider him his brother. But the gifts never seemed
to be everything Soto wanted and brotherhood did not keep "the governor" from
regarding the Indians as little more than hostlers or beasts of burden. After
resting and fattening his horses in one town the Gentleman of Elvas says, "in
consequence of the importunity of some who wanted more than was reason, the
governor asked thirty women of the chief for slaves." The cacique replied he
needed time for consideration and used the delay to get his people out of town.

Being an on the scene observer the Gentleman of Elvas does not fall totally
into romanticism. De Soto's trek was more the stuff of barbarity. He tends to
write prosaically, presenting the Indians he fought without laudatory or pre-
judical words but their eloquence, apparent graciousness and courage still come
through his pages. Soto had a large well armed force which the Indians had not
seen the like of before but they were also fighting on their own ground. The
Gentleman of Elvas describes Spanish valor and hardship (for instance troops
were frequently obliged to carry their own gear because Indian porters, for
whom Soto remembered to provide chains but forgot clothes, died of cold).

On one of several occasions when he decided to attack a town (this called
Mauilla) the Indians urged their chief to leave advising: "As things in war are
so subject to fortune, that it was never certain who would overcome the other,
they wished him to put his person in safety; for if they should conclude their
lives there, on which they had resolved rather than surrender, he would remain
to govern the land; but for all they could say he would not go. . ."

We get a gristly account of a fight to the finish in which "the Indians fought
with so great spirit that they many times drove our people back [and] many
Christians, weary and very thirsty, went to drink at a pond nearby, tinged with
the blood of the killed." Finally the Indians were fighting from their houses

which the Spanish put to the torch. The Indians still resisted up preferring to smother and burn. Soto lost eighteen men and twelve horses, 150 which received 700 arrow wounds. 2,500 Indians died.

Writing over a decade after events he described we wonder what our narrator thought about his adventure. His Indian oratory was clearly manufactured for the printer. Accounts of bravery might have been accurate but how did he know about that Indian council when they advised the chief to leave? Not being Spanish he felt little need for *apologia* but there is something more. He had returned the *Old* World with its decadence and strife and contrasting gracious, brave Indians with Soto's arrogance and cruelty also imagined a different place.

The 16th Century northern visitor who stayed the longest time, seven years, and wrote about it was Alvar Nunez Cabeza de Vaca. He joined a party under Pamfilo de Narvaez which reached Tampa in 1528. Narvaez sought to trek overland with 300 men and came to nothing. Only four members of his march saw civilization again, an infantry captain, Andres Dornantes de Carranca, his Blackamoor slave Estevan, Castillio Maldonado and Cabeza de Vaca who gives an interesting account of the experience. Narvaez fought Indians, who had seen enough Christians to be sick of them, as far as the top of the Florida peninsula when he was forced to sea in handmade boats. Cabeza de Vaca's craft, with all aboard asleep and debilitated washed up on an island off Texas.

Apropos of meeting a hundred armed barbarians he says, "If they were not large our fears made giants of them." This is part of his of his tone, a simple no frills narrative, which while pious and even inspirational stays away from the sensational. He is an exception for recognizing the Indians for what they are, some are good, some bad but he does make them into something they are not for his own purposes. At one point some of the survivors tried to put to sea again but their boat capsized and they washed on shore:

> naked as they were born with the loss of all they had; and although the whole of it was of little value, at the time it was worth much, as we were then in November, the cold was severe and our bodies so emaciated the bones could be counted with little difficulty, having become the perfect figures of death. . . The Indians, at the sight of. . . our suffering and melancholy destitution, sat down among us, and from sorrow and pity . . . . all began to lament so earnestly that they might be heard at a distance, and continued so doing more than half an hour. It was strange to see these men, wild and untaught, howling like brutes over our misfortunes. . . Holding us up they carried us with all haste. Because of the extreme cold. . . least anyone should die or fail by the way, they caused. . . . large fires to be placed at intervals, and at each the warmed us; and when they saw that we regained heat and strength, they carried us to the next so swiftly that they hardly let us touch our feet to the ground. In this manner we went as far as their habitations, where we found they had built a house for us with many fires in it. An hour after our arrival they began to dance and hold great rejoicing. . . although for us there was no joy, festivity or sleep, awaiting the hour they should make us victims. In the morning they again gave us fish and roots, showing us such hospitality that we. . . lost somewhat the fear of sacrifice.[11]

As Cabeza de Vaca learns more of his hosts he discovers they "love their offspring the most of any in the world and treat them with the greatest mildness. When it occurs that a son dies, the parents and kindred weep, as does everybody; the wailing continues for a whole year."

But Dorantes and a few others made another attempt to return to civilization and in the process fell into the hands of a tribe where Dorantes with his slave Estevan became a slave himself. These Indians: "abused [the captured Christians] as slaves never were, nor men in any condition have ever been. Not content with frequently buffeting them, striking them with sticks, and pulling their beard for amusement, they killed three of the six for only going from one house to another." He says they often kill their male children on account of dreams and cast away daughters at birth for fear they would marrying into another tribe, all of which were their foes, and thereby increase their numbers. To marry among their own tribe would be incest. (Its a little hard to understand how this tribe propagated.)

Cabeza de Vaca goes on to describe a famine ridden land where the cuisine includes, "spiders and the eggs of ants, worms, lizards, salamanders, snakes, and vipers. . . the dung of deer, and other things that I omit to mention; and I honestly believe that if there were stones in that land they would eat them." He finds the Texans a bit misogynistic, forcing their women to bear heavy burdens while the men carry none and working them eighteen of the twenty-four hours. He also accuses some of them of the "sin against nature." The majority are thieves for "on turning the head, even a son or father will take what he can. They are great liars and also great drunkards. But Cabeza de Vaca refuses to deny these slobs their humanity and he is confident that they will soon be raised to the level of Christians, once the missionaries arrive.

MORE SAVAGES

As far as books about America are concerned the big sellers were stories about cannibals. Vespucci is a good example but just as good is Hans Staten. In 1557 he published in Marburg a work entitled: *True History and Description of a Country of Wild, Naked, Cruel, Man-eating People in the New World of America.* Imagine a book with a title like that coming out today. It sounds like one of those best sellers about people who meet extra-terrestrials.

Staten was a Hessian mercenary in the service of the Portuguese. He was helping fortify a settlement near Santos when one day towards the end of 1553 he fell into an ambush and captured by a party of Tumpinamba. They stripped him to their own state of nakedness and took him to their village, making him shout out as he entered, "Here I come, your food." For nine months he remained prisoner under constant threat of being killed and eaten.

In addition to being as good an adventure yarn as his century could produce Staten's story is a tale of simple piety and a lively account of Tumpinamba life at a time when it was barely touched by European influence, and under the circumstances it is hardly surprising he dwells on cannibalism.

ABOVE: Title page and a cut from Staten's Marburg edtion. BELOW and PAGE 155: Like he did for so many other groups of Indians Theodore de Bry gave Europe its most vivid image of the cannibals when he selected Staten for inclusion in the third volume of his America series in 1592. These are two of the forty-five plates he prepared.

Although he was no university man he had a good basic education, fine native intelligence and good powers of observation. In addition to preparing the text for his *True History* he designed more than fifty woodcuts for the book (some prepared in the old fashion of depicting successive events as though they were happening simultaneously) which he observed the xylographer did not execute quite to his satisfaction. The pious element of his story comes in after he had erected a cross which the Indians subsequently pulled down. Soon afterwards rain began and the Indians came to his hut and asked him to persuade God to stop the downpour for it would impede planting. Staten replied, "it was their fault; they had angered my God by taking away the piece of wood near which I was in the habit of conversing with Him." The Indians helped him erect a new cross and, "immediately the weather cleared although it had been stormy all morning. They marvelled believing my God would do what I wished." Staten made no claims for his own powers but explained God accomplished the miracle but from now on he was in less fear of being turned into gruel.

Now in good stead with the Indians he was able to move about only to be repulsed by sailors on a French vessel who told him if they allowed him to escape on their ship they would alienate the Brazilians. When a second French ship arrived and finally consented to rescue the German the crew played an elaborate trick, based largely on hair color, to convince the Indians he was a relative and by that stratagem got him back to Europe in 1555.

For our purposes the significance of Staten is the immediate and enormous popularity of his book of two years later which achieved seventy some editions, a clear indication of back home fascination with cannibals and Amazons. As Richard Eden put it in his 1555 translation of Martyr, "there is no man able to behowlde them, but he shall feele his bowells grate with a certain horroure, nature hath endewed them with soo terrible menacynge and cruell aspecte."

The savage got some interesting literary treatment from the French who had a tendency to say more than they knew. After Cartier their next effort to find a place in the colonial sun focused on Brazil. This was a colony lead by Chevalier Nicolas Durand de Villegaignon. In his propaganda Villegaignon excused the well advertised cannibalism of Brazilians on grounds of lack of missionary zeal on the part of the Portuguese who, "had never spoken a single word about our Lord Jesus Christ to the poor people of that country." And if Europeans were occasionally eaten by Cannibals it was because the Portuguese offended and outraged them by their boundless avarice. However, aside from his recruiting campaign Villegaignon displayed little concern over the souls of the natives. His "colonists" tended to be treasure hunters and the best known religious figures associated with the colony, Thevet and Lery, spent more time writing about savages than converting them.

Villegaignon's first group arrived Guanabara Bay (site of present Rio de Janeiro) in 1555 where they were joyously greeted by Indians who turned out "in large numbers to welcome them with gifts of food and curious things in order to enter into perpetual alliances with them." But Villegaignon sought to keep as much distance as possible establishing his camp on an island. His reasoning seemed to be supported when the familiar European pestilence spread to the Indians killing more than 800 of them. The Brazilians naturally blamed the French and relations quickly deteriorated but the island location deterred open hostility.

Villegaignon's poorly administered colony miraculously survived for five years and in the process inspired two important works. The first was by Andre Thevet, a Franciscan monk (b. 1502) whose education, although superficial, inspired him with a desire to see the world. He had spent some time in Italy and five years in the Eastern Mediterranean before he set off with Villegaignon's first party. His title: *Les Singularities de la France Antarctique...* at first glance suggests he was a little vague about which side was up since it includes not only Brazil but Canada. More importantly it implies France was as firmly established in the New World as Spain and Portugal. Apparently popular, it was printed by la Porte in 1557 and again in '58 and again in 1558 by Christopher Plantin. It also has the distinction of being one of only three pieces of Americana printed in English between Eden and Frobisher (1568).

Unfortunately Thevet fell ill shortly after arrival, took the bed and returned to France after only two or three months. The result: after echoing Oviedo and others by announcing, "experience is the mistress of all things," he goes on to devote much of his book to hearsay. He creates a farrago of fabrication, with some anecdotes, a little original observation, descriptions of flora and fauna, cannibals and monsters (like the "haut," a creature with a human face and legs as big as a small elephant which lived on air).

The contemporary historian, de Thou, complained the monk, who was now the king's official cosmographer, was motivated by vanity to compile extracts from other authors and easily available guidebooks: "In fact, he is ignorant beyond anything one can imagine, having not knowledge of literature or of antiquity. . . he uses the uncertain for the certain, the false for the true, with astonishing assurance."

Thevet despite wide travels and official position was neither learned nor sophisticated and could not resist trying to say more than he knew. To flesh out *Les Singularitez* he falls back on comparison with ancient customs, a common

LEFT: A Cocoa tree and Brazilian family from LES SINGULARITEZ. ABOVE: Tumpinamba King Quoniambec from the cosmography.

PAGE 158: Top left, Cooking dinner. Top right, An Amazon execution. Bottom left, The "Haut." Bottom right making fire and smoking a cigar, all from LES SINGULARITEZ.

enough practice by now, Martyr, Oviedo, Casas *et al*. He says Americans "make their haire grow as Monkes were wont to doe, the which passeth not their ears." Alright. He has described a haircut but he has to push the comparison back in time. "It would be thought," he explains, "if these wilde men have frequented Asia, they should have learned this of the Abantes... Also Pluutarke sheweth in the like Theseus, that ye custome of the Athenians was they were... bound to offer lockes of heare... to the god in the Island of Delphos." Commenting on Indian nudity he recalls the same custom had prevailed among the original barbarian inhabitants of Europe as well as ancient Rome, as shown by their undressed statues "reared up in their temples all naked." To those who charged the Indians with other regrettable practices Thevet responds that they were simply conducting themselves in the manner of the complainant's own ancestors.

If Amerindians ate their parents they were merely following a practice known among the Romans under conditions of warfare; if they ate their enemies so had many ancient peoples. If they were at variance with European morals they were in company with the ancients and Thevet tediously recites chapter and verse. He finds they have some knowledge of the soul's immortality and in this respect finds Brazilians, despite some of their odious habits, more tolerable than the Protestants he sailed with.

Not content to only write what he did not know about Brazil he devotes the last eight chapters of his book to Canada which he writes about as if he had been there - which he had not. But he knew Cartier and had met Donnacona and from them received considerable information. He finds the Americans the most hospitable in the world. In speaking of Canada he says: "returning from the southern lands, we had difficulty meeting barbarians. A knight in animal skins, accompanied by several persons, thinking that we were worried and that we feared them, spoke to use in a friendly manner in this language. . . 'Come, come, my bothers and friends. Come and drink of what we have. We swear to you by the heavens, by the earth, by the moon and the stars, that you will suffer no more harm than we ourselves.' Seeing the goodwill and affection of this old man, we stayed with him the whole day. . ."

(The Gentleman of Elvas published the same year. One wonders who had been reading who.)

He adds he would sooner trust them than Moors or Turks. Cartier was hardly as enthusiastic, Fonteneau thought the exact opposite and Villegaignon, still down in Brazil, was getting thoroughly disgusted with the natives.

Thevet built up Norumbega into a castellated city and managed to work up a conversation out of Cartier's Iroquois vocabulary and attributes it to Norumberans on the Penobscot which Cartier never got anywhere near. He does add information the captain had neglected to print but again he gets confused. He notes in war, Canadians smoked out their enemy and used poisoned arrows. (Was he thinking of Brazil?) The weapons of the Canadians were such that they fought wars in the manner of the ancients. He follows earlier writers in citing vengeance as their cause for war since they did not fight over territory. But he does not see that they can be blamed for vengeance anymore than Christians. He also exonerates the Canadians of cannibalism.

Thevet is not without value though. His constant comparisons between some of the least civilized of the Amerinds and Old World ancestors guarantied them membership in the human race less than a decade after Casas had been yelling his head off in futile debate and was still dashing off reams of manuscript trying to prove they were something more than semi-human. Furthermore many of his observations tend to compliment and confirm Lery, Staten and Cartier.

One of the most interesting features of *Les Singularitez* is the inclusion of seventeen woodcuts. Some, if not all are attributed to the mannerist painter, Jean Cousin the Younger who provided illustrations for Thevet's *Cosmographie Universal* of 1575. Of greater purity of style than any until now that presumed to depict America they provide depth to the work. A good picture is worth a thousand words and Cousin's classicism neatly compliments Thevet's. Following the custom the of time he tends to portray figures in classical poses but they depict many details based on Brazilian reality. However illustrations of Amazon warriors (again a classical theme) are imaginary as are, presumably, a few depictions of Canada. A captive killing is copied from a Staten woodcut and a picture of a buffalo is lifted from Gomora.

Thevet's two folio *Cosmographie Universale* repeats most of these cuts along with much of the information contained in *Les Singularitez* throwing in a few more for good measure. There are new Tumpinamba views including a portrait of "King" Quoniambec and "un roy du Canibales." He also added a view of Trinidad, totally made up and maps of the four continents which he claimed to have drawn himself but in fact copped from Ortelius.

In 1584 Thevet published a large volume of copper engraved portraits: *Les Hommes Illustres.* . . which again said more than he knew but contributed to a eurocentric image of an American state. Like other illustrators of his day and later he was perfectly prepared to include imaginary portraits of "Atablatha, Roy du Peru," and "Montezuma, Roy de Mexique." He also included a picture of the King of Cannibals with a headdress resembling de Bry's engravings after first hand observer le Moyne and a figure of the King of Florida which also resembles de Bry so presumably he saw le Moyne's pictures and copied them.

One of those Protestants Thevet found so inferior to the Brazilians was Jean de Lery. He was born in Margelle Burgundy in 1534 and studied theology at Geneva. He sailed with a second group of colonists from Honfleur in 1556. Unable or unwilling to endure Villegaignon's tyrannical administration of the colony Lery and a few companions managed to escape Fort Coligny (as Ville-gaignon christened his settlement) and were concealed by Indians. Lery made it back to France in 1557. He was later pastor of several French churches during the religious wars and died in Berne, Switzerland in 1611.

Lery initially did not plan to write a relation of his voyage but several motives changed his mind. First he wanted to expose Villegaignon's tyranny. Second he claimed friends' interest in the narrative and the fact that Thevet's book was full of lies. *Histoire d' un Voyage fait en la Terre du Brazil* finally appeared in 1578.

Lery writes in a slightly Montaingesque manner recognizing that customs while different are not necessarily abominable. While sharing the common astonishment at naked Indians he represents this as the result of innocence and simplicity rather than the curse of Ham, from whom he thought they were descended. He admired their good looks as well as their restrained habits of eating reporting that they ate first and drank afterwards. This habit caused the French to ask, "Are they then like horses?" In describing Brazilian women's care of babies he suggests European women would do well to emulate some of their practices. He gathered other evidence of Tupimamba culture he considered worthwhile including some of their music which he published in the 1585 and

Illustrations from Lery: Brazilian dancing, a Timpumba family and cannibal warriors.

'86 Geneva editions of his book. During nearly a year in Brazil Lery came to realize danger to Europeans from Amerinds often resulted from misunderstanding. Personally he would entrust himself more willingly to Indians than certain (presumably Catholic) Frenchmen, as in fact he did when he fled Fort Coligny. As for cannibalism he observed nothing less after the St. Bartholomew's day massacre and notes apropos of the same event Indians only warred against their enemies.

Lery follows his contemporaries in claiming the Brazilians had no religion but unlike them does not use this to argue their lack of reason. (An interesting juxta-position from later centuries.) He uses an anecdote to illustrate their logic. Noting the Indians were afraid of thunder the French took the occasion to tell them it was God speaking in order to prove his power to shake the heavens. To this the Indians replied that if God had to frighten them to prove that his position must not be very secure.

Lery's vivid account is full of moralizing and mirroring. While Indian nudity is deplorable it is no more conducive to lust than the stylish wigs and provocative blouses of French women. And reprehensible as cannibalism is it is hardly worse than European usurers who suck blood and marrow from so many widows and poor people, eating them alive when it would be kinder to cut their throats immediately. In this respect they are crueler than savages who despise avarice.

In face of widespread fascination with the savage Lery does his best to illustrate them with five well done woodcuts. Two years later his second edition added three stylistically inferior scenes derived from Thevet, a battle between cannibals, the sacrifice of a captive and a strange looking animal which is actually a sloth. Meticulous in his determination to present as accurate a picture as possible he goes on to provide a description:

> Now first of all, following this description, you will want to imagine a savage. Imagine a naked man, well built and well proportioned of limb, with all his body hair plucked out, the hair of the head shorn away like in the way I have described (that is, like a monk), the lips and cheeks split, with pointed bones or fresh quarried stones set into them, the ears pierced, with rings in the holes, the body daubed with paint, the arms and legs blackened with paint... necklaces made from innumerable tiny pieces of... shell hung around the neck. You will imagine him as he usually is in his country, and his physical appearance is as you see him portrayed below, wearing only the highly polished bone crescent on his chest, the ornament in the hole in his lip, and, to keep himself in countenance, his loose bow and arrows in his hands.[12]

Lery's version of a cannibal battle copied from Thevet who never saw one.

A dramatic enough verbal picture, equal to Staten who Lery acknowledges as accurate while damning Thevet who he sometimes echoes but by the time he published the French Brazilian adventure and one other were history.

Two years after Fort Coligny fell to the Portuguese the French tried their hand again. This time in sunny Florida. According to Hakluyt Jean Ribault reported the Floridians were: "of a good and amiable nature, which will obey; yea be content to serve those that shall with gentleness and humanitie goe about to allure them, as it is needful for those that thither hereafter to allure them, as I have charged those that be left there to do, to the end they may aske and learne of them where they take their gold, copper, and turquesses, and other things yet unknown to us. . . For if any rude or rigorous means would be used towards this people, they would flie hither and thither through the woods and forests, and abandon their habitations and countries."

Maybe, but just as in Canada and Brazil the French were soon up to their necks in Indian trouble. John Hawkins who briefly visited the colony attributed the problems to the fact that most of the colonists were soldiers who "desired to live by the sweat of other men's brows." They would not even make the effort to catch fish as long as they could depend on Indian allies. In Florida as well as Canada and Brazil the French unwittingly debased their coin. To use the title of Patricia Olive Dickason's book the French suffered from "the myth of the savage." Despite ample evidence to the contrary they could not get it through their skulls that Indians, however uncivilized, were not simple silly children of nature but had customs, social patterns and minds of their own which they were perfectly capable of using once they knew the name of the game. Beads, knives and other trinkets tendened to deflate rapidly causing the French to complain of prices Indians demanded for food. As Hawkins put it the French, "made the inhabitants weary of them by their daily craving for maize, having no wares left to content them withall, and therefore they were forced to rob them, and to take away their victuals perforce, which was the occasion that Floridians (not well contented therewith) did take certain of their company in the woods and slew them; whereby there grew great warres betwixt them and the Frenchmen."

In any event the pathetic colony never got a chance to get off the ground. The Spanish wiped it out in 1565.

THE FRENCH PERSPECTIVE

America entered French consciousness in a very different fashion from the Spanish. Mostly through luck the Spanish reduced lands they entered almost immediately. Although speculation on the nature of the Indians began early Spanish occupation of "their land" was a *fait accompli*. Efforts to understand the Indians were primarily devoted to organizing them into a colonial framework and converting them to Christianity. Denuded of their own cultural base the Indians rapidly became second class citizens.

The French, on the other hand, during their extremely limited exposure to Americans were obliged to deal with free men. Instead of wiping out entire cultures with a single blow they were forced to trade for bare necessities. Such continuing experience they had in Canada between Cartier and Champlain was based on trade, not conquest, necessitating at least some recognition of equality, however it may have been understood.

All this is not to say the Spanish, French and finally the English did not approach America with eurocentric perceptions. Europeans had received varying receptions and discovered dozens of different cultures which they generally failed to recognize as such. It took uneducated Cieza de Leon and finally Father Acosta to realize they were dealing with a very large and variegated place. Most writers preferred to lump the entire population into a single group, "savages." Even Aztecs and Incas fell into this category because of idolatry.

Of course the French never encountered states in any way comparable to Europe like Mexico or Peru. Their most popular Americana authors were Lery and Thevet, writing about the savage cannibals that had fascinated readers ever since Vespucci's lurid accounts started coming off the press.

Returning to Ms. Dickason's point, "the myth of the savage" and my own, fear of idolatry it would be a mistake to underestimate the classification of New World men as savages whether they were living in an ancient golden age or wallowing in bestiality. They lived, according to most information available in France, *sans roi, sans loi et sans foi* representing anti-social forces that need to be brought under control.

Ms. Dickason quotes Thomas Hobbes by way of making her point. Writing in his *Leviathan* (1651) he explained: "During the time men live without a common power to keep them in awe, they are in that condition which is called war. . . [they have] no knowledge of the face of the earth; no account of time, no arts; and danger of violent death; and the life of man, solitary, poor, nasty, brutish and short. . . The savage people in many places of America. . . live at this day in that brutish manner."[13]

I cite this later writer because it reflects a common 16th. Century attitude. Acosta said about the same thing sixty years before. Amerinds collectively were probably less bellicose than Europeans. (Champlain was disgusted with Indian allies, who having taken a few prisoners in battle decided the fight was over and decided to go home.) But stories about Brazilians, Vespucci, Staten, Thevet, *et al*, described them as warlike. Even Lery who claimed to have witnessed only two violent incidents, followed Thevet by throwing in an imaginary illustration of Brazilian warfare and Thevet, for good measure, added an equally fictions picture of Canadian wars. A fete finale celebrating Henry II's entry into Rouen was an Indian battle and Jan Mostaert's famous painting "West Indian Landscape" seems the very essence of chaos.

This garbled image appears in a novel set in Canada, the first to use North American Indians as characters: Antoine du Perier's *Les amours de Pistion* (Paris, 1601). It is old time European fantasy with Indians resembling wildmen lurking

This American allegory engraved by Philip Galle around 1580 is an early recognition of New World variety with his Indians ranging from Eskimo's to Brazilians.

in the woods, straight out of medieval mythology. They possess a rustic grace but on the other hand they were "poor men having nothing human but the form; living with beasts like beasts. . . I only call them men because they spoke. . . Living without delights in this world, they will be suffering in the next because of the devils they worship." Du Perier then forgets his description and makes his Canadians act like Europeans. Instant transformation. Apparently popular the novel was adopted into a play by Jacques du Hamel in 1603.

This keeps us on a problem we have been trying to help renaissance man deal with all along, cultural diversity. It has often been pointed out that during the Renaissance man discovered himself but at the same time he discovered an entirely new type of man. Rational voices were occasionally raised in defense of cultural relativism: "The Aethiopian thinketh the blacke colour to be fairer than the white: and the white man thinketh otherwise. . . and the bearded man supposeth hee is more comely than hee that wanteth a beard. As appetite therefore moveth, no reason perswadeth, men run tinto these vanities, and every province is ruled by its own sense." (Martyr) "For there is nothing where in the world differeth so much as in customes and lawes. Some things are here accounted abominable, which in another place are esteemed commendable." (Montainge) The Indians "are nothing more strange to us than we are to them; savages we call them, because their manners differ from ours, which we think the perfection of civility: they think the same of us." (Benjamin Franklin)

These voices, unfortunately, were an extreme minority. The backwardness of the Indians, lack of artifacts and ignorance of the True God was ascribed by Jean Bodin to their "wandering far from their first fountaine, and leaving no sufficient monument to instruct their posterity." Le Roy made a similar remark in his *Vissitudes*. . .

For Bible readers these migrations were not meritorious. Movement always seemed to be the result of sin. The Old Testament is full of banishments starting with the Garden then Cain then Ham then Babble. By the third quarter of the century the Garden of Eden had moved back across the map to someplace around Palestine so Martyr's view that the Caribbean was some sort of a blessed place no longer held water because obviously the Indians had wandered further than all.

The Renaissance for all its blossoming, was not a period of tranquility or peace of mind. Rather it was a violent time when even as fragmenting spirituality gave way to the corporeal a sense of danger prevailed. Everything new, be it a painting technique, invention or discovery pointed away from a sublime spirituality and every change was a threat to the orthodoxy that offered tranquility. American discoveries exacerbated the fear.

Cultural diversity was held as a process of decay. Presumably Golden Age mankind had possessed a uniform ideal culture. Somewhere along the line, maybe at the time of Babble, this culture started to break down. As *The French Academy*, the mid-century encyclopedia of ethics, put it, "The nature of man desirous of diversity and novelty, suffereth itself to be easily overcome. . . of diversity and naughtiness rather than goodness." Differences between Spanish, French and Germans were bad enough but the Indians were just too much.

Albertus Magnus noted that plants and animals grew either larger or smaller as they moved from one climate to another. Bodin picked up on this to declare, "We see men as well as plants degenerate little by little when the soil has been changed." He discusses this in his *Methodus*. . . and *Republic*. . . largely following Ptolemy's theory of latitude determining coloration and temperament. He adds that according to Spanish observation the Chinese in the East were the most ingenious and cautious while Brazilians at the extreme West were the most barbarous and cruel. Unfortunately the widely read jurist only knew of three books on America. However this influential author manages to redeem himself slightly by conceding that social conditions could modify the effect of climate.

Although le Roy proudly announced "we can now actually affirm that the entire world has been made manifest and the whole human race known" he did not seem to understand it himself when he also adopted Ptolemy's theory of latitude changing human characteristics. Columbus had long since noted that Amerinds living on the same parallel as Ethiopia were not of the same color and by the time le Roy and Bodin wrote American travellers had depicted a consistency of hair and skin color throughout the hemisphere. This did not stop one of those travellers, Thevet, from using Ptolemy to explain that the Indians of the North were more courageous than those of the South but without Ptolemy to tell him how could he have known? As late as 1609 Marc Lescarbot in his *Histoire de la Nouvelle France* wondered why the hair of Americans was black while that of French living on the same latitude was not. Martyr speculated these puzzling discrepancies arose from the particular disposition of land in relation to the heaves in the American tropics. All this lead to questions about why Negroes carried into Europe did not turn white or whether American colonists would eventually evolve into savages.

Meanwhile the Europeans were well aware of their technological superiority. By mid century those American artifacts Martyr had so admired were floating around Europe as doubloons and escudos and writers like Gomora and Xeres dwelt on *pesos de oro* rather than culture. Cieza and later Acosta could only speculate on ruins. And, while Asia and parts of Africa were recognized to possess civilizations las Casas spent his life trying to convince his countrymen the Indians were better than mules.

The same Louis le Roy who had to use Ptolemy to explain physical and cultural difference breaks away from the idea of a deteriorating world and places his own eurocentric age at the height of civilization dismissing, along with Bodin, the idea of a golden age of classical purity. Stressing the importance of printing, the mariners' compass and gunpowder he contrasts the ancients' limited conception of the world with what had been revealed by the voyagers.

This theme of European superiority appears allegorically on the title page of Ortelius' atlas. Europe sits at the top of an arch with her crown and scepter presiding over Asia in flowering silks on one side and a semi-clad Africa offering a flowering branch from the other. Both seem to be looking down sadly at a nude America, recumbent at the base with her spear, arrows and a severed head. America, the last continent, seems not yet awake.

The idea of a superior and inferior order of men was no stranger to the French than it was to the Spanish despite my above remark about them having to deal with the Indians on more equal terms. Bodin in his *Theatre de la Nature* (1576-'97) explaines, "almighty God himself... divided the mingled parts of the rude Chaos and so settled everything in its due and proper place and order." He points out that just as there are some parts of the human body like feet which are called upon to labor and carry about "the whole bulk of the body" so there were slaves and lower orders who were "kept under... the most heavy burdens and commands of other citizens."

Dress in the 16th. Century, more than today indicated rank. Envision Bodin's hierarchy. At the bottom was the semi-clad slave then the unadorned farmer and laborer. There followed the suited merchants then wigged and robbed judges. At the top of this sartorial ladder was the king, so weighed down with ermine jewelry and finery he could barely move. During this increasingly rigid period clothing both identified position and symbolized law and authority. Thevet's slant on the subject in his *Singularitez. . .* was that in the manner of clothed civility God "uniquely favored Europe over other parts of the world." This obviously did not auguer well for the Amerindian image.

Simply organizing the savage into a chain of being did not stop speculation on his nature. Odd customs and dubious origins confuted and confounded ancient and biblical authority and contrasted wildly with European social structure which on one hand was considered a degeneration from classical purity and on the other the epitome of civilization.

Pierre Charron's *De la Sagesse* of about 1600 pointed out nudity had been the original condition of man: "Nature did not teach us that certain parts are shameful; we did that ourselves through our own fault." De Bry visually expressed this sentiment about ten years earlier when, with no sense of incongruity, he included a full page plate of Adam and Eve in the Garden in one of his *America* volumes. While Charron placed clothing as a devolution from a purer time his remark was a double edged sword. Once that step out of nudity was taken it was inconceivable man could be so shameless as to revert to his previous naked state, unless perhaps they had not shared in the experience of the Garden. Herrera used this heresy as justification for Indian enslavement.

Lery came closest to Montaigne in understanding a culture in direct opposition to Europe. He was surprised that even whips used to make Brazilians wear clothes were only partially effective: "As soon as night fell they took off the clothes we had given them for the pleasure of strolling naked around the island before going to bed." But he sympathized with their logic, clothes interfered with bathing. "At every spring and stream they come to, they splash water on their heads, wash themselves and plunge into the water like dogs, on some days more than a dozen times. They say it would be too much trouble to undress so often. How about that for a good and pertinent reason?" Thevet added Brazilians were annoyed by clothing because it interfered with movement.

After Lery it fell to Montaigne to describe Americans and in so describing try to rid the renaissance mind of the curse of diversification. "I have divers times wondered," he wrote, "to see in so great a distance of times and places, the sympathy or jumping of so great a number of popular and wild opinions, and of extravagant customes and beliefs." Speaking of the people of the New World he says nations have been found "which (as far as we know) had never heard of us," yet "where our crosses were in several ways in great esteem." There was also found "a very express and lively image of our penetiteniaries [i.e. priests, pilgrimages, etc.], the use of mytres, the priests' single life; the art of divination by the entrails of sacrificed beasts; the absence of all sorts of flesh and fish, for their food [during fasts or for other religious reasons] ; the order among priests in saying of their divine service, to use, not the vulgar but a particular tongue. . . There were places found, where they used the persuasion of the day of judgement. . ." They also "used traffic by exchange. . . and had adorned but one God who heretofore live man, in perfect virginite, fasting and penance, preaching the law of Nature and the ceremonies of religion. . ."

At first glance Montaigne seems to be echoing the multitude of writers who compared Amerinds with ancient Jews and pagans with such droll results. But his purposes are different. He is trying to introduce the idea of comparative ethnology and discover comparisons and universal cultural similarities. In his famous essay *Of Cannibals* of about 1580 he deliberately broke away from scholastic epitomizations and cultural data he could crib from ancient literature.

He had read Thevet, Lery, Benzoni and Gomora but he knew the informant was the weakest link in the flow of information so he preferred oral testimony of men who had lived in Brazil and he talked to Brazilians in France. He found these "simple and rough hewen" men more "fit to yeild a true testimony." Learned men might be curious and take in more but subtle men Montaigne feared: "the better to perswade, and make their interpretations of more validite. . . cannot chuse but somewhat alter the stoie. They never represent things truly, but fashion and maske them according to the visage they saw them in; and purchase credit for their judgement, and drawe you on to believe them, they commonly adorne enlarge, yea, and hyperbolise the matter."

The result was a description, new and fresh in spirit framed in language Montaigne insisted was "natural and unaffected. . . not pedantical, nor friar-like, nor lawyer-like." But for all his interest in cultural comparison and his complaint that learned men try to draw you in Montaigne fell into the same trap. He could not resist the temptation to compare Indians with the first men who went "naked, unshod, unbedded and unarmed." As a result Montaigne, along with le Roy finds it necessary to frequently invoke the word "No." There were no letters, no laws, no kings, judges, government, rule, commanders, no arts, no commerce or agriculture, no money, no personal property or clothes.

This frequent emphasis on the negative had a double connotation. For le Roy's readers if not Montaigne's it conjured images of the rapacious tribes that overran Europe to crush the Roman Empire. Furthermore the idea of a savage being possibly good outside of the Christian system was insulting to European conscience. In fact it was almost out of the question.

Even le Roy who by stressing the superiority of European technology and civilization almost single handedly broke the mood of rennaisance pessimism discovered a doctrine of compensation. While Europe had attained enlightment and superiority over anything that had gone before or existed elsewhere these great accomplishments were offset by terrible afflictions: epidemic syphilis, constant warfare and the erruption of religious strife. This leads us back to the positive implication of "No."

If le Roy could detect flaws in his society Montaigne was up to his ears in them. He found himself saying it was impossible to imagine a better society than existed in America, "with so little artificce and human solder." Intentionally or unteniionally the early rationalist becomes a Utopian. He echoes More and his narrator Hythlodaeus in fearing his readers will be skeptical, but unlike More Montaigne is telling no fairy tale. He makes his point ironically, recalling an enounter with Brazilians he met in Rouen nearly two decades earlier. When asked what they found most interesting or hard to understand about Europe he recalls two answers: 1) The Americans were amazed at the enormous power held by unworthy persons. 2) They were even more uncomprehending that property was not held in common with some Europeans "full and gorged with all sorts of good things" while others were "emaciated with hunger and poverty."

Montainge consistantly contrasts the virtues of barbarian America with corruption and decadence in civilized Europe. He confutes le Roy by praising Americans who have not yet been led astray because:

> The laws of nature still rule them, very little corrupted by ours; and they are in such a state of purity that I am sometimes vexed that they were unknown earlier, in the days when there were men better able to judge them than we. I am sorry that Lycurgus and Plato did not know of them; for it seems to me that what we actually see in these nations surpasses not only all the pictures in which poets have idealized the golden age and all their inventions in imagining a happy state of man, but also the conceptions and the very desire of philosophy. They could not imagine a naturalness so pure and simple as we see by experience; nor could they believe that any society could be maintained with so little artifice and human solder. This is a nation, I should say to Plato, in which there is no sort of traffic, no knowledge of letters, no science of numbers, no names for a magistrate or for political superiority, no custom of servitude, no riches or poverty, no contracts, no secessions, no partitions, no occupations but leisure ones, no care for any but common kinship, no clothes,

no agriculture, no metal, no use of wine or wheat. The very
words that signify lying, treachery, dissimulation, avarice,
envy... [are] unheard of. How far from this perfection would
he find the republic that he imagined? [14]

Theodore de Bry's illustrations for Harriot's VIRGINIA and Laudonniere's FLORIDA. PAGE 171: An old man of Pomeiock who looks like a Roman senator and one of the chief ladies of Secota. ABOVE: A Virginia chief who looks the very essence of a Roman warrior. BELOW: A Florida king with all the dignity of a European monarch.

For all his nascent ethnology and cultural comparison Montaigne along with the rest fails to understand that New World society was not based on the logical creation of nature but was as riddled with habit and custom as the Old. For him the noble savage is back, happy, good and brave to show up Europeans for the moral and psychological pygmies they had been since the end of the golden age.

Montaigne was unwittingly confirmed by his contemporary, the masterful engraver Theodore de Bry who probably did as much to enoble the savage with his pictures as anyone of his century. De Bry was a classicist by training. Whatever he knew about Indians did not make much difference. Like Martyr, who probably could not write differently to save his soul, de Bry knew only one way to engrave. The result is most evident in the famous plates in the first two volumes of his *Grand's Voyages* Harriot's *Virginia* and Laudonniere's *Florida*. In the case of Harriot on the scene drawing's made by John White survive in the British Museum. They depict some relatively scrofulous Indians, cooking snakes and otherwise engaging in primitive unappealing activities. Although de Bry follows the drawings carefully they become Greek gods under his burin.

Of course all Europe, except apparently Montaigne, considered the Indians in error. They were rightfully disgusted by cannibalism and human sacrifice. Idolatry was unthinkable while nudity, unsatisfactory eating habits and oft mentioned sodomy were condemned. But Montaigne articulated a theme that ran through fractionalized Europe's century like an underground stream, a romantic longing for a world without history and deadly sins that might start up again. Although most of Europe was not even thinking about America it lurked as an alternative that eventualy broke out.

THE SPANISH PROBLEM

Stay at home philosophers and day tripping visitors could write whatever they wanted about the savage. The Spanish had a job to do and the Indians were not helping. Put in the best light possible they were there with a license from the Pope to win the land to Christ, by force if necessary. This required missionaries, soldiers and administrators, none of whom in the discharge of their duties produce food, clothing or shelter. Somebody had to do it or pay for it. And if they tended to exploit the Indies a little all that wealth was going to serve Ferdinand and Charles, the last crusaders.

The Spanish approach on entering a land was reading of the *requerimento*. Although it had been used since the time of Columbus Enciso prided himself on rendering into its finest legal form around 1510. The *requerimento* was a summons enjoining the Indians to recognize the Holy Trinity, Jesus' investiture of the Pope and the Pope's authority to grant new lands to Christian lords in order to spread the True Faith. All very logical. If rejected this endowed violent conquest and enslavement of the vanquished with the character of a just and holy war. If the document was probably incomprehensible to most Indians who heard it the problem seems to have been overlooked at the time.

Even though he was a pragmatist to the core Enciso insists on draping the conquest in the garb of a religious crusade. He maintains the great purpose of the enterprise is enlargement of Christendom. The Spanish are the new apostles sent to the ends of the earth to preach the Gospel; if their words are rejected the idolaters' ingratitude toward God deprives them of any right to the lands they occupy. All accounts of the conquest have to be read against this pandemic attitude.

Enciso freely admits the *requerimento* had its limitations. In his *Suma de Geographia* he gives the response of a cacique who did understand it. The chieftain replied that the idea of a single God sounded reasonable enough but "the Pope must have been drunk when. . . he gave away something that was not his to give [and] the king. . . must be some sort of madman because he was asking for something belonging to someone else." Let the king come and try to take their land and they will stick his head on a pole "as they had done with some of their other enemies whose heads they showed me stuck up on poles." The cacique also pointed out that they occupied the land and "had no need of any other lord."

Enciso again threatens the cacique with war and enslavement but the reply remains unchanged. A scuffle ensues and the Indians are overwhelmed. He concludes with a description of a captured cacique: "I found him an honorable man of much truth. . . who kept his word and. . . could see bad as bad and good as good." Realizing he reduced this honorable man to slavery the zealous gold seeking Christian bitterly concedes: "that is the way most wars are conducted conducted there."

Enciso is sympathetic to the Indians but needs to get on with the job. In the course of it he discovers what the Indians believe, their rites and customs and pays attention to what they do and why they do it. He does not denigrate their intelligence and respects their craftsmanship. He occasionally sees them with amusement as in the case of an *In hoc signe vinces* story he told Martyr. As Enciso puts it the Indians regarded the Virgin as a helper of Christians. She was a "very beautiful woman who came to help [Christians] with a stick and beat [the Indians] all to death." But in the end they recognized her as a true goddess and a "good cacique." And although few learned the whole prayer they obliged every Christian they met to recite the *Ave Maria* whether he wanted to or not.

Enciso wrote *The Sum of Geography* to encourage exploitation of the Indies. Unfortunately his approach which totally erased a pre-existing culture base had some very debilitating results.

It was not that the Spanish did not try to understand the Indians. The view that the Indian mind was a *tabula rasa* ready to receive the faith held by Columbus and many others who made initial encounters fell apart fast. For purposes of learning their language and customs Columbus, belatedly recognizing Luis Torres limitations as a translator, on his second voyage carried the father of American ethnology, Father Ramon Pane. The good father probably realized he had bit off more than he could chew. The Spanish were totally preplexed by patterns of behavior that failed to conform to any European concept of civilization or society. This prompted officials in Spain to encourage government officals and ecclesiastics to study the Indians more closely, resulting in the preparation of numerous reports which went largely unpublished at the time. This body of linguistic, archeological and ethnological material is both contradictory and generally impossible to assess in face of the preconceived notions of the reporters. One of the earliest reports was Toribio de Motolinia's *History of the Indians of New Spain* prepared by order of the Franciscan chapter in Mexico. Completed in 1541, Motolinia's work provides an account of the life and beliefs of pre-conquest Mexicans and the labors of the Franciscans since their arrival in 1524. He added information about rivalry between Dominicans, Franciscans and Augustinians and some frank remarks on oppression of Indians and Spanish avarice.

The zealot, Diego de Landa, who tortured Indians and burned their books to eradicate idolatry, also carefully studied their customs and religion. He investigated every phase of Mayan custom and wrote the first description of their hieroglyphics and religion. Even though he condemned their practices he admired aspects of their culture and knowledge including the calendar, ability to cultivate fields, a quasi-Christian baptism, fear of death and the beauty of some of the women. However he has no reluctance to see this stamped out by the conquest which had brought them the great advantage of Christianity.

The Franciscan Father Bernardino de Sahagun produced the most complete and systematic study of Aztec life in his *General History of the Things of New Spain*. Sahagun was an able and attractive friar (in his early years his superiors kept him out of the pulpit because his good looks distracted women in the congregation from religious matters) who began to collect information in 1547. Ten years later his provincial ordered him to prepare a history. He spent 1558-'60 in the village of Tepepulco conferring with the oldest and most knowledgeable Indians he could find. He used a carefully prepared list of culture elements as the basis for his investigation and the Indians drew many pictures to explain their history. During 1560-'61 he visited Santiago Tlatelolco and checked his information with a fresh set of informants. He spent the following three years organizing his material into a manuscript of twelve books, a methodically arranged mass of carefully verified information on Indian gods, celebrations and ceremonies, ideas on immortality, astrology, medicine, philosophy, government, economics, arts and crafts, vices and virtues along with a natural history of the country and the Indian view of the conquest. Even las Casas could not equal his determination to find out what Indians thought.

Sahagun's labors were opposed by some Franciscans, on grounds that it was inappropriate for a man of God to devote so much attention to the ways of the Devil. He defended his work, attacking Motolinia and others for avoiding too deep an examination of Indian life least failure to understand minds so alien would strengthen Indian loyalties to ancient custom. To be a doctor you have to know the disease. In any event his work lay in manuscript for centuries.

Despite all this investigation by mid-century the prevailing view, in Spain at least, can be summarized by the story of the 19th. Century English traveller, who returning from some exotic land wrote a book on his experiences including a chapter on "Customs and Manners" consisting of four words: "Customs: beastly, manners: none."

In 1556 Francisco Tamara translated Johann Boemus' *Manners, Laws and Customs of all Nations* into *El Libro de las Costumbres de todas las Gentes de Mundo y de las Indias*. Although originally ignored by Boemus Tamara managed to add about 200 pages on America. Unfortunately he, like practically every other writer on relative manners and customs of the time, ignored the issue of social influences and fell back on Ptolemy's theory of latitude as determining human characteristics. Ptolemy let Tamara casually dismiss a few disenfranchised, landless Indians remaining on Hispaniola as "Vicious, lazy, idle, melancholic, cowardly, base, evil intended, mendacious and given to wicked and abominable sins [sodomy]."

This view brought out the aristotelians, one of whom was the Spanish jurist, Juan de Matienzo, who in his *Government of Peru* (1567) pronounced all Indians to be "pusillanimous and timid" and ascribed these defects to their melancholic humor: "Men of this type and complexion are, according to Aristotle, very fearful, weak and stupid," he explains and were: "naturally born and brought up to serve. And it can be known that they were born for this because, as Aristotle says...such types were created by nature with strong bodies and were given less intelligence, while free men have less physical strength and more intelligence. So it can be seen they carry burdens on their backs of twenty-five to fifty pounds and walk along beneath them without difficulty."

Matienzo concludes the stronger you are the stupider you are. (Unfortunately we have no idea of his physique.) Just as Aristotle described barbarians as irrational and living only by their senses like beasts Matienzo finds the Indians "animals who do not even feel reason but are ruled by their passions." He tells us the Indians ate and drank without a thought for tomorrow. (An interesting juxta position to Martyr who found this a virtue.)

Matienzo was no armchair philosopher condemning the Indians to natural servitude from a well stocked library back in Spain. He was a pragmatic official with six years experience in Peru but classical authority seemed to overwhelm him. Apparently more ignorant of the successful Incan communism the Spanish had so effectively numbed than he should have been, Matienzo also finds a solution to the problem in Aristotle. "It is not surprising," he argued these poor Indians should be idle and take no trouble to work, because untill now they had no private property, but everything in common." Aristotle said attachment to private property made men work so Matienzo suggests offering the Indians plots of land and wages for labor, get a specie economy going so they could buy goods. This he believed would gradually transform them into civilized men.

A similar view was held by another Peruvian official, Hernando de Santillan who maintained that while Indians were "of little understanding and civility" they were not as brutish as the Spanish made them out to be. Wages would create in them acquisitive instincts and the consequent propensity to work.

As the century wore on Spanish settlers increasingly needed apologists. The argument that they were cross bearers was getting shaky in face of the growing and obvious enslavement and destruction of Indians. This took the form of paternalism. Early on Martyr reluctantly concluded the necessity lest the Indians lapse back into their old ways. The theme was spelled out by Pedro de Feria, bishop of Chiapas, in a memorandum submitted to the third Mexican Provincial Council of 1585: "We must love and help these Indians as much as we can. But their base and imperfect character requires that they should be ruled, governed and guided to their appointed end by fear more than love. . . These people do not know how to judge the gravity of their sins other than by the rigor of the penalties with which they are punished."

The most famous aristotelian was Juan Gines de Sepulveda who penned a Latin dialogue: *Democrates Atler, Sive Justis Belli Causis Apud Indos*, upholding the "just causes of war against the Indians" and their subsequent enslavement because forcible conquest was the only way to jamb Christianity down Indian throats. Fortunately for the Indians he was seeking a license to print when las Casas returned to Spain on one of his periodic complaining missions. A clash was inevitable. It began with Bishop Casas' successful attempt to block publiccation of *Democrates Atler*. . .

Casas claimed Sepulveda's book was based on information derived from Spaniards guilty of destroying Indians, designed to rationalize forcible conquest and slave holding (in opposition to laws promulgated in the 1540's to defend the Indians) colored as a defense of royal title to the Indies.

Denied a license to print in Spain Sepulveda sent his manuscript to friends in Rome who printed it in the form of an "Apology" to the Bishop of Segovia who had helpfully corrected him on some religious matters. Learning of this Charles V ordered all copies of the *Apology*. . . in Spain seized. Undaunted Sepulveda got out a "Summary" for circulation in Spain prompting Casas to dash off about 500 pages of manuscript defending the Indians against it.

These were opening shots in a controversy that became so fierce the emperor, his conscience belatedly troubled over how to carry out the conquest, ordered a suspension of all expeditions in America while a junta of foremost theologians, jurists and officials was convened in Valladolid to listen to arguments. The debate, of course was academic - by now Spain had crushed Mexico and Peru and had no intention of restoring country to Indians or abandoning products of their mines. But the encounter produced historic literature none the less.

It began late in 1550 with Doctor Sepulveda appearing at the first session and summarizing the main points of *Democrates Alter*. . . He justified conquest on four reasons: 1) The gravity of Indian sin (including good old sodomy). 2) Rudeness of the natives which made it appropriate for them to serve more refined Spanish. 3) Necessity of spreading the faith which previous subjugation simplified. 4) Protection of Indians, liable to human sacrifice or cannibalism.

Las Casas took the stand next and spent five days reading his manuscript. While Sepulveda painted Indians as irrational sub humans Casas argued they had many skills and possessed a culture worth respect. He cited agricultural methods and irrigations systems. He demonstrated their ingenuity by the way they derived twenty-two products from the maguey tree and contrived delicate ornaments. He drew special attention to their capacity to master Old World crafts, describing their cleverness as painters and hand lettering which was so fine sometimes it could not be distinguished from printing. About the only thing he found an Indian could not do as well as a Spaniard was shoe a horse.

The bishop got a little carried away when it came to Indian religion. He argued the most religious people were those who offered most to their god, and those who offered human beings must have a very high opinion of their deity indeed. Indian fasts, mortification of the body, sacrifice of men were clearly superior to the paltry sacrifices of ancient pagans. Under the ghoulish aspects of such rites Casas discerned a depth of religious devotion which could be directed to higher ends and enlisted in the service of the True God.

Casas relied heavily on the papal bull which insisted all people in the world were men, emphatically rejecting static and hopeless barbarism. He declared God would not allow a nation to exist "no matter how barbarous, fierce or depraved in their customs" which might not be "persuaded and brought to a good order and way of life" provided the persuasion was peaceful. He further insisted the only justification for Spanish presence in the New World was Christianization by peaceful means. *De jure* he was right, citing papal authority chapter and verse. *De facto* he was dangerous nonsense, not only to Spanish colonists but the emperor himself who was spending every ounce of American gold he could get his hands on to stamp out Protestants and other threats to the Holy Roman Empire.

After the debate the judges prepared a summary. Sepulveda wrote a twelve point rebuttal to which Casas gave the same number of answers.

As to the outcome both Casas and Sepulveda claimed victory. In fact no formal decision was made and none could have been. But if the old conquistadors hoped to loosen up laws the bishop had fought for most of his life they failed on the strength of Casas' disputation.

In 1550 seventy-seven year old las Casas resigned his duties as Bishop of Chiapas and took up residence in the Dominican College of San Gregorio at Valladolid where he became a publisher. He began with a series of eight quarto tracks which saw print during his lifetime which we will discuss elsewhere. He spent the next ten years collecting and editing books and manuscripts about the Indies. The result, finally finished about 1561, was his *Historia de las Indias* and *Apologetica Historia* which he had begun in 1527 at the Dominican monastery of Peurto de Plata on Hispaniola.

Although these works were not published until the 19th. Century las Casas is rivaled only by Oviedo as a participant historian fortunate enough to have lived through this seminal period of American history. He gives extensive details of the discovery period down to 1520 based on original documents and personal acquaintance with many of the participants. An offshoot of the history was the *Apologetica Historia, Summaria de les Gentes destas Indias* or "Apologetic History." Begun as a descriptive aside to the general history it was finished as an elaborate encyclopedia to prove Indian capacity by aristotelian principals and comparison with antiquity - as if Sepulveda was still nipping at his heels.

The first twenty chapters of the *Apologetica Historia* describe the "provinces, quality, amenity and prosperity" of Hispaniola. Chapter twenty-one sketches in the geography and climate of the other islands. Chapter twenty-two is a geographic throwback that tries to prove "the Western Indies are part of India." The remaining 245 chapters are a formal defense of the Indians based on Father Bartolome's extensive studies and observations. His method of doing this is the familiar technique of comparing them with ancient pagans but las Casas has a slightly different slant, devoting nearly a fifth of his book to practices of ancient Greeks, Romans, Egyptians and others in an effort to prove the Indians were no less corrupt than any other nation "without the light of faith." He gives chapters to pagan orgies, sacrifices and depravities concluding: "They equaled many nations of this world that are renowned and to none were they inferior. Among those who they equaled were the Greeks and Romans, and they surpassed them in many good and better customs. They surpassed also the English, French and some of the people in our own Spain; and they were incomparably superior to countless others, in having good customs and lacking many evil ones."

A rather sweeping dictum. But Casas did marshal conclusive evidence of Indian capacity. Were it not for the fact that accusations of racial inferiority have been made to our own day it would seem remarkable that all this would seem necessary seventy years after Columbus and forty years after Cortez.

It was not until century's end that a lone voice, again crying in the wilderness, began to understand the problem of cultural disenfranchisement. In 1591 a young doctor, Juan de Cardenas, a native of Mexico City, published *Problems and Marvelous Secrets of the Indies*. He describes the Chichimeca of Northern Mexico as "as savage and barbarous people, never subjected or tamed by any other nation." They live among rocks and crags, wore no clothes and stank to heaven. They have no God, no rites or customs and publicly committed every bestial act imaginable. Their entire life was given over to killing animals and men. But Cardenas concedes that, despite a repulsive diet, in their own country they were brave, healthy and strong.

Capture a Chichimeca, try to civilize him and what happens? He languishes and declines. Cardenas found an explanation for the sad change in environment and custom. Spanish food was unnatural to men whose regular diet was roots and berries. The decline and death of Chichimecas in civilization he ascribes to "change of air, diet, custom and way of life, so that one can say with justice of them that change of custom is equivalent to death."

Cardenas' opinion did not change anything.

CIVILIZED INDIANS

The first and best American archeologist and anthropologist is a self solving mystery. His name: Pedro de Cieza de Leon. His biography is as interesting as any of the conquistadors but since this has already been provided by Harriet de Onis and Victor Wolfgang von Hagen we can confine it to a few lines. Twelve year old Pedro was in Seville on January 9, 1534 when the galleon *Santa Maria del Campo* wharfed carrying most of Atahualpa's ransom, millions of pesos of gold and silver. This alone must have been enough to fire young Pedro's imagination since he came from the Estremadua province of Spain, a harsh land that gave America many of its conquerors like the Pizarros and Belalcazars. It was one of those places that breed greed, hunger, do or die megalomania and zeal producing hard bitten peasants prepared to brave the New World rather than their own rude land. 1535 found Pedro with a force "disemboweling" graves along the Suni river in search of gold. Later he joined an army of exploration and conquest into the Uraba area, the same place Columbus briefly thought he had found his strait and where Enciso, Oviedo, Balboa and others founded the first continental settlement. Things had not changed much since Enciso. The Spanish were still looking for a strait and fighting Indians. A topographical map of the Atrato River shows what they were impossibly trying to do but Cieza wrote with some pride that after months of hacking and hammering at walls of vegetation "We were the first Spaniards to travel this route to the Southern Sea."

In 1537 Cieza transferred to an expedition that promised to take him deep into the interior where rumor held a lord named Natibara surrounded himself with golden luxury. They pooled up a "Green River" not knowing where they were going, always hungry, chopping at tree roots that obstructed passage and avoiding, whenever possible, poisonous snakes. The Indians were still giving trouble. War horses emerged from skirmishes with enough arrows stuck in them to look like porcupines, worse still were darts dipped in deadly curare. Pedro describes enormous water snakes, "one twenty feet long which Pedro Jimon ran through with a lance. . . which in its belly they found a young deer. . . The Spaniards were so hungry they ate the fawn and even part of the snake."

The golden chieftain (perhaps the original El Dorado) was never found but the expedition resulted in the settling of Antioquia, about 150 miles inland from the Gulf of Uraba. In 1541 Cieza joined a new captain to settle regions further up the valley and having pacified or at least terrorized the country Cieza settled down in a garrison for the next six years.

It was here in autumn 1541, he began writing and the dual mysteries of his book(s) began. What mysteries? First, how did Cieza who came to America at thirteen to be reared in the theater of war, write such an articulate work from such astute observation? The second question largely resolves the first. How could his manuscript, virtually unique at the time and clearly seminal, a closely examined account of Amerindian customs virtually devoid of conventional bias, be written in the first place?

Cieza obviously had little opportunity for formal education and was there-fore free of excess baggage that encumbered other writers. He had read Erasmus and occasionally tosses around names like Herodotus, Cicero, Alexander, Hector, Livy, Valerius and even Diodorus Siculus, usually in direct relation to points he is making. But these authorities could be gleaned from a half dozen books which were the *sine qua non* of the period so, unlike his contemporaries, he is not so steeped in educated prejudice and authority that he cannot see the forrest for the trees. He is Montaigne's "simple and rough hewen" reporter rather than an Oviedo who claims everything he says is based on observation then worries if Pliny knew about it or a Thevet who says the same thing then goes on to des-cribe some ancient Mediterranean tribe or an Acosta who has to get everything into an organized picture. And if Cieza is not a university man neither is he a theologian. His work is not devoid of the usual religious kant that sometimes smothers Acosta. He is undoubtedly pious and can see the hand of the Devil in the behavior of the Indians and speculate on God's involvement in the affairs of men but not to the extent his writing becomes turgid beyond meaning. Nor is he an apologist clothing every act in the need to subjugate barbarity. He is capable of frank remarks like: "there was little need for the killing, for it was only for the sake of getting this accrued gold from them." And he routinely confutes fellow writers who insisted that at best Indians were human failures.

The result is a book that tells us almost all we know about the prehistoric tribes of Columbia. All that exists on the costal tribes of Ecuador was set down by Cieza but more interesting he made the first methodical study of the Inca realm and distinguished between tribes within it. The same astuteness applies to his observations of natural history. He describes the remarkable countryside and carefully details flora and fauna, describing, for instance, vicunas and llamas which he fellow writers simply called "sheep" and he learned everything he could about Inca culture itself.

1548 found Cieza in the service of Pedro de la Gasca who had been sent out from Spain to put down a rebellion led by Gonzalo Pizarro. La Gasca was no soldier. He had studied law and theology but he seemed to know what he was doing. On April 9 1548 he faced Pizarro on the plains of Xaquixahuana and crushed his enemy.

When the last shot was fired and Gonzalo Pizarro appropriately beheaded Cieza changed his armor for the cloak of an historian and sharpened his quill. He promptly came to the attention of Gasca who must have been impressed with a soldier who not only wrote but even carried his papers into battle. (At Xaquixahuana he lost some of his notebooks which he later wrote he sorely regretted.) At any rate Gasca read what Cieza had written and while he was giving out rewards to the deserving and assorted punishments to those who had the misfortune to lose Cieza was appointed *Cronista de Indias*.

He was allowed access to Gonzalo Pizarro's captured correspondence and wearied himself copying complaining, "my mind is so confused in trying to com-prehend. . . the affair which we yet have to deal with, and my body so weary through the long journeys and protracted vigils I have passed through." All this arm weariness did not keep him, however, from returning to the cordillera to continue his search into history. Cieza traveled as far as the silver mountain of Potosi which he wrote fulsomely of but his burgeoning manuscripts could take in no additional territory. He had covered an immense amount of territory. No writer before him had seen such a variegated mass of America.

Finally, when Cieza was ready to return to Spain, he arranged a marriage contract with Isabel Lopez who was apparently from his native village. He wrote the last words of his manuscript "in Lima, City of Kings, in the Kingdom of Peru on the 18th. of September, 1550, when the author was thirty-two years old, having spent seventeen of them in the Indies."

Back in Spain Cieza set about an ambitious publishing plan, an eight volume history of the discovery, conquest and civil wars in Peru. In 1553 the first folio volume: *Parte Primera de la Cronica del Peru* came off the press. This was the only volume to appear until the 19th. Century for death in various forms was at hand. In the first months of 1553 his young wife died. Cieza himself became ill soon after. There is no indication of his aliment, it could have been a tropical infection which slowly consumed him. But illusions sustained him to the last as slowly dying he continued preparation of the remainder of his work for eventual publication.

In his will Cieza enjoined his executors to have his remaining works published or if they did not see fit "I order it to be sent, with the Injunction that he print it, to the Bishop of Chiapas." He must have been out of his mind! Las Casas who Cieza had met at court in 1552 and obviously shared sympathy with, was still influential enough and may have used some of Cieza's material in his final battles for Indians in Peru but the father of the Black Legend probably could not have gotten a license to print a restaurant menu. But with or without Casas there was more reason not to print the book than print it. In the face of the racket the bishop made during his own brief publishing career the Spanish were getting increasingly testy about their public image. Reports of Spanish rapacity, the dubious legitimacy of sizing territory of foreign monarchs, the clergy's reluctance to see descriptions of American religion in the hands of laymen, Cieza's all too obvious admiration for Incan culture in face of Spanish need to justify a policy of paternalism and his audacity in occasionally critic- izing the emperor himself were raspy enough to keep his manuscripts gathering dust for centuries. Finally the first (published) part of the chronicle and a second (manuscript) part dealing with the Incas exclusively were organized into a single volume by Harriet de Onis and Victor Wolfgang von Hagen in 1959.

Cieza's account reads like a travelogue down the Royal Highways of the Incas and already we see his admiration for their achievements in that miracle of engineering, the road itself:

For if it were a question of a road fifty leagues long, or a hundred or two hundred, we can assume that however rough the land, it would not be too difficult, working hard, to do it. But these were so long, one of them more than 1,100 leagues, over mountains so rough and dismaying that in certain places one could not see bottom, and some of the sierras so sheer and barren that the road had to be cut through the living rock to keep it level and the right width. All this they did with fire and picks. In other places the incline was so steep and rough that they built steps from the bottom to ascend to the top, with platforms every so often so that the people could rest. In other places there were piles of snow, and this was the most dangerous, and not just in one spot but in many, and not just a little, for there are no words to describe or tell what they were like when we saw them...

Having described how these roads ran and how good they were, I shall tell how easily they were built by these people, without the work occasioning death or undue hardship. When a Lord-Inca had decided on the building of one of these famous highways, no great provisioning or levies or anything else was needed except for the Lord-Inca to say, let this be done. The inspectors then went through the provinces, laying out the route and assigning Indians from one end to the other to the building of the road. In this way, from one boundary of the province to the other, at its expense and with its Indians, it was built in a short time.[15]

He says the road was constantly maintained, kept free of snow and rubbish and lined with lodgings, storehouses and other necessary posts concluding: "Oh, can anything comparable be said of Alexander, or any of the mighty kings who ruled the world, that they built such a road, or provided the supplies to be found on this one! The road built by the Romans that runs through Spain and the others we read of were nothing in comparison to this. And it was built in the shortest space of time imaginable, for as the Incas took longer to order it than their people in carrying it out."

Knowing that idle hands are the Devil's plaything Cieza says elsewhere, noting it as an example of good government, "Huayna Capac often remarked that to keep the people of these kingdoms well in hand it was a good thing, when they had nothing else to do or busy themselves with, to make them move a mountain from one spot to another."

On his trip down the highway he questions Indians about their ancient history and beliefs and usually gets and repeats the Inca version of the situation: The Incas were the great culture givers and introduced a purer, less idolatrous religion but Cieza is astute enough to recognize some of the ruins as having been built by civilized men who antedated the Incas and speculates they might have been wiped out by wars. As for the Indian mythology he collected he says, "I have laughed often to myself at what I have written [of the myths of] these

Indians yet I have set down what they have told me," and fearing to tax his readers' credulity adds "omitting many things and not adding a single one."

He necessarily deplores Indian religion, first on the grounds that it was not Catholic and second on the more rational grounds that it involved human sacrifice and entombment of wives and servants of dead nobles. But he concedes that "beneath their general blindness they believed in the immortality of the soul." He also defends the Incas against sodomy. He had seen enough to know there are different strokes for different folks but says the Incas firmly forbade it and punished it severely when it was discovered, citing this as a futher example of Godliness.

And he is fulsome enough in praise of their temples. Of course by 1550 they had been thoroughly vandalized and Cieza laments, "all the palaces and dwellings and other marvels [the Incas] possessed have fallen into ruin and in their present state only their outlines can be seen and the remnants of their buildings. But as they were of beautiful stone and finely constructed they will endure for time and ages without wholly disappearing." In his admiration for Cuzco he finds the ruined temples and major buildings so amazing that "In all Spain I have seen nothing that compare with these walls and the laying of the stones except the tower known as Calahorra, the bridge of Cordoba, and a building I saw in Toledo. . . [and] although these [Peruvian] buildings somewhat resemble those I have mentioned they are finer." But, given the mood of the time, he necessarily contradicts himself saying, "their old temples. . . are all cast down and profaned, and the idols broken, the devils driven from these places. . . In truth we Spaniards should be eternally grateful to our Lord for this."

Cieza approaches the Incan administration exactly as he would describe a similar European state investigating civil and judicial procedures and officers,

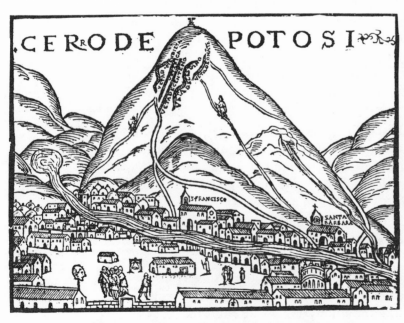

First printed depiction of Potosi from Cieza.

Cieza's rendering of an Inca.

the military and various devices used to implement commerce, conquest and administration. This part of the book is a virtual manual on how to run an empire. Unfortunately: "In the days of the Incas there was very little arable land in these kingdoms that was not under cultivation, and all as thickly settled, as the first Spaniards who entered this realm can testify: to be sure, it is a sad thing to reflect that these idol worshiping Incas should have such wisdom in knowing how to govern and preserve these far flung lands, and that we, Christians, have destroyed so many kingdoms. For wherever the Spaniards have passed conquering and discovering, it is a though a fire had gone, destroying everything in its path."

He describes golden statues and icons based on what earlier Spaniards told him and things he had seen himself when the *Santa Maria del Campo* arrived in Spain, invariably admiring the quality of workmanship. But Peru is so amazing Cieza again fears his readers' incredulity so he says, "I make no mention of the silver work, beads, golden feathers and other things which, if I were to describe them would not be believed."

One thing he finds particularly curious was the Incas' ability to remember history, do accounts and send lengthy messages without writing. Consequently he devotes a chapter to how bards were taught to chant Incan history, adding a new stanza each time one of the Incas died. This and other feats were accomplished through the use of *quipas* (strings of beads of various sizes and colors which served as mnemonic aids). Cieza professes amazement but he asked a cacique to use one to read off a record of everything that transpired since Pizarro was first sighted and he did it without a single mistake.

While Cieza describes wonders and natural prodigies of Peru in a way that astonished the 16th. Century reader and fascinates the 20th. Century visitor it is the people who receive the most notice. He gives much attention to religious and burial customs (the latter perhaps because the Spanish were still opening tombs to dig out buried treasure). He describes temples, feast days and the corresponding calendar, monasteries, convents, ceremonies, sacrifices and even the way they raise children. In short he touches on every aspect of Indian life he can dig up. And it is hard to overestimate the impartial uncluttered quality of his vision. He had been in America long enough and seen enough variety he could say of Amerinds collectively;

> There are people who say very harsh things of these
> Indians, comparing them to animals, saying their habits and
> way of living are more like those of beasts than men, and that
> they are so evil that not only do they commit the abominable
> sin, but eat one another, and although in this chronicle of
> mine I have written something of this, and other evils and
> abuses of which they are guilty, I want to make it clear that
> it is not my intention to say that this is true of all. On the
> contrary, it should be known that although in one province
> they eat human flesh and make human blood sacrifices, there
> are many others where they abhor this sin. And if in others

they indulge in the sin against nature, in many they hold it
to be a foul thing, and never commit it but, on the contrary
loathe it. Therefore, it would be unjust to condemn them all.
And even these evils which they committed have the excuse
that they lacked the light of our Holy Faith, and for that
reason they were unaware of the wrong they were doing, like
many other nations, especially the Gentiles in olden times,
who, like these Indians, lacking the light of faith, made as
many sacrifices as they did and more. And if we consider the
matter fairly, there are many [Europeans] who profess our law
and have received the waters of baptism, who, led astray by
the Devil, commit grave sins every day.[16]

Thus he can describe Indians in the province of Cajamarca as well man-
nered, skilled, with loving women (some quite beautiful) caring little for vain
honors and gracious to Spaniards. In a Martyr-like sentence he says if this
lifestyle was elective, i. e., Christianized it would be ideal. On the other hand
his manuscripts describe experiences in Columbia with hostile Indians in
fortified villages with fighting towers mounted above "on top of which hung
the heads of their enemies. . . a fearsome sight to behold." He says any Spaniard
who had the misfortune to fall into their hands was destined for the cooking
pot. "These Indians are so given to eating human flesh that they are known to
seize women on the point of giving birth. . . and swiftly cut their belly. . . and
extract the child. . . which they roast and eat." He adds, "Once the Spanish found
a big cooking pot full of boiled meat. They were so hungry that their one
thought was of eating. . . when they had eaten their fill, one Spaniard fished out
of the pot a hand with fingers on it." Prisoners whether Spanish or Indian were
not immediately killed but placed "in a very large pen or cage. . . and well fed,
and once they were fattened, they brought them out. . . killed them with great
cruelty, and ate them."

Following Cieza the next American anthropologist to see print was Father
Acosta. If Father Joseph's *Natural History* seems like a step backward in the
scientific revolution his *Moral History* is a great leap forward. Acosta tells us
why, "Human beings have much resemblance in themselves, and some grow wise
by that which happeneth to others. There is no nation, how barbarous so ever,
that have not something in them good and worthy of commendation; nor
commonweale so well ordered, that hath not something blameworthy. . . If
therefore, there were no other fruit in the history and narration of the deeds
of the Indians but this common utility. . . it deserves to be received as a
profitable thing, neither ought it be rejected, for as it concerns the Indians."

Obviously not everybody agreed, including Acosta's Italian translator's boss
who must have ignored this passage, but Father Joseph has more to say on his
motives. He explains he is out: "to confute that false opinion many do commonly
hold of them, that they are a gross and brutish people, or that they have little
understanding so as many excesses and outrages are committed upon them using
them like brute beasts, and reputing them unworthy of any respect; which is so

common and dangerous an error. . . . And moreover, for the small regard many make of these Indians, who presume to know much, yet are commonly the most ignorant and presumptuous. I find no better means to confound this pernicious opinion, than relating their own laws."

He now falls back on the familiar classical comparison defense noting that while Indian religion might have been introduced by the Devil the admired philosophers of Greece and Rome were also idolaters and the Indians like them, have institutions worthy of respect. "But we at this day little regarding this, enter by the sword, without hearing or understanding; persuading ourselves that the Indians' affairs deserve no other respect, but as venison that is taken in the forrest, and brought for our use and delight." He adds with Sahagun and Casas that in order to bring Americans into church it is necessary to understand their mentality. Furthermore, "ignorance of these laws and customs hath bred many errors of great importance, for that governors and judges know not well how to give sentence, nor rule their subjects. And besides, the wrong which is done on them is against reason, that it is prejudicial and hurtful unto ourselves; for thereby they take occasion to abhor us, as men both in good and evil always contrary unto them."

These lines alone absolve Acosta of being a mere Spanish apologist lauding greedy zealous bigots for reducing infidels to the slavery Sepulveda thought they so rightly deserved. He even has the audacity to suggest that Indians might have some customs Europe might benefit from. Except for the Utopians and Noble Savage romanticists this remark was hardly uttered for centuries.

He begins his description of Amerindian institutions with the Mexican and Peruvian calendars then gets off on one of his digressions about the alphabet, apparently with the ultimate intent of demonstrating Indian intelligence. He explains Americans instead of letters use pictographs "not unlike those of Japan and China," although they are not as complex. He notes the Chinese use a single symbol for any given thing so to be perfectly literate a Chinese must know above "six score thousand" characters. As a result literacy in China is obviously low. Curious about how the Chinese system worked he asked a Chinaman he met in Mexico to write, "'Joseph Acosta has come from Peru'. . . whereupon the Chinese was long pensive but in the end did write it, the which other Chinese did after read, although they did vary a little in the pronunciation of the proper name." From this Father Joseph concludes "an Indian. . . that hath learned to read and write knows more than the wisest mandarin. . . for the Indian with four and twenty letters. . . will write all the words in the world, and a mandarin with his hundred thousand letters will be troubled to write some proper name, as Martin or Alonso."

Turning to other customs Acosta follows Cieza closely enough to at least make it obvious he had read the earlier writer and as far as Peru is concerned generally what can be said for one can be said for both. For Mexico he had the assistance of a fellow Jesuit who had convened elderly Indians in Mexico City where they showed him their surviving books, calendar stones and the like and explained how they were read enabling Acosta to provide a description.

On the matter of government Acosta says tyranny is the true measure of barbarism, "for the more men approach reason the more mild their government." Among barbarians the lords are tyrants, "using their subjects like beasts and seeking to be reverenced like gods." Then he makes a series of curious remarks: "For this occasion many nations of the Indies have not endured any king or absolute or sovereign lords, but live in commonalities, creating and appointing captains and princes for certain occasions only, to whom they obey during the time of their charge then after they return to their former estates." He puts this group on a certain level which is based on the council of the many. This is no utopian vision, however, because he likens them to another group, less civilized, who recognize no authority but live in anarchy, "having no other things, but will violence, un-reason and disorder."[17]

At first glance these seems to indicate the Americans are incapable of any form of government except tyranny, but of the Incas he has much good to say: "The affection and reverence this people bare to their Kings Incas, was very great for it was never found that any one of his subjects committed treason against him, for they proceeded in their government with good order and justice, suffering not many to be oppressed. . . therefore such as have any understanding thereof hold the opinion that there can be no better government for the Indians, nor more assured than that of the Incas."

He finds in their "works of great labor" abundant evidence of civilization, marveling at their ability to join stones of "great bigness." And in the course of his examination of their social system discovers an admirable communism where "They every year divided these lands of the commonality, in giving to every one that which was needful for the nourishment of their persons and families. And as the family increased or diminished so did they increase or decrease his portion."

Mexico, says Father Joseph, was also a well ordered realm with selfless subjects loyal to their king. He offers the example of "a man, the best of the Mexicans [who] refused the realm seeming unto him to be very expedient for the Commonweale to have another king." He admires Mexican zeal in instructing their children. Like las Casas he is impressed by their devotion to their gods. He echoes Casas, Oviedo and Motolini with a story about a priest who complained "that the Indians were no good Christians." to which "an old Indian answered 'Let the priests. . . employ as much care and diligence to make the Indians Christians, as the ministers of the idols did to teach them their ceremonies; for with half that care they will make us the best Christians in the world. . .' Wherein he spake the very truth to our great shame and confusion," Acosta says, having pointed out twice within a couple of pages the Christians were not all they could be.

CONCLUSION

Acosta, Cieza and Casas covered the most American landscape and saw the widest group of Amerindians as any who saw print during the century. Most efforts of of the last two failed to see print for centuries. Others had met very different people and saw them through naive eyes. The result was media failure both in terms of American nature and Indians. The world map had changed by 1600 but concepts could not keep pace.

The confused American image received expression from Shakespeare early in the next century. His *Tempest* has three characters who seem to exemplify Amerinds. First is the wise old counselor Gonzalo who says:

> Had I plantation of this isle my lord...
> I' th' commonwealth I would by contraries
> Execute all things: for no kind of traffic
> Would I admit; no name of magistrate;
> Letters would not be known; riches, poverty,
> And the use of service, none; contract, succession,
> Bourn, bound of land, tilth, vineyard, none;
> No use of metal, corn, or wine, or oil;
> No occupation; all men idle, all;
> And women too, but innocent and pure;
> No sovereignty.
>
> (Act II, i.)

Unfortunately another occupant of this same island is Caliban of whom Prospero complains:

> ... Abhorred slave,
> Which any print of goodness wilt not take,
> ... I pitied thee,
> Took pains to make thee speak, taught thee each hour
> One thing or another. When thou didst not, savage,
> Knowing thine own meaning, but wouldst gabble like
> A thing most brutish, I endow'd thy purposes
> With words that made them known. But thy vile race,
> Though thou didst learn, had that in't which good natures
> Could not abide with.
>
> (Act I, ii.)

The third character is wondering Miranda, amazed at the brave new world she discovered from a European. She resembles nothing more than Stradanus' allegory of Vespucci awakening America out of her hammock or the comatose figure on Ortelius' title page.

Stradanus' allegorical depiction of Vespucci awakening a sleeping America out of repose.

This view of Amerinds, still so imperfectly known after a century of speculation along eurocentic lines, increasingly separating into two opposing views of the same reality, was argued through the 19th. Century. The simple lack of clothing and of ABC (as Montaigne put it) were used by ancients which depicted virtue as a nude figure suggesting lack of concern for riches, customs and willingness to share. The opposing theme of bestiality was also symbolized by nudity and apparent lack of customs. Such individuals warred with each other, ate repulsive food had loathsome sex habits and worshiped the Devil. As positive and negative views of the Indians crystallized the former would create a literary genre of the noble savage while the latter became a guide for practical politics.

The Quest

THE ROMANCE OF CHIVALRY

A general feeling of impending calamity hangs over all. . . people saw their fate and that of the world only as an endless secession of evils. . . insecurity was further aggravated by obsession with the coming end of the World and fear of Hell, sorcerers and devils. The background of all seems black. . . somber melancholy weighs on people's souls. Whether we read a chronicle, a sermon, a poem, a legal document even, the same impression of immense sadness is produced. . . It was fashionable to see only suffering and misery, to discover signs of decadence and the near end - in short to condemn the times and despise them.[1]

These words Johan Huizinga used to describe the closing of the Middle Ages. If you like pictures better than books simply look at the print "Dance of Death" or pratically any other engraving produced during this late period. There was an alternative, a grail-like quest, most popularly remembered by legends of Arthur, a vision of sublime heroism in the face of doom, human frailty and threatening infidels.

The New World had all the components necessary for a romance of chivalry and was not only perceived as such but gave the genre a new lease on life. Such romances were set in the long ago or far away and involved heros in violent clashes with bizarre forces in the course a search for the grail. Although in this case the grail seems to have been made of gold it was the stuff of 16th. Century America. As Martyr put it in his first letter about Columbus, the admiral had "with only three ships, penetrated to that province which he believed to be legendaiy."

The stage was already set when Columbus sailed towards the mysterious Orient and discovered instead some equally mysterious islands. It started with Ulysses who was supposed to have been the first to sail through the Pillars of Hercules, hungering after "experience beyond the sun, of the world without people" says Dante in *The Inferno*. (Dante's opinion that the sea was without people was recalled in the introduction of Vespucci's *Four Voyages*. An equally explicit reference is etched into a plate by Stradanus showing Vespucci studying stars of the Southern Hemisphere reminding the viewer of Dante's "Oh widowed world of the North, forever deprived of the sight of them.") Where exactly did Ulysses want to go? Presumably to one of those Elysian lands that speckle literature from time immortal and through the quasi-mystical medieval mind made it onto the map.

Stradanus' allegory of Vespucci studying the stars with Dante's lines about southern stars.

Ulysses was not the only person who wanted to travel out of the world. Medieval Irishmen made voyages and their literature abounds in *imrama*, descriptions of voyages embellished with marvels and miracles. The best of these is the *Navigatio Sancti Brendani Abbatis*, a 6th. Century monk who with the aid of God overcame incredible hardships to discover an island which was "The Promised Land of the Saints." The story enjoyed enormous popularity in the middle ages rivaling *The Song of Roland* and the legends of Arthur.

Another Briton, Prince Madoc, wearied of the civil wars that broke out in Wales on the death of his father was believed to have sailed West in 1170 with 120 of his more dovish countrymen to discover an island where strife did not reign. Leaving them he returned and fitted out an expedition of ten ships and passed out of view presumably preferring to remain in this new Elysium.

The Irish, during their brief and peculiar renaissance produced one other island named Hy-Brazil ("Land of the Blessed"). Never still, it is occasionally

Illustrations from the marvelous adventures of St. Brendan and his monks at sea which appeared in an Ulm, 1499, edition of his romance. UPPER LEFT: They meet a siren. UPPER RIGHT: A Holy Man floating on the ocean. LEFT: They are attacked by a sea monster.

sighted by a goat herder on a hill or glimpsed through the fog. No living man ever set foot on it but it was on Angelino Dulcer's chart of 1325 and wandered around the map for another four centuries.

The most interesting mythical isle is Antilla (rough translation: alternate or opposite), also refereed to as the "Isle of the Seven Cities." It appears on a Portuguese nautical chart of 1424 and is generally cited by chauvinist Portuguese historians as evidence of pre-Columbian discovery of America. Whoever drew the map spotted it with seven cities with outlandish names. Martin Behaim put it on his 1492 globe, writing against it: "In A.D. 734, when the whole of Iberia had been won by the African heathen, the above island, Antilla, called Seven Cities, was occupied by an archbishop from Oporto with six other bishops, men and women who had fled thither from Spain together with their cattle, property and goods. In 1414 a Spanish ship got nearest to it without danger."

Ferdinand Columbus includes the story of these seven bishops, unwilling to serve under the heathen who took refuge beyond the horizon's rim in his biography of his Father. Casas picked it up in his history saying in Columbus' notebooks he found a story about a storm driven ship landing on the Isle of Seven Cities in the time of Henry the Navigator. The crew was welcomed by Portuguese, anxious to hear news from home. On the way home they found gold in sand they had taken for their cook box. When they reported to Henry he scolded them for not procuring more information and ordered them to return but they refused.

These elysian islands were identified with America through the century. Caribbean islands became "The Antilles" almost immediately. When the seven cities failed to appear they moved to the middle of the continent inspiring

De Bry's allegory of Magellan sailing through his strait reeks of fantasy.

Coronado's expedition in search of the Seven Cities of Gold (or of Cibola). They never found anybody in Colorado or Kansas who spoke Portuguese but that only proved the seven cities were there for, as Gomora put it, when the Spanish approached the Indians hid them by enchantment and enchantment kept them on the map along with all the other mythical kingdoms. Peru was routinely identified with Ophir and Oviedo, for the convenient political purpose of legitimizing Spain's title to the New World, claimed the Antilles were the mythical Hesperides, property of the Visigoth kings of Spain. In the process he earned the animosity of Ferdinand Columbus who was petitioning the crown for redress for the shabby treatment his father had received. Hakluyt and Sir Humphery Gilbert did the same thing for Madoc; the latter even got the old prince down to Mexico to become Quetzacotatl. Brazil escaped identification with the wandering Irish isle, deriving its name from the dye wood, but it is almost the exception. When the Spanish reached Baja California they naturally identified it with the domain of the mythical amazon, Queen Califa.

Meanwhile there was the Asian connection. As long as the mainland was identified with Asia visitors expected to see bizarre creatures out of Marco Polo and Sir John Mandeville's romance and often as not they were not disappointed. Polo's Anan which Columbus heard of on his first voyage changed its name to Anian and along with its sister kingdom, Quivera, moved across the map until by century's end it made it to Alaska. Equally romantic, and suggestive of grail like spirituality is Columbus' conviction that he reached the foot of the mountain of Purgatory and that he would meet up with the mythical Christian King of Africa, Prester John.

Visitors saw what they expected. Wilcombe Washburn uses the example of Oviedo expressing his inability to describe American prodigies in words and wishing a fine Italian painter was on hand to do the job to suggest the New World, to some extent at least, could only be perceived in the light of romantic fantasy. Equally tongue tied Martyr and Cieza, unable to put their admiration for American crafts, into words offer similar examples. And if Europeans were seeing what they expected to see they were hearing what they expected to hear. Local myth, and tall tales of fantastic kingdoms "just a little further on" gained credence just because they were already part of medieval mythology. Martyr hears tales of Amazons which he suspects are fables but he accepted, along with Acosta and others giant stories and a kidnapped Carolina Indian, christianized Francisco, told him about many provinces ruled over by a giant who had his bones stretched since childhood. His subjects had domesticated deer in their houses to provide milk and cheese and lived near a race with rigid tails who, when they sat down, needed to dig a deep hole to accommodate these curious appendages.[2]

One of the first suckers was Ponce de Leon who, in 1512, set out to find the Fountain of Youth. According to Herrera, writing ninety years later, Ponce heard of the fountain from Caribbean caciques who had visited and one old codger with barely strength to endure the journey came away so completely restored as to resume "all manly exercises. . . take a new wife and beget more children." Herrera adds that would be native patrons from the Greater Antilles had searched every "river brook or pool" for their hopefully rejuvenating drink without much success.

Sounds like a fairy tale but Ponce was the companion of Columbus who imagined a similar fountain flowed into the Gulf of Paria. He probably shared with his erstwhile captain the *idea fixe* that he was in the enchanted Orient where such a fountain was more likely to exist than not. On hearing of Ponce's quest Martyr devotes a lengthy digression to the probability of such a fountain. He quotes Aristotle, Pliny, Homer and the legend of Medea for authority. He uses some garbled natural history about nature rejuvenating animals to support so fantastic an idea saying: "If therefore, all these things are true; if Nature, that astonishing creatrix, graciously shows herself so munificent and powerful towards the dumb animals. . . how should it be astonishing for her to create and nourish in her bounteous breast similar phenomena in a superior order?" Of course we a discussing a credulous period. Prodigies and miracles could also be found in Europe but reports from America repeatedly described the different and necessarily had to do it in terms that would be understandable to folks back home.

Early on More had used Vespucci's discoveries as a location for his fantasy. Another example of how America could be understood in terms of romance is the ease with which one book slipped into print.

The Italians were rightfully proud of having provided most of the trans-Atlantic navigators. Genoa boasted Columbus and Cabot. Florence had Vespucci and Verrazano, only Venice, Queen of the Adriatic, was left out. This serious omission was corrected in 1558 when a Venetian publisher got out an attractive little book with the, englished, title: *The Discovery of the Islands of Frislanda, Estotiland, Iceland, Greenland and Icaria: Made by Two Brothers of the Zeno Family: viz; Messire Nicolo, The Chevalier and Messire Antonio. With a Map of the Said Islands.*

The title page was adorned with three flying nudes involved with a floating ribbon inscribed: *Veritas figlia temporis.* Perhaps, but one wonders in this case. Fortunately, for the Zenos at least, America was an easy place to write about few had visited and there was plenty of space to fill. The Zeno narrative did its best.

The work is a little choppy as its editor, Nico Jr. admits, explaining;

> These letters were written by Messire Antonio to Messire Carlo his brother; and I am grieved that the book and many other writings on these subjects have, I don't know how, come sadly to ruin; for, being but a child when they fell into my hands, I, not knowing what they were tore them in pieces, as children will do, and sent them all to ruin: a circumstance which I cannot now recall with the great sorrow. Nevertheless, in order that this important memorial should not be lost, I have put the whole in order, as well as I could, in the above narrative; so that the present age may, more than its predecessors have done. .. derive pleasure from the great discoveries made in those parts where they were least expected; for it is an age that takes a great interest in new narratives and in the discoveries which might have been made in countries hitherto unknown, by the courage and great energy of our ancestors. [3]

Already Nico Jr. is protesting too much but since he promises to do the best he can the least we can do is give him a little space. He begins with a tedious account of his family's illustrious history but once past that he gets around to:

> Nicolo, the Chevalier, being a man of great courage, after the aforesaid Genoese war... which gave our ancestors so much to do, conceived a very great desire to see the world and to travel and make himself acquainted with different customs and languages of mankind, so that when occasion offered, he might be the better able to do service to his country and gain

for himself reputation and honor. Wherefore having made and
equipped a vessel from his own resources, of which he possessed in abundance, he set forth out of our seas, and passing
the Strait of Gibraltar, sailed some days on the ocean, steering
always to the North, with the object of seeing England and
Flanders. Being, however, attacked...by a terrible storm, he
was so tossed about for the space of many days with the sea
and wind that he knew not where he was; and at length when
he discovered land, being quite unable to bear up against the
violence of the storm, he was cast on the Island of Frislanda.
The crew, however were saved, and most of the goods that
were in the ship. This was in the year 1380.

So far so credible. Venetians made routine trips to Flanders, storm tossed
ships were common enough and Junior freely admits they did not know where
they were. If it was not for the accompanying map the narrative would not have
made much of a story. But "Frislanda," an island about the size of Iceland
appears some place around the traditional "Ultima Thule," one of those places
even Dante's characters failed to attain. It must have been quite a storm.

The Inhabitants of the island came running in great numbers with weapons to set on Messire Nicolo and his men, who
sorely fatigued with their struggles against the storm, and not
knowing what part of the world they were in, were not able
to make any resistance at all, much less defend themselves
with the vigour necessary under such dangerous circumstances; and the would doubtless have been very badly dealt with,
had it not fortunately happened that a certain chieftain was
near the spot with an armed retinue. When he heard that a
large vessel had just been wrecked on the island, he hastened
his steps in the direction of the noise and outcries that were
being made against our poor sailors, and driving away the
natives, addressed our people in Latin, and asked them were
and whence they came; and when he learned that they came
from Italy, and that they were men of the same country, [Does
this mean the chieftain was an Italian?] he was exceedingly
rejoiced.[4]

This chief was named Zichmini. Now Zichmini decided to take these "good
men and true," on a voyage of conquest but: "This sea through which they sailed
was full of shoals and rocks; so that Messire Nico and the Venetian mariners
not been their pilots, the whole fleet, in the opinion of all. . . would have been
lost. . . and there was no talk but of them and the great valor of Messire Nico."
Etc. etc., etc., And on land, again thanks to the Venetians, Zichmini was
everywhere victorious against savages who ran around nude although they
"suffer cruelly from the cold." Damn right they did. The Zeno map has the
Arctic Circle running right through the middle of it.

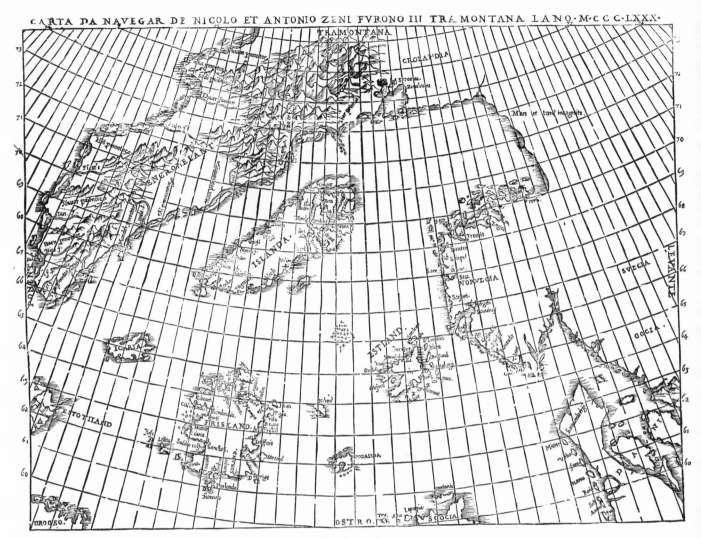

The Zeno Map.

Now Nico wrote to his brother Antonio who arrived "after a long voyage in which he encountered many dangers." Meanwhile Nico had been discovering the West coast of Greenland but not being accustomed to such severe cold, fell ill, and after returning to Frislanda died.

As it happened there was an ancient mariner on Frislanda who twenty-six years earlier had been blown a thousand miles West to the Island of Estotiland where: "The inhabitants are very intelligent people, and possess all the arts like ourselves; and it is believed that in time past they have had intercourse with our people, for he said that he saw Latin books in the king's library, which they at this present time did not understand. They have all kinds of metals but especially they abound in gold. . . [and to the South] there is a great and populous country [Droego] very rich in gold."

Unfortunately for the aging Sinbad's comrades there were cannibals about and they got eaten but not before visiting "a fair and populous city." Zichmini, recognizing a good man when he saw one, dispatched Antonio with a few small vessels westward in search of these places which he duly recorded on his map which Junior regrets was sadly faded with age.

Too bad about Junior tearing up his ancestors' report of their adventures. A further account of Venetian discovery of America would have been interesting. It is also a shame about that map fading so badly because Junior seems to have had a little trouble copying it. Greenland looks about the same as it did on ptolemaic maps except for the settlements on the West coast Junior attributed to the industry of his ancestor. Greenland was hardly news. Hanseatic merchants knew all about it. Adam of Bremen in his chronicle of 1070-'75 even mentions Vinland and coincidentally, in 1492, Alexander VI lamented Greenland had not been visited by a Christian priest for a century. But gradually it became the "Ultima Thule" of medieval romance. Shortly after 1200 Wolfram von Eschenbach put three allusions to it in his *Parzival* and another in *Willehhalm*.

The problem with the Zeno map is an assortment of other islands. Frislanda, Estlanda and a few small islands can be excused as the Orkneys or Faroes but Estoninland and Drogeo are unforgivable, especially since the last two run conveniently off the edge of the page to give Venetians credit for discovering Newfoundland and probably New England.

For the time being Junior got away with his hoax, shivering cannibals and all. Patriotic Venetians were delighted and cartographers got a couple of new islands to draw on their maps. Twenty years later Frobisher carried the map on his initial voyage and mistook some of his landfalls as previously discovered by the Zeni. In 1582 Hakluyt, who should have known better from what he knew about Frobisher's experience, included the narrative in his *Divers Voyages*.

Writing style also contributed to the romance of chivalry. The ideal of chivalry assumed violence with jousts for the honor of a lady, impossible quests in the face of hostile forces and slaying of dragons. Martyr's classical style neatly complimented this romance. Evidence his account of Balboa's discovery of the Pacific. He begins with a description of Balboa's singularly unruly behavior:

> We have messengers from the New World. Vasco Nunez de Balboa, with the aid of his followers and against the will of authorities appointed by the King, has usurped the Government in Darien, driven out the Governor and thrown into prison the lawyer Enciso, who was the official charged with rendering justice. Balboa has attempted and accomplished a deed so great that not only has be been pardoned for his treasonable conduct, but distinguished by honorable titles. The rumor had prevailed among the colonists of these lands that beyond the high mountains lying in sight of them was another ocean, richer in pearls and gold; but the Kings of the lands situated in between proposed to defend them sharply. Moreover, to break their power it would require an armed force of one thousand men. Pedro Arias was sent on in advance at the head of these warriors to open a way by force.

> In the meantime, while these things were preparing in Spain, while the army was collecting and arming and the ships were building, Vasco Nunez de Balboa himself decided to put fortune to a great hazard. He set out from Darien with 190 men of the first day of September in this last year 1513, and began his journey. Partly by force and partly by conciliations and by pacifying the native Kings with our presents, he scaled the mountains and saluted the ocean. Thus he stole away from Pedro Arias and his companions the fame and glory of this great enterprise. Wonderful things are written!

Balboa also encountered a cacique named Pacra he found so:

> deformed and, so dirty and hideous that nothing more abominable could be imagined. Nature confined herself to giving him a human form, but he is a brute beast, savage and monsterous. His morals were on a par with his bearing and physiognomy. He had carried off the daughters of four neighboring caciques to satisfy his brutal passions. The neighboring chiefs, regarding Vasco as a supreme judge or a Hercules, a redresser of injuries, complained of the debaucheries and other crimes of Pacra, begging that he should be punished by death. Vasco had this filthy beast and three other caciques, who obeyed him and shared his passions, torn to pieces by dogs of war, and the fragments of their bodies were afterwards burnt.[5]

According to Martyr Balboa for all his barbarious religiosity and conniving, had "changed from a ferocious Goliath into an Elias; He was an Antaeus; he has been transformed into a Hercules, conqueror of monsters. From being foolhardy, he became obedient and entirely worthy of royal honors and favor." Martyr's view that anybody who advanced the cause of Christianity was a hero praised the rascal for having "subdued cunning man eaters in immense tracts of country abandoned and unknown to the Christian religion and now your Holiness will call to yourself these myriads of people as a hen gathers her chickens under her wings."

Sycophants also exaggerated the valor of chivalrous knights. For Francisco Lopez de Gomora (1511 - 1556 or '7) "The discovery of the Indies, what we call the New World, is excepting the Incarnation and Death of Our Lord, the most important event since the creation of the world" and Cortez was its hero. Around 1540 he met Cortez in Spain where the latter was engaged in the countless legal battles he had been fighting since 1528. He became the conquistador's chaplain and served in that capacity until Cortez' death in 1547, after which he entered the service of his son, Martin.

During the last seven years of his life embattled, embittered Cortez had ample opportunity to describe his glorious achievement. These reminiscences appeared in 1552 under the title: *La Conquista de Mexico* followed a year later by an expanded work including Pizarro's adventures called *Primeria y Segunda Parte dela Historia General de las Indias*. Of the two parts that dealing with Cortez is by far the longest and most detailed. Peru is simply sketched out from secondary accounts.

Gomora produced an instant best seller that went through nearly fifty editions in various languages in as many years. But for all its popularity the book of the hour was viewed by the Spanish government with very different eyes. In November, 1553 Prince Philip put his signature on a *cedula* ordering all copies of the book seized "because it is not fitting that this book be read or sold or that other copies of it be printed."

The Prince/King of Spain was sufficiently imperious to see no need to explain his motives. A number of possibilities suggest themselves. The most likely is Gomora's extravagant praise of his master at the expense of Spanish officialdom and the clergy caused the suppression. The monarch had already snatched the Viceroyalty of New Spain from Cortez and his heirs, who, along with those of Columbus, were pleading for relief from their fading fortunes. No point in improving their case. Cortez' own reports were designed to emphasize his value and he was careful not to put forward his lieutenants lest one be selected to supplant him. Anything unfavorable to his advantage he suppressed while elaborating his own achievements. Gomora was his echo. Another conquistador, Diaz del Castillo, grumbled "Where he [Gomora] has written 80,000 read 1,000."

The same Bernal Diaz del Castillo saw fit to prepare his own history which while hardly sycophantic was no less romantic and although his manuscript of 1568 was not published until 1632 he is too interesting to ignore. He arrived in the New World about the time Santa Maria del Darien was being settled and participated in the conquest of Panama. He sailed with Cordoba (1517) and Grijalva (1518) to the Yucatan and accompanied Cortez on his voyage into history. In 1523 Diaz participated in the conquest of Guatemala where he remained to become and alderman of the city of Santiago de los Caballeros (an interesting name suggesting a self conferred encomium by the conquistadors) and an *encomendero*.

For half a century Diaz had talked and thought of the glorious period which witnessed the destruction of the Aztecs. Whenever he encountered a fellow conquistador they would sit and reminisce and people gathered to listen. By 1568, when he started to write only five men who originally sailed from Cuba were alive and Diaz says, "we are very old, and bowed down with infirmities, and very poor, and with a heavy charge of sons to provide for, and daughters to marry off, and grandchildren to maintain, and little rent to do withall ! And thus we pass our lives, in pain, in labor and in sorrow." Diaz regarded himself as spokesman for his dead comrades; except for the five survivors the rest were gone and record of their valiant deeds was buried with them. He set himself with the patient determination of a man emersed in his subject to write *Historia Verdadera de la Conquista de la Nueva Espana* with every intention of giving credit where credit was due or to use his own words: "I say also that Cortez did everything that ought to be expected from a wise and valiant general, and that he owed his success, under God, to the stout and valiant captains, and us brave soldiers, who broke the force of the enemy, and supported him by fighting in the manner we fought."

Stylistically the *True History* is as much a romance of chivalry as the tales of Charlemagne or the re-conquest of Spain itself. Diaz boasts of having fought 119 battles and casually dressing his wounds with strips of hide cut by his sword from the dead foe's rump. Along with Gomora he attributes the victory of a handful of Christians over a multitude of Indians at Ceula in Tabasco to the intervention of St. James although he admits with Christian humility he was too miserable a sinner to see the miraculous apparition. He has the romantics's admiration for a brave enemy along with a continuing suggestion of a voyage into the fantastic. His description of the Aztec capital is famous:

> We saw so many cities and villages built on water and other great towns on dry land, that straight and level causeway going towards Mexico, we were amazed and that it was like the enchantments they tell us in the legend of Amadis. . . And some of our soldiers even asked whether these things that we saw were not a dream. It is not to be wondered at that I write it down in this manner, for there is so much to think over that I do not know how to describe it, seeing things as we did that had never been seen before, not even dreamed of.

He continues "When I beheld the scenes that were around me, I thought within myself that this was the garden of the world!" but sadly "all is now destroyed and that which was a lake is now a tract of Indian corn. . . and so entirely altered that the natives themselves would hardly know it."[6]

Francisco Pizarro is probably the most glorious and cruddy noble knight of medieval chivalry to come to America and he had a sycophantic secretary, Francisco de Xeres, to detail his adventures. At the beginning of the story we find Pizarro in Panama, "possessing his house, his farm and his Indians, as one of the principal people of the land. . . having distinguished himself in the service of His Majesty. [enslaving Indians and raiding tombs on the plains of Sinu] Being at rest and repose but full of zeal to . . . perform other more distinguished services for the royal crown, he sought permission to discover the coast of the sea to the Eastward."

Xeres describes Pizarro's first abortive voyage down the coast during which several of his men died of starvation. He pitched camp at a place he christened Port Famine where he subsisted on seaweed. (Sounds like poor planning to me but Xeres does not seem to think so.) A second expedition of 160 under Pizarro and his friend Diego de Almagro sailed for three years "suffering great hardships from hunger and cold" and losing 110 of their force to starvation. But they turned up traces of Incas and gold. Unable to proceed further they camped North of the present Columbia-Ecuador border awaiting reinforcement. Meanwhile the governor of Panama who thought Pizarro somewhat rash, dispatched a ship to rescue anybody who wanted to come home on the assumption "that it was impossible to endure more hardships than they had suffered during the last three years."

On its arrival illiterate Pizarro, according to Garcilasso de la Vega (writing ninety years later), seeing his men return to the ship:

> drew his sword and made a long line on the ground with the point. Then turning to his men, he said: "Gentlemen! This line signifies labor, hunger, thirst, fatigue, wounds, sickness and every other kind of danger that must be encountered in this conquest, until life is ended. Let those who have the courage to meet and overcome the dangers of this heroic achievement cross the line in token of their resolution and as a testimony that they will be my faithful companions. And let those who feel unworthy of such daring return to Panama; for I do not wish to put force on any man. I trust in God that, for his greater honor and glory, his eternal Majesty will help those who remain with me, though they be few, and that we shall not feel the want of those who forsake us." On hearing this speech the Spaniards began to go on board with all speed, lest anything should happen to detain them.[7]

Herrera describes the event in a slightly different manner and Xeres confines it to a few sentences but I like Vega, having the governor play Sancho Panza to Pizarro's Quixote. Vega might have written Pizarro's speech for him but the violent chivalrous ideal, loathing of the infidel, the worth of specie in the face of Spain's and Christendom's plight and geographic confusion makes Pizarro into the new St. George. Some, like practical Oviedo, were not buying any of it and some missionaries had a different view but the fact remains it would be another eighty years before Cervantes lampooned barbarous chivalry.

In any event Xeres says sixteen men crossed the line. The rest returned to Panama. With his remaining party Pizarro gathered more trophies which he carried to Panama.

Pizarro began his voyage of conquest in January 1531. He spent his first year in Ecuador and Northern Peru, terrorizing and subduing the country, organizing settlements and arranging part of the colonial empire. During this period he learned of the central Peruvian monarchy. Realizing that by conquering the Inca he could quickly bring the entire realm under control he set out to find him in September 1532 with sixty-two horsemen and 102 infantry with three guns and twenty crossbows.

In the course of the trek Xeres, whose purpose was to glorify and rationalize his captain's actions has little eye for the country. The best he can say for some costal Indians is: "These people are dirty. They eat flesh and fish raw. . . They have other filthy things in the way of sacrifices and mosques, which they hold in veneration. . . Each month they sacrifice their own children, and with the blood they anoint the faces of the idols, and the doors of the mosques."

That Xeres uses the word "mosque" here and everywhere in describing Indian temples is revealing. He is still thinking about Moors forty years after their expulsion from Spain. The *reconquista* simply never ended. Similarly he with most other writers generally refers to the Spanish as "the Christians" and the Indians are savages, cannibals (whether they were or not), infidels or barbarians. This gave any and all aspects of any venture God's approval.

As Pizarro proceeded towards Cuzco he exchanged messages with emissaries from the Inca which were a combination of friendly intentions and braggadocio but leery Pizarro was receiving conflicting reports of the Inca's intentions. The only thing he knew for sure was Atahuallpa had a large army in readiness. Xeres estimates it at 30,000 to 40,000 troops. Finally the two met in a town called Casa Marca. Pizarro kept his entire force, cavalry as well as infantry inside houses with orders to sally forth at the cry of *Santiago!*

> Having made these arrangements, the Governor waited for the appearance of Atahuallpa; but no Christian was in sight except the sentry... The Governor and Captain-General visited the quarters of the Spaniards seeing that they were ready to sally forth when necessary, saying to them that they must be of good courage, and make fortresses of their hearts, for that they had no hope in but in God who would help those that worked in his service even in their greatest need. He told them that though for every Christian there were five hundred Indians, yet they must have that reliance which good men find on such occasions, and they must trust that God would fight on their side. He told them that at the moment of attacking, they must break through the enemy... Those and similar exhortations were made by the Governor and Captain-General to the Christians, to raise their spirits, and they were more ready to come forth than remain in their lodgings. Each man was ready to encounter a hundred, and they felt little fear of seeing such a multitude.[8]

Once again Arthur and Roland pale in comparison, but Xeres was there so we will let him finish the story. Around sunset Atahuallpa entered the town square on a litter, leading a procession of dancing, singing, colorfully dressed Indians who Xeres claims had weapons concealed under their clothes. He had waited out most of the day on the assumption that horses, which the Indians feared as if they were tanks, could not operate after dark. At that point Pizarro sent a priest to speak to Atahuallpa, precipitating a famous incident. The priest: "advanced, with a cross in one hand and the Bible in the other, and was going amongst the troops up to the place where Atahuallpa was, thus addressing him: 'I am a priest of God, and I teach Christians the things of God, and in like manner I come to teach you.'

"Atahuallpa asked for the book, that he might look at it and the priest gave it to him closed. Atahuallpa did not know how to open it, and the priest was extending his arm to do so, when Atahullpa, in great anger, gave him a blow on the arm... Then he opened it himself... and threw it away from him five or six paces." This of course was sufficient justification for further events in the face of Pizarro piety.

Then the governor put on a jacket of cotton, took his sword and dagger, and with the [four] Spaniards who were with him entered among the Indians most valiantly... he came to the litter where Atahuallpa was, and fearlessly seized him by the arm crying out *"Santiago."* Then the guns were fired off, the trumpets sounded, and the troops, both horse and foot sallied forth. On seeing the horses charge, many of the Indians... fled and many fell over each other. The horsemen rode them down killing and wounding and following in pursuit. The infantry made so good an assault upon those that remained that in a short time most of them were put to the sword... Then the Spaniards made such a slaughter amongst those who carried the litter that it fell to the ground and if the Governor had not protected Atahuallpa, that proud man would there have paid for all the cruelties he had committed... During the whole time no Indian raised his arms against a Spaniard. So great was the terror of the Indians at seeing the Governor force his way through them, at hearing the fire of the artillery, and beholding the charging of the horses... they thought more of flying to save their lives than of fighting... It was a wonderful thing to see so great a lord taken prisoner in so short a time. [9]

The entire episode took about half an hour; 2,000 Indians died and 3,000 were captured. One horse received a slight wound.

Next came the ransoming. Ransoming was completely compatible with the chivalrous code of honor. It was the frankly avowed purpose of the noble knight to make his way by arms and Froissart's *Chronicles* never fail to enumerate the profits a successful enterprise produced for its heros, giving amounts down to the last ducat. Presumably the greater the ransom the more illustrious the deed and in Atahuallpa's case it was very large indeed. He offered to fill a room twenty-two feet long, seventeen feet wide and eighteen feet high with gold half way up the wall and as for silver he would fill the same chamber twice over. He endeavoured to do this within two months.

Atahuallpa about to toss the Bible on the ground. Title cut from an anonymous TRESLADO DE UNA CARTE of 1534.

But even as gold was being gathered there was treachery afoot. Atahuallpa was allowed continued communication with his subjects. According to Xeres, who by now is lying through his teeth, Pizarro learned of a large army forming to free their master. Pizarro accused the Inca of treachery but the cunning heathen laughed at the accusation. Pizarro sent de Soto with a scouting party ostensibly to check out reports of mutinous Indians, but apparently to get him and such particular conquistador ethics he possessed out of the way. Then he assembled a kangaroo court with the predictable verdict. Death.

Two days after the execution de Soto returned to report there was no Indian army nearby or evidence of insurrection. He found Pizarro, by way of mourning, wearing a felt hat slouched over his eyes. Indignant De Soto said, "Sir, you have done ill. It would have been best to wait for our return; for the accusation against Atahuallpa is false." Pizarro replied, "Now I see I have been deceived." And Pedro Pizarro claimed, "I saw the Marquis [His brother Francisco] weep with sorrow at not being able to spare his life by reason of his escaping."

Incredulity leaps off the pages. A weeping Pizarro? But it is all consistent with chivalry. Lancelot was a regular crybaby. In any event the same Soto who would soon make himself so loved and admired by American Redskins joined eleven others to protest that Pizarro had no jurisdiction over a foreign king and killing a prisoner whose ransom had been received would bring dishonor on Spain. They appealed to the emperor for justice.

Cervantes did not write any of the above but neither did Xeres. The latter operating on the simple assumption that history is written by the victors confines himself to claiming Atahuallpa was put to death for the treason he committed and on his death his troops would disperse. Anyway that's the way the Marquis' secretary saw it.

We can get rid of Xeres, for the time being at least, with the first page of his book where he asks if any nation is greater the Spanish who "cause joy to the faithful and terror to the infidels. . . and whose deeds can be compared with those of Spain? Not surely those of the Jews, nor the Greeks, nor even the Romans," etc., etc., *ad nauseam*. Fawning yellow journalism for sure but he had a point. Spain and the chivalrous quest were on a roll.

THE CROSS BEARERS

Most of the historians, Oviedo, Casas, Martyr, Cieza, Gomora wrote with a sense of the importance of what was occurring and many participants in the American drama may have considered themselves part of an historical process. For an idea of what that process was conceived as we can look at the *Nuremberg Chronicle*, among the weightiest and commonest items of incunabula. After tracing world history down to 1493 it leaves six blank pages about three quarters of the way through the book so purchasers could record any significant events that occurred between then and - What?

The Bible tells us in several places, notably *Revelations* XX, 7 - 8. Satan will be loosed from his prison to go out and deceive the nations of the earth with Gog and Magog to gather them together in battle. They will encompass the camp of the saints and attack the beloved city. Then fire will descend from heaven and consume them and the beast will be cast into a brimstone lake to suffer eternal torment. Only the godly will remain, released from their weary venal world to the innocence of Eden. After those six blank pages the *Chronicle* goes on to confidently describe a new Heaven and Earth.

Ironically the *Chronicle* came out three months after the initial appearance of Columbus' letter and news of the discovery had not reached the printer. But biblical eschatology seemed to be borne out by the facts. Infidels had not only attacked Jerusalem but occupied it and laid Christendom under siege. The final battle was in process and the conquistadors were the new crusaders.

"God made me the messenger of the new Heaven and the new Earth of which he spoke in the *Apocalypse* by St. John, after having spoken of it by the mouth of Isaiah; and he showed me the spot where to find it," Columbus wrote to one of Isabella's ladies in waiting. And in a letter to the sovereigns he wrote "it was clearly predicted concerning these lands by the mouth of the prophet Isaiah in many places in Scripture that from Spain the holy name of God was to be spread abroad."

The millennium was at hand or at least would be when the entire world worshiped Christ. By and large I believe pronouncements like the above should be understood as sincere, an expression of the times which went hand in hand with chivalry. As evidence consider the fact Spain required depositions American immigrants were neither Jews, Protestants or other undesireables. Francis I, who was slightly more ecumenical, allowed Cartier to scrounge prisons for his colony of 1540 so long as his recruits had not been convicted of counterfeiting, *lese majesty* or heresy.

For many the ideal of a world state ruled by a single emperor worshiping one God seemed an attainable goal. Enciso in the preface to his *Sum of Geography* reminds young Charles V that he ruled more territory than any previous monarch and was destined to rule more. Later with this idea in mind quixotic Philip II sailed off to marry Mary Tudor to bring apostate England back into the fold.

With this sentiment the Hapsburgs back in Vienna heartily agreed. About mid century they adopted a motto fitting the vowel ordered acronym AEIOU which is the first letter of "Austria's Empire Is Ordained Universal" in German, Latin and coincidentally English.

This theme floated around Europe, showing up here and there in various forms. An interesting example was added to the third edition of Ariosto's *Orlando Furioso* which appeared in Ferrera in 1532. It consists of a digression in which Andronica gives Astolfo a geography lesson, explaining the explorations in context of Charles' gloriously expanding empire. Astolfo learns the navigators, "following the sun's circular course [found] new lands and a New

World." The poet personally presented his creation to the emperor in reward for which he was created poet laureate.

Iconographicaly we pick up the idea in the woodcuts prepared in 1517-'19 by Hans Burgkmair the elder for his "Triumph of Maximilian I" where the peoples of the world follow a series of kings in service of the emperor. Verses prepared for but not cut into the blocks (on account of Maximilian's death) echo the implications of the conquest even before it happened:

> The Emperor in his warlike pride,
> Conquering nations far and wide,
> Has brought beneath our Empire's yoke
> The far-off Calcuttish folk.

PAGE 208: Brazilians marching in the parade led by Maximilian according to Hans Burgkmair.

LEFT: Triumphal Arch. Woodcut from Giovannii Albicante's TRATTATO DEL' INTRA IN MIILANO DI CARLOS V...

The cartouche of Gemma Frisius' world map suggests the same ideal on a classical model with Charles V sitting next to Zeus on top of the world. More bellicose but in the same vein is an illustration in a fete book commemorating Charles' entry into Milan in 1541. A crude woodcut shows Charles astride a horse trampling a Turk, a barbarian and an Indian. The accompanying verse explains, "Our age will be more perfect with the New World discovered and Vanquished."

Similar motifs were picked up in 17th. Century allegories which often show the world bathed in the light of Heaven and feminine representations of the continents carrying tribute to Europe. Long after Christendom was totally fractionalized several writers still entertained the vision. One of them was Tommaso Campanella, the same magician-author who produced *Citta del Sole* in 1623. Three years earlier he had published *Monarchia di Spagna* which predicted the Spanish king would become a world ruler under whom there would be universal peace and justice. (But Campanella spent most of his time trying to get out of jail so there is a suggestion of pandering there.)

Only slightly less pandemic was the burning desire on the part of many clerics to establish a New Jerusalem in America. Protestantism had shattered the unity of European Christendom but many yearned to accomplish in the New World a bright and shining spiritual conquest. Some writers even noticed that Luther and Cortez were born in the same year, one the anti-Christ, to destroy Christian unity in Europe and the other to make possible a New World free of the distentions that were splitting Europe asunder. This dream would come true when the souls of the Indians were won. An interesting parallel to this showed up after Villegaignon's ecumenical Brazilian colony fell apart. It lead to mutual recriminations that it fell because a false faith had been introduced in America.

All this is by way of explaining the religiosity that peppers 16th. Century Americana. It peppers it the way you pepper your sandwich when somebody forgot to screw the lid on the shaker. Although other examples are spotted through our text one writer, Xeres, can serve as an example for all, partially because he is so ironic and partially because I frankly love to listen to Pizarro talk. After his horsemen ran down Atahuallpa's army (if in fact it was an army) Pizarro had the Inca sit next to him and:

> soothed his rage and agitation at finding himself so quickly fallen from his high estate. Among other things the Governor said to him: "Do not take it as an insult that you have been defeated and taken prisoner, for with the Christians who come with me, though few in number, I have conquered greater kingdoms than yours, and have defeated other more powerful lords than you, imposing upon them the dominion of the Emperor, whose vassal I am, and who is King of Spain and the universal world. [Where else can you find better hyperbole?] We come to conquer this land by his command, that all may come to a knowledge of God, and His Holy Catholic Faith; and by reason of our good object, God, the Creator of heaven and earth and of all things in them, permits this, in order that you may know him and come out from the bestial and diabolical life you lead. It is for this reason that we, being so few in number, subjugate that vast host. When you have seen the errors in which you live, you will understand the good we have done you by coming to your land... You should consider it to be your good fortune that you have not been defeated by a cruel people, such as yourselves, who grant life to none. [This last remark was, of course, far from the truth but our narrator, Xeres, has a proclivity for ignoring Incan customs and blarney.] We treat our prisoners and conquered enemies with kindness, and only make war on those who attack us, and being able to destroy them, we refrain from doing so but rather pardon them... [he goes on to explain that in this case he had to make an exception to the no first strike rule] because you threw the Book to the ground in which is written the words of God. Therefore our Lord permitted that your pride should be brought low, and that no Indian should be able to offend a Christian.

Next Xeres has the great cross bearer explaining the evils of idolatry to Atahuallpa pointing out that all this time he had been receiving his advice from the Devil. A few pages later the priest of the temple of Pachacamac was brought to Pizarro's camp and Atahuallpa begs for the privilege of putting him in chains because the priest had advised war with the Christians. "He had also told his father, the Cuzco [Xeres has a gift for getting things wrong, in this case consistently confusing the Inca with the city, variously referring to the "old Cuzco" or "the other Cuzco."] when he was on the point of death, that he would not die of that disease. The governor ordered the chain brought and Atahuallpa put it on. . . Atahuallpa told the [priest] he wished the riches of the mosque to be given to the Christians because the idol was a liar; and he added: 'I wish to see whether this you call your god will free you from your chains.'"[10]

Apparently Atahuallpa was a bit of a religious chameleon. And Xeres? If Gomora thought Cortez was the best thing that ever happened to the Mexicans Xeres outclasses him by making Pizarro the patron saint of Peru. I almost forgot to mention that Pizarro did Atahuallpa one other favor. He told him he would be burnt at the stake if he did not accept baptism but if he became a Christian he would only be garroted. Atahuallpa converted.

An interesting exception to all this piety is the Gentleman of Elvas who refuses to clothe de Soto in the garb of cross bearer. About the only time he mentions religion is apropos of a scuffle where the Spanish lost the implements necessary for mass (chalice, censor, etc.) but he claims these were a small loss compared to what de Soto wanted. But then again he did not much like Soto so maybe this exception proves the rule.

I don't want to leave this chapter without letting a couple of pacifists get in a word or two. Las Casas repeated recited his experiences, notably in Central America, where he was capable of reducing a "Land of War" to Christian peace without violence but before him there was Cabeza de Vaca who is too interesting to ignore partially because he is another example of the pious idea that God invariably protected the Christians.

Shortly after his party washed up on the "Isle of Misfortune," as they dubbed their camp, disease broke out among the Indians decimating their population. The Indians blamed Spanish witchcraft and, not for the first time, Cabeza de Vaca was in fear of his life. But sorcery is a two edged sword. It can cure as well as kill. So, as Cabeza de Vaca put it, the Indians "wished to make us physicians without examination or inquiring for diplomas." He describes the local medicine man's techniques and says the Indians ordered them to do the same. He says, "We laughed at what they did telling them it was folly [and] that we did not know how to heal." The Indians were so adamant that they withheld food until the Spanish complied adding a new element: "Our method was to bless the sick, breathing upon them and recite a Pater-noster and an Ave-Maria, praying with all earnestness to God our Lord that he would give health and influence them to make us some good return. In his clemency he willed that all those for whom we supplicated, should tell the others that they were sound and in health, directly after we made the sign of the blessed cross over them. For this the Indians treated us kindly; they deprived themselves of food that they might give it to us, and presented us with skins and some trifles."[11]

The result was that Cabeza de Vaca became a faith healer and trader among the Indians. He plied this trade for about five years journeying inland and

along the coast for as much as 150 miles. After a series of vicissitudes he was
reunited with Dorantes, Moldonado and the Moor and they determined to try
to reach civilization. In the course of his peregrinations we start to pick up
stories of faith healing again and his story takes on an increasingly spiritual
tone which leads to the denouement of the book. Although his travels are
impossible to follow (because he did not know where he was going) his final
journey probably began at a spot between San Antonio and Laredo. The four
Christians walked across the Sierra Madre and zig-zaged through Chiuahua and
Sonora to a place near the present town of Ures (about fifty miles Northeast of
Hermosillo). They passed from tribe to tribe, their reputation as healers always
preceding them. Like Staten, Cabeza de Vaca nowhere claims special powers to
himself but only to the grace of God. In this way the Spanish became missionaries. On hearing a superstition of a creature called "Badthing" who entered
their huts and inflicted wounds on them: "we laughed and ridiculed and they
seeing our incredulity, brought to us many they said he had seized; and we saw
marks of the gashes made in the places according to the manner they described.
We told them he was an evil one, and in the best way we could gave them to
understand, that if they would believe in God our Lord, and become Christians
like us, they need have no fear of him. . . At this they were delighted and lost
much of their dread."

Near Ures the Christians first encountered other Spaniards, in the form of
a military party of slave hunters. Not surprisingly the natives were hiding in
the hills and:

> We found it difficult to induce the Indians to return to their
> dwellings, to feel no apprehension and plant maize. They were
> willing to do nothing until they had gone with us...for if they
> returned without doings so, they were afraid they should die,
> and going with us, the feared neither Christians no lances.
> Our countrymen [the slavers] became jealous at this, and [told]
> the Indians that we were of them, and for a long time had
> been lost; that they were the lords of the land and must be
> obeyed and served, while we were persons of mean condition
> and small force. The Indians cared little or nothing for what
> was told them; and conversing among themselves said the
> Christians lied: that we had come whence the sun rises, and
> they whence it goes down; we healed the sick they killed the
> sound; that we had come naked and barefoot, while they had
> arrived in clothing and on horses with lances; that we were
> not covetous of anything, but all that was given to us we
> directly returned to give, remaining with nothing; that the
> others had the only purpose to rob whomsoever they found,
> bestowing nothing on anyone...Even to the last, I could not
> convince the Indians that we were Christians; and only with
> great effort and solicitation we got them to go back to their
> residences.[12]

A few pages later he is explaining his God to the Indians. Using the convenient combination of the Soul and the Sword he tells them those who do not believe in God, "He casts beneath the earth into the company of demons and a great fire which is never to go out." But if they became Christians the Spanish "would cherish them like brothers and behave towards them very kindly... they would give no offense nor take from them their territories, but be great friends. If the Indians did not do this, the Christians would treat them very hardly, carrying them away as slaves into other lands."

The Indians knew a good thing when they saw it and agreed to be baptized whereupon the captain of the slavers "Made a covenant with God, not to invade nor consent invasion, nor enslave any of that country."

The *Relation du dio Alvar Nunz Cabeza de Vaca* (Zamora, 1542) has a point to make: "God in his infinite mercy is pleased that in the days of your Majesty, under your might and dominion, these nations should come to be thoroughly and voluntarily subject to the Lord who has created and redeemed us. We regard as certain that your Majesty is he who is destined to do so much [it will not be] difficult to accomplish [by peaceful means]."

But things were not working out quite that way and this brings us to our next chapter.

Brazilian man and woman from Antonius Silvius' OMNIUM FERE GENTIUM (Antwerp, 1572).

The Black Legend

THE other side of the romantic chivalry coin was violence and barbarity and Spain got blamed for it all with good reason.

History books attribute foundation of the "Black legend of Spanish cruelty" to Bartolome de las Casas. Ironically this man who never touched a sword and only published eight short tracts harping on a single subject in his lifetime has come down through ages with more lustre than any conquistador.

Casas is one of those figures whose life and writing are so intertwined it is impossible to discuss one without the other. Bartolome (b. 1474) was the son of Pedro de las Casas who sailed with Columbus on his second voyage to become one of the first colonists on Hispaniola. Most biographers believe Bartolome was a student at Salamanca then; he came to the Indies in 1502. His *Historia de las Indias* relates many incidents that occurred on Hispaniola during the following decade but Casas speaks of his activities only incidentally. He participated in slave hunting expeditions and later admitted with shame he had an *encomienda* (a land grant to conquistadors, with Indian slaves to work it).

About 1510 he was ordained a priest, for he speaks of celebrating his first mass that year. This did not stop his joining Diego Valasquez in the conquest of Cuba in 1512. Valasquez' first task was to pacify Indians who had fled Hispaniola to Cuba. He established his first settlement there and soon subdued the rebels by capturing and burning their chief. Casas was not present at the incident but heard the story from a friar who offered baptism to a condemned cacique only to have it denied on grounds he might find Spaniards in Heaven.

With the island pacified there followed dividing up. Casas with a friend received his share, a "good big" *encomienda* on the Ariamo River, the richest in gold yet discovered. Of the two partners Casas' friend gave himself up largely to spiritual matters while Casas worked the Indians, planting crops and washing sand for gold. He later admitted he spent more time doing this than teaching the faith.

Encomiendero that he was Casas' views were suffering a change. Traveling around Cuba he visited villages asking how the natives were and getting the same answer: "Hungry, hungry, hungry!" Able bodied men were worked to death in mines and those he found were barely able to stand. Women with suckling babies were so debilitated milk dried in their breasts so their infants died. In this way Casas says 7,000 children died within three months. Insensitivity was not one of Casas' weaknesses and what he witnessed preyed on his mind, slowly arousing his conscience.

Casas was not alone in noticing this barbarity. Among the first was a Dominican friar, Antonio de Montesinos who, in 1511, thundered from a pulpit in Hispaniola: "Tell me, by what right or justice do you keep these Indians in cruel servitude? On what authority have you waged a detestable war against these people who dwelt quietly and peacefully on their own land?... Are these not men? Have they not rational souls?"

Montesinos was seconded by other friars whose protests so alarmed colonists they sent their own monk to Spain to offset these shocking charges. Other clerics responded with their representative. A distressed Ferdinand convened a junta to discuss the matter. The conclusion was promulgated as the Laws of Burgos in December, 1512. The new edict endorsed a sort of benevolent slavery. Indians and land could be parceled out and Indians forced to work for Spaniards but they were to be fed, housed, clothed and not worked so hard that they droped. Of course they were also to be instructed in Christianity. But even if the wish-washy Laws of Burgos were composed with benevolent intent their vagueness and lack of enforcement left the Indians no better off than they were before.

In 1514 Casas finally decided to join Montesinos' cause. Memories of native misery began to cloud his mind. On hearing of the Hispaniola Dominican's denunciation of native servitude he remembered one of his order had refused to confess him because he held Indian slaves. He thought about his continuing sin as he still held them. Apparently he spent the summer of 1514 pondering the matter until the veil of ignorance was lifted and he saw "the same truth" at last. The entire system of allotments was unjust and tyrannical. He too would denounce it. On August 15 he delivered a sermon which was the turning point in his life. He set forth the sin in which Spaniards were living by holding Indians and the restitution to which they were bound, and announced he was giving up his own *encomienda*. This was the first of several sermons in which las Casas repeated his new conviction but his words fell on deaf ears.

In 1515, despairing of effecting any reform in Cuba, Casas returned to Spain to present his case. This was the first of at least six crossings of the Atlantic and ceaseless peregrinations around the Caribbean, Terra Firma, Central America and Mexico during which he argued his cause before settlers, the king and even fellow clergy. In the course of his adventures he was frequently in risk of bodily harm and even his life. As early as 1516, in connection with a royal inquiry, he was appointed "Protector of the Indians" with a salary of a hundred pesos a year. "Not so little," he later commented, "as that hell of Peru had not yet been discovered which with its multitudinous quintals of gold has impoverished and destroyed Spain."

For thirty years Casas' eloquent efforts to secure better treatment for the Indians were largely ineffective. Vague edicts which he clearly influenced were issued in Spain only to be ignored by colonial officials 3,000 miles away. It was not until 1542 with the promulgation of the "New Laws" that his voice was effectively heard and we find his anonymous hand behind a printed document. Although the New Laws fell short of Casas' proposals they made sweeping changes in the way Spanish colonies would be administered.

The New Laws began mildly with measures for administrative reform, including an order that courts be scrupulous about good treatment of Indians.

Then, mounting to a crescendo, followed new policies for dealing with natives. First came a flat edict forbidding taking of slaves in future either by war, under guise of rebellion or barter. As for existing Indian slaves the crown ordered a swift inquiry. Whenever owners could not show legitimate title or had mistreated an Indian the Indian was to be freed. Furthermore, Indians could not be used as pearl fishers or carriers, except when it was unavoidable, and then they had to be paid and not overloaded or used against their will.

After these preliminaries came the real bombshell - the law abolishing *encomiendas* by slow stages. All *encomiendas* held by officials from the viceroy down, the clergy, monasteries, treasury, etc. were revoked and these Indians placed under the crown at once. In Peru "principal persons" involved in the civil wars were to be deprived of their Indians forthwith. In Mexico excessive estates were to be reduced to moderate size. No new *encomiendas* would be created and existing ones would escheat to the crown on the death of their owners. Heirs would receive a moderate pension. New discoveries could not include the taking of slaves or the taking of anything from Indians except by barter and priests must accompany the expeditions.

Las Casas returned from this series of deliberations as Bishop of Chiapas to find his parishioners seething with the animosity raging through the Indies. When the New Laws were read in Peru the royal emissary barely escaped with his life. The conquistadors were violently aroused because the laws effectively spelled their doom. They had gained the land and parceled it and the Indians out among themselves. Now everything these patriots who had done so much for Spain and themselves would have their spoils taken away. The next Spanish official to arrive in Peru was a Knight of Avila, Blasco Nunez Vela, who when asked to consider some alleviation of the laws replied frigidly, "I have come not to tamper with the laws nor discuss their merits, but to execute them." But Vela instead of executing the New Laws was executed by them. Gonzalo Pizarro defeated him in battle and he was stabbed to death on the field. It took the Pedro de la Gasca, who Cieza served under, to defeat Pizarro and finally bring the realm back under control. In Mexico a similar catastrophe threatened only to be moderated through the influence of Viceroy Mendoza. According to Gonzalo de Aranda 600 disgruntled settlers sailed back to Iberia and he feared not enough old conquistadors would remain to hold the country in the face of so many Indians who even if they seemed good Christians were basically evil and born to be subjected. Casas himself narrowly escaped violence at the hands of his parishioners. The upshot of all this disturbance was a new edict of 1545 which severely modified the New Laws. Meanwhile aging las Casas, unable to accomplish anything in America and meeting opposition everywhere he went returned to Spain for the final time in 1547. It was then his debate with Sepulevda occurred.

Now the former Bishop of Chiapas began his publishing career. In 1552 - '53 he printed eight quartos that would make his name famous to the ends of the earth. The first and most appalling appeared on August 17, 1552. It was the

damning *Brevissima Relaction. . .* or to give it the full title it ultimately found
in English: *A Relation of the First Voyages and Discoveries made by the Spaniards
in America. With an account of their Unparalleled Cruelties on the Indians, in the
Destruction of above Forty Millions of People; together with the Propositions offered
to The King of Spain to Prevent the Further Ruin of the West Indies, By Bartholomew de las Casas, Bishop of Chiapas, Who was an Eye-witness to their
Cruelties.*

The blood curdling "Brief Relation" had been prepared back in 1542 for his
battle for the New Laws along with the next track to come off the press, *Entre*

LEFT: Title page of the
BRIEF RELATION. The fol-
lowing pages contain
examples of the gristly
illustrations de Bry
prepared for his edition
of the work. They hardy
require explination.

los Remedios (Eight Remedies). The eighth was fundamental, abolishment of allotments of lands and Indians and placement of all Indians under the crown. Next came his *Tratado Sobre los Indios se han henco esclavos* (Treatise About Indians Who Have Been Made Slaves). Here he insists all Indians enslaved since the conquest and that those still alive were mostly held by Spaniards with bad conscience. This powerful document reviews the gristly annuals of Indian enslavement, methods of the slavers and the depopulation of entire provinces by raiders. Next he printed a paper he had prepared during his tenure as bishop which had created much friction back in Chiapas: *Avisos y Reglas para los Confesores* (Advice and Rules for Confessors). In this he maintains slave holders cannot receive confession. Even deathbed confessions may only be heard after the penitent executes a legal document restoring his property to the Indians since he took it from them in the first place. He allows some provision might be made for heirs but children of New World Spaniards had no right to property stolen by their fathers. Then came two more just title tracts defending it. He recalls his dispute with Sepulveda in a seventh tract generally summarizing the positions of the two parties for public consumption. An eighth tract was a statement of principals for use in disputes in order to protect Indian rights.

Las Casas might have continued his career as a pamphleteer indefinitely and in fact had a ninth tract ready for the printer but he had boldly issued them without the all important "privilege" or license showing it had been examined and approved. Manuscripts had to run the gamut of the King's Council, the Holy Office of the Inquisition, Council of the Indies and frequently the Royal Board of Trade. Casas' boldness did not go unchallenged. The former Bishop of Chiapas was denounced to the Inquisition. Little is known of this episode but the trouble was probably instigated by New World colonists or Sepulveda. In any event Casas apparently got off by promising to behave himself and get out of the publishing business.

The ninth tract was published posthumously in 1571 under the title: *Erudita et Elegans Explicatio* (Learned and Elegant Dissertation). It was picked up by a German named Griestetter who had lived in Spain and published in Frankfurt on Main. This work, along with the eighth tract, argues that kings, although sovereign, do not have unlimited powers. People make kings who must rule for the popular good. From this doctrine Casas attacks grants of fiefs without consent of the feudatory. He rests this denial of royal authority to grant allotments on a sweeping doctrine of popular rights. Under the "natural rights of man" he asserts all men are free and are to be ruled only for their own benefit. The king is the administrator of the goods of the state and is responsible for public welfare but is without power to arbitrarily dispose of personal goods, communal lands or native kingdoms. Strong words that would not be heard again until Jean Jacques Rousseau echoed them two centuries later.

Casas died in July 1566 at the ripe old age of ninety-two but not without first prophesying:

God in His goodness and mercy saw fit to choose me as his minister, though unworthy, to plead the cause of the people of the Indies. . . against unimaginable oppressions and evils and injuries received from our Spaniards. . . and to restore them to the primitive liberty unjustly taken from them. . . and free them from the violent deaths they still suffer and die as they have died; and by this cause many thousands of leagues have been depopulated, many in my presence. And I have labored in the court of the kings of Castile going and coming from the Indies many times, for about fifty years. . . only for God and from compassion at seeing perish such multitudes of. . . peaceful humble, most amenable and simple beings, well fitted to receive our holy Catholic faith. . . Now I say and hold certain. . . that all crimes committed by the Spaniards against these people. . . with such perverse cruelties, have been against all the pure and most righteous law of Jesus Christ, and against all reason, and to the greatest infamy of His name and the Christian religion, and the total obstruction of the faith. . . And I believe that for these impious and ignominious works, so unjustly committed. . . God will pour forth His fury and anger on Spain if she does not perform a great penance. . . And I fear that she will do this later or never, because of the blindness that God has permitted in great and small alike. . . who think themselves wise and presume to rule the world. . . a denseness of understanding still current that after they started robbing and killing and exterminating those nations. . . even today they have not yet realized that such massacres and captivities. . . and universal desolations have been sins and the greatest injustices.[1]

If las Casas was the foundation of the Black Legend Girolamo Benzoni was its cement. He was twenty-two when, in 1541, he left his native Milan for the New World. For the next fourteen years he traveled around the Antilles, the Main, Central America and Peru practicing his trade as a silversmith and taking part in several expeditions. He returned home in 1556 so delighted to have seen "so many novelties, so much of the world and so many strange countries" he decided to write about his experiences. His *Historia de Mondo Novo* appeared in Venice in 1565 and was reprinted there in a slightly larger edition in 1572.

As an historian Benzoni offers little new. His work consists of wholesale borrowings, largely from Gomora, interspaced with anecdotes, some probably fanciful, such as the story of Columbus and the egg. (According to Benzoni Columbus, in council with Spanish ministers, bet he could make an egg stand on end and then showed them how it could be done. He cracked it slightly at the bottom.) In another he says some Indians believing the Spanish to be gods decided to find out by killing one and revive him and explain it had only been a joke. To their amazement he did not revive.

Benzoni does add somewhat to our and his century's picture of America by including seventeen woodcuts in his book, one of plants, the rest illustrating Indian activities but the locations depicted are often hard to determine.

The real importance of his book is his echoing of las Casas. He may have been a closet Protestant, perhaps before he left his Spanish dominated city of Milan, or became one during his American wanderings. Somewhere along the line he developed a violent anti-Spanish bias. About a third of his history is devoted to Spanish cruelty, harping continually on their abuse of Indians and thirst for gold. In one (again possibly fanciful) anecdote he gleefully recounts how some Indians wrecked poetic justice on their masters by capturing one and pouring molten gold down his throat. Elsewhere he repeats the oft told story of Indians killing themselves in preference to serving the Spanish.

The same Catholic chronicler, Andre Thevet, who we accused a few pages earlier of making other's experiences his own complained of Benzoni's plagiarism, his consistent anti-Spanish attitude and some of his little stories and questioned whether Benzoni ever set foot out of Europe. He labeled Casas' and Benzoni's books "little tracts of falsehood used by men who would not dare to say these things for fear of losing their skins, and so pass off their impostures under the names of men who supposedly travelled in those countries in order to give weight, color and authority to their own ridiculous fooleries." To confute Thevet the modern historian Hose Torbio Medina, discovered a document describing Benzoni's appearance before the Mexican Inquisition on a charge of heresy, so at least we know he was there.

HOW BLACK IS THE LEGEND?

There are two charges against las Casas making his *Brief Relation* the most violently debated book in American history. The first is that he was responsible for the introduction of Black slavery in America. It is true that he suggested at one point Spanish laborers and Negro slaves could be brought to America to replace the fast perishing "frail" Indians. However there were Black slaves on Hispaniola long before he made the suggestion. Furthermore Casas was largely working within the system and slavery was legal. If African tribes warred among themselves and took captives they could either ransom them back to their own tribe or sell them to the Spanish. What Casas maintained was illegal was aggressive wars which resulted in the seizure of other people's land and their subsequent enslavement. Later he came to realize that slavery in any form was wrong and became a virulent polemicist against it. This makes him far from the introducer of Black slavery in America, but the first to denounce it.

The second charge is that Casas grossly over exaggerates the decimation of the Indian population and Spanish cruelty. It is true that his estimation of the pre-Columbian native population of America was too high. (He gives Hispaniola an original population of three million, probably three times too many.) This problem was exacerbated by subsequent editions of *The Brief Relation* which threw figures around randomly. It is also indisputable that many Indians died from the introduction of previously un-encountered viruses which Casas little understood. To some extent this may account for his continuing descriptions of the Indians as frail compared to Spanish and Blacks. But Casas' percentages remain accurate. By century's end only about ten percent of the native population in Spanish occupied areas survived and some were completely decimated.

As for Spanish cruelty, the Black legend could have gotten along without Casas. Back in 1525 Martyr regretted that when Columbus discovered Hispaniola and Jamaica there were at least a million souls but now "on account of the cruel treatment by the Spaniards [who] forced these poor unaccustomed men to dig for gold, on account of the despair driving them to their deaths, or because mothers killed their children there are almost none left." He goes on to describe how "both men and women fought fiercely to regain their liberty" and how kidnapped captives on Hispaniola, desperately homesick, fled to the North coast of the island where the winds of their homeland blew and familiar constellations shone and there, throwing their arms wide with mouths panting to catch native breezes fell senseless to the earth of their insufferable exile.

The Gentleman of Elvas also gives a live free or die anecdote in his description of Cuba. He says the island still abounds in gold but there are few slaves left to mine it, "many having destroyed themselves because of the hard usage they receive from the Christians. . ." The overseer of one mine, "having understood that his slaves intended to hang themselves, went with a cudgel in his hand and waited for them in the place at which they were to meet, where he told them. . . that he had come to hang himself with them, to the end that if he gave them a bad life in this world, a worse would he give them in that to come. This caused them to. . . return to obedience."

Although a declared enemy of las Casas Motolinia condemns his countrymen as bitterly as his rival. He claimed Spaniards killed so many Indians in Mexican mines that "for half a league around and for a great part of the way one could scarcely walk, except over bodies or bones, and the birds and crows that came to feast on the dead bodies. . . greatly obscured the sun."

Another enemy of Casas, Oviedo, hardly an Indian lover - one of his tasks was branding Indian slaves for work in the mines - also finds rape of the Indies destroying the colonies. His reasons may have been more pragmatic but he recognizes rapacity by conquistadors, in one case observing that de Soto was too fond of killing Indians for sport. He notes with moral satisfaction that the gold seekers resemble those Spaniards who go back to Spain with faces the color of gold "though not of the same luster but looking like citrons, the color of saffron or jaundice, and so sick they quickly succumb." He grumbles along with Casas and Acosta about lack of zeal in teaching the faith and for good measure throws in clerical greed: "Very few of these fathers have I seen without covetousness, and [no] less inclined to gold than me or any other soldier. . . through they are cleverer and quieter about keeping it because they hold it as a piety that everyone should give to them for the love of God." He complains priests seize their converts gold, wives, children and other goods and, "left them nominally baptized, but without any understanding of the benefit of the lofty sacrament they had received. . . I have now seen a great number of these Indians in the thirty-five years I have been acquainted with these parts. . . and not one perfect Christian have I found among them."

And there were terrorist tactics. Cortez had the nasty habit of cutting off hands, among other things, to keep natives in order. Cieza describing his experience in the pacification of Columbia says, "The natives took such horror of us that they and their women hanged themselves from the trees by their hair and belts." But these are just a few examples among scores.

The Spanish badly needed an apologist but after Sepulveda about the best they had was Father Acosta who cannot understand anything incompatible with divine plan. He says during an Incan rising when the Spanish were besieged in Cuzco Indians threw torches on their straw roofed houses, "yet nothing set on fire. . . a woman did quench it presently, the which the Indians did visibly see and were amazed. It is certain by relations of many. . . that in diverse battles which the Spaniards had. . . their enemies did see a horseman in the air. . . fighting for the Spaniards. . . Other whiles they did see the image of Our Lady, from whom the Christians have received in these parts incomparable favors."

Because the time for conversion of the Indies had come, "we ought not to condemn all these things the first conquerors did. . . as some religious and learned men have done, doubtless with good zeal but too much affected. For although. . . they were covetous men, cruel and very ignorant. . . the Lord of all (although the faithful were sinners) would favor their cause. . . for the good of the infidels, who should be converted unto the holy Gospel by this means."

Acosta usually saw the forrest, missing the trees, but everybody is entitled to their opinion.

A NEW TWIST

Apparently it started in England, after Bloody Mary, with Elizabeth seated firmly on her throne finishing up the Protestant reformation. With only minor exceptions the English had no interest in America and less in Indians. Catholics were a different matter. During the two decades between Eden and Frobisher only three Americana books appeared. There was a translation of Thevet's *Les Singularitez*. . . The other two were anti-Catholic/Spanish polemic. One was penned by the first Englishman to visit America and subsequently write about it, the great buccaneer, Sir John Hawkins. Sir John began his career with a slave raid on Guinea in 1562. Seeking to cash in on American treasure he made two subsequent voyages to the Caribbean. During the second he succored the wretched French colony in Florida. On his third an event occurred which was to have a profound effect on Anglo-Hispanic relations.

Starting home after a successful trading venture his five ships were storm driven into Vera Cruz. The following day a Spanish squadron showed up at the mouth of the bay and after cautious negotiations with the English entered. Days later the Spanish turned on Hawkins' little fleet without warning. Out- numbered and taken by surprise, three English ships were disabled. Hawkins barely escaped by transferring to from his flagship, the *Jesus,* to another. The only other ship to escape was commanded by Hawkins' kinsman, Francis Drake. They left a hundred men behind where, as Protestants, they fell into the hands of the Inquisition. British historians claim that day Drake swore revenge which he took so thoroughly that for a century after he was described in Spanish annals as "The Dragon."

The disastrous incursion ended when Hawkins and Drake "arrived in. . . Cornwale y XXV of [January, 1569]. . . praised be God forever." The same year he published an account of his voyage: *A True Declaration of the Troublesome voyage. . . to Guynea and the West Indies. . .* To a modern reader Hawkins' narrative is reminiscent of some ironic, pious kant we have already heard. Sailing a slaver called the *Jesus,* doing clandestine business in waters foreigners had been warned out of he complains of Spanish treachery. And, while every other sentence contains a phrase like "thanks to God" or "God preserved us" or "God had mercy upon us" one searches in vain for Christian charity for the four or five hundred slaves he carried except to the extent he expected them to "countervail our charges with some gains." Hawkins' Christian virtues seem to have been confined to faith (that he could outwit the Spanish) and hope (of making a bundle).

But by the time Hawkins wrote the English were primed for Catholic perfidy, at home and abroad. 1566 saw an immediate translation from the French of the brutal Massacre of Laudononniere's Florida colony written by a survivor, Nicholas le Challeux: *A True and perfect. . . description of the last voyage. . . attempted by Captain J. Rybaut. . .* The second English book on America since Eden. More polemic.

With the Reformation in full swing and small but influential colonial parties developing in England and France the printing press took on a life of its own. Las Casas' *Brief Relation* turned up in Flanders in 1578, in England in 1583 and Germany in 1597. Now all Europe was reading about timid enfeebled natives lashed to work in mines and thousands crowed together like sheep awaiting slaughter. People read about caciques who, having offered gifts of gold were asked for more. When they could not produce it they were wasted at the extremities by torturing fires until, after hours of agony, they turned their dying gaze on their tormentors rather in amazed dread than rage. Mutilations of hands, feet, ears and noses jumped off pages. Protestants (note the publication locations) learned it was a common sport among the cavaliers of Spain to lay wagers as to who could cut a pedestrian in half with a single sword stroke while riding him down in the street. In one case two dozen were killed before the effective stroke was delivered. Stories of gallant soldiers delighting in ripping babies from their mothers' breasts, tearing them apart and throwing them to dogs also made juicy reading. Las Casas would be printed and reprinted, frequently with such embellishments as his editors saw fit, as yellow journalism as late as the Spanish American War. He became a media event in the propaganda war against the very country he was trying to save from perdition.

Better yet there was Benzoni. Back in Geneva there was a Calvinist minister named Urbian Chauveton. After attending the University of Geneva he held various posts around the city. His initial venture into Americana occurred when he helped Nicholas le Challeux with his *Discours de l' Histoire de la Florida. . .* (Dieppe, 1566).

Later he encountered Benzoni. He says he read most Spanish accounts of the conquest and found himself wondering why chivalrous Spaniards failed to make a peaceful entry into the New World which they claimed they were there to Christianize. At first, as Spanish writers would have him believe, he attributed the wars and atrocities to the wild untameable nature of the barbarians. Then he read Benzoni. Now he has found an impartial historian and the air clears. No longer is every conquistador a brave cross bearing general carrying Christianity and civilization to unappreciative Indians.

Benzoni, he explains, disillusioned with corrupt European civilization and weary of oppressive strife flew to the New World, called there by reports of wealth, temperate skies and antique simplicity. But even as he beholds this marvelous new place the aspect darkens. He sees natives driven from their homes into enslavement while the Spanish wage unceasing raids in search of more labor to satisfy a rapacious lust for gold. The barbarians retaliate, bringing on fresh horror.

For the convenience of his readers Chauveton divided Benzoni's continuous narrative into chapters followed by his own notes. He used these additions for two purposes. First, painfully aware of Benzoni's literary borrowings, he makes an attempt to correct discrepancies. More importantly he uses them to indicate his own partialities. His two initial translations (Latin, 1578) and (French, 1579) were a *machine de guerre* against Spain. He wrote when Admiral Coligny's dream of uniting Protestants and Catholics in colonial expansion and a patriotic war against Spain still might become a reality. Thus Chauveton dwells on the wealth of the Indies and potential exploitation (by Frenchmen). A note on the pearl fisheries is thirteen pages long and four pages are devoted to the sugar industry on Hispaniola. Others deal with cattle raising, vines, olives, wheat and so on.

Of course the pastor cannot neglect the apparently primary purpose of the American adventure, conversion of heathens. Taking every opportunity to damn the Iberians for failure to do so he quotes an unnamed French captain who said French merchants involved in the Brazil trade could have made more progress in subduing Brazil in five years than the Portuguese had in seventy. In other words French sailors made better missionaries than Portuguese priests. But for all his religiosity Reverend Chauveton is more an opportunist than a missionary. What he wanted was religious toleration in France. It was against this background previous French ecumenical colonial ventures had been launched.

Not content with a mere annotated version of Benzoni Chauveton went on to expand Challeux' story of the Florida colony and its destruction by the Spanish. He justifies this addition by noting it deals with virtually the same subject and that it will tear off "the fine mask of zeal and religion with which the Spanish have covered their barbarous acts in the Indies."

Chauveton recites the Spanish *apologia* in the form of a dialogue. The wars were fought against cannibals whose only resemblance to men was physical say the Spanish. Chauveton asks why then massacre French in Florida, emissaries of a nation that had formerly been considered the most civilized on earth? (The "formerly" was apparently a snide allusion to the St. Barthomew's Day massacre.) The Spanish explain they were Protestant heretics harassing Spanish shipping lanes while they thumb their nose at the King of Spain who is the rightful owner. And, the Spanish argument continues, the Pope granted the Indies to them and it was their's by right of conquest anyway. To this Chauveton replies that the Pope had given away something that was not his to give. (If America belonged to the Indians France had no more right there than Spain but this point escapes Chauveton who reduces the natives to mere weapons in his defense of French's right to the colonial sun.) Besides, he continues, the Pope made the award for purposes of Christianization and one could search the Indies in vain for a native who truly knew Christ or a Spaniard who had properly announced his name so the papal grant was voided anyway. If the Spanish held the Indies by right of conquest, which Chauveton reminds us is unjust, France has just as much right to areas Spain failed to occupy.

To cap off this bit of patriotic polemic Chauveton added a "Petition in the form of a supplication" addressed to the French king for relief of "the women, widows, grandchildren, orphans and others who were so cruelly invaded by the Spaniards in the French Antarctic called Florida."

Benzoni's history, usually in Chauveton's version, achieved enormous popularity going through dozens of editions into the 18th. Century. It must have delighted the cockles of Theodore de Bry's Huguenot heart when he got hold of it. He used it for three volumes of his *Grands Voyages*, picking up on Benzoni's crude illustrations and adding as many gristly ones he could think up himself to give his customers, even if they could not read, a clear picture of Spanish brutality. Graphically Bry with a little help from Casas, Benzoni and Chauveton probably did as much for the Black Legend as he did for the noble savage.

Woodcut from Benzoni's original (Venice-1565) edition showing Indians pouring liquid gold down Spanish throats and otherwise taking revenge.

The Colonial Impulse

SPAIN had little need for colonial propaganda. Columbus' announcement that she had reached the Indies combined with the gold he returned on his first voyage insured a steady flow of adventurers. About the only exhortation for Spanish conquest I can find is Enciso's *Sum of Geography* of 1519 which was written with the avowed purpose of encouraging exploitation and providing a geography to help Spanish pilots get on with the job. With the discovery of Mexico and its spoils even that was redundant. America was the place to make a bundle. By the 1560's an estimated 25,000 immigrants had sailed from Spain.

Spain had other advantages to distinguish her from England, France and even Portugal, luck and zeal. From the very first she always seemed to have enough men on hand to do the job. They did not even think in terms of colonies. They walked in, took over and established viceroyalties. England and France had no such luck. All they could find was cold weather, Indian troubles and no gold; all of which naturally contributed to lack of enthusiasm.

In his letter to Francis I Verrazano, on the assumption he was near a water route to Cathay and finding Indians amenable to trade, suggested the possibility of an outpost but since the same report indicated North America might be more of an obstruction than an asset his words went unheeded. Even after Cartier returned to France with tales of Saguenay he had to scrounge the prisons to find settlers. After his effort to establish a colony resulted in nothing more than two miserable winters in Canadian wilderness and no gold enthusiasm dwindled.

But things were still going on back home and by way of digression I might point out that colonial experience, especially seminal colonial experience, has to be viewed in light of what was happening in the mother country. In France there were two things. One was a developing economy that might have use for American products (not the least of which was gold). The second was the Reformation. This resulted in a colonial party and colonial propaganda. For some of the latter the expansionists depended on prompt translations from the Spanish. A good example is Xeres whose *Verdadera Relacion de la Conquista del Peru* of 1534 which appeared in France the same year under the somewhat naive title: *Nouvelles Certaines des Isles du Perou,* certainly an inducement to go exploring.

At mid century the only thing France had from its own explorer was Cartier's *Brief Recit. . .* of 1545 but its anonymous publication three years after Cartier had gotten thoroughly sick of Canada smacks of colonial propaganda. One imagines a publisher anxious to strengthen the colonial cause asking Cartier for a book and the captain throwing a pile of field notes from his second voyage at him and saying, "Take this but don't put my name on it." The dedication to the king refers to the Indians' "good will and gentleness," somewhat contrary to Cartier's experience and opinions. It repeats the existence of golden

Saguenay long after his "gold' and "diamonds" had been assayed as worthless. It describes a lush land which Cartier did seem to appreciate, but nothing about the third expedition and subsequent colonial fiasco appears.

Lacking useful material from their own explorers the French developed fantasies. They had been involved in the brazilwood trade since 1520 (at least) and developed considerable interest in the country. The principal beneficiaries were garment makers in Rouen who used it as dye so it is not surprising they stressed the issue in 1550 when King Henry II and Catherine visited. The events are described in a fete book commemorating the occasion: *C'est la Deduction du Sumptueux Ordre Plaiantz Spectacles et Magnifiques Theatres, Dresses, et Exhibes.* . . . (Rouen, 1551). Like most fete books this one is sumptuous, containing twenty-nine woodcuts commonly attributed to the same Jean Cousin who worked for Thevet. The most interesting picture in the book is the finale, a field of three hundred "Brazilians" in simulated habitat, complete with thatched huts, hammocks, canoes, bows and arrows, parrots, monkeys and trees decorated with exotic fruit, painted red to resemble the real article.

Fifty of the "Brazilians" were natives brought back by ships engaged in the Brazil trade. The remainder were sailors and young ladies appearing nude, save for a cover of red dye, despite modesty and chill of November air. The fete capped off with a mock battle in which the "Toupinabaux" and the "Tabareres" assailed each other firing the grass huts. We hear the "king's eye was joyously content with the scene." The commemorative book came complete with a poem addressed to the king asking him to expel the Portuguese from Brazil. (The Brazilians living in Rouen were one of the city's curiosities for a long time. They were the ones Montaingne interviewed in 1562 when they were presented to Charles IX and they obviously left a vivid image in his mind.)

Religious tension in 16th. Century France was also an incentive for New World colonies. France needed an outlet for Protestants or a form of religious toleration. Cartier's third expedition carried as its supreme commander the Protestant Sieur de Roberval. Now it was wavering Protestant, Chevalier Nicholas Durand de Villegaignon's, turn. His was to be a colony where toleration would reign. But despite enthusiastic propaganda Villegaignon and Cartier both had to resort to convicts to fill out his first compliment of colonists. Presumably the threat of being abandoned in a permanent American colony was unappealing to craftsmen and laborers who preferred a known evil to an unknown good. He solved this problem a year later by promising subsistence to his colonists along with passage back to France if required. Now so many applied his three ships could not accommodate them all. This second group, far from wanting to establish a permanent colony, were bent on making a fast buck and returning home as soon as possible. Instant contradiction; the haven for the prosecuted became a Mecca for treasure hunters. They even neglected necessary implements for agriculture when they sailed.

Stuck with what he had Villegaignon, like Roberval, resorted to terrorist tactics. He drown dissidents and according to Lery totally turned against the

Brazilians in a forest-woodcut from C'EST LA DEDUCTION DU... ORDRE...

Protestants when religious strife broke out. Somehow the colony held together for five years but one wonders how. After it fell to Portuguese assault Villegaignon attempted to raise a retaliatory force against Portuguese settlements in Brazil but his words fell on deaf ears. The colony had only marginal interest to Catholics and the Protestants felt betrayed.

More interesting in terms of subsequent events was the Florida colony. Despite two expensive failures Admiral Coligny was still determined to plant Frenchmen in America for the dual purposes of placing France in New World competition with Spain and providing an escape valve for Protestants. This latter motive prompted Francois de Belleforest, writing in his frenchified version of Munster's cosmography (Paris, 1575), to observe sourly that France's overseas fortresses were erected to protect heretics. But Belleforest was either enough of a patriot or had read enough of the Gentlemen of Elvas to explain Coligny selected Florida because the Spanish had managed to so antagonize the natives it had become their "cemetery."

As a result of the admiral's plan on May 1, 1562 a ship emerged from the ocean mist near Savannah flying the Royal Blue of France and commanded by the famous Protestant sea dog Jean Ribault. There he constructed a wooden fort, christened Charlesfort. Leaving a garrison of thirty men he with his second in command, Rene Laudonniere, also a Huguenot, sailed back to Dieppe which they found under siege by a Catholic army. When it fell Ribault fled to England where Queen Elizabeth listened with interest to her fellow Protestant and offered to return him to Florida in English ships. But Ribault wanted Florida for the Huguenots not the English so he declined, for which he got thrown in the Tower of London.

Meanwhile his tiny colony languished in the wilderness waiting for relief. Isolation gave way to despair. The commander became homicidal, hanging one man with his own hands and sentencing another, named Lachere, to slow starvation on an island. His exasperated men mutinied, killed him, freed Lachere and named Nicholas Barre to command. They made a boat of pine and moss which everybody climbed aboard except a seventeen year old who said he would take his chances with the Indians.

The pitiful craft somehow made it into the open Atlantic where it lay becalmed for three weeks. The sailors ate their clothing, drank their own urine and finally "made the motion that it was better that one man should die than so many. . . should perish." The fatal lot was drawn by the twice-doomed Lachere whose "flesh was divided equally among his fellows." By the time the ship of horrors approached Europe the sailors were too debilitated to land and were picked up by an English patrol vessel. Nicholas Barre was interviewed by Elizabeth and clapped in the Tower along with Ribault.

Undeterred, Ribault's old shipmate Laudonniere led another expedition to Florida. Among the 300 men and four women he carried was the artist, Jacques le Moyne de Morgues, who would provide originals for de Bry's famous pictures.

The Spanish, determined to keep the French out of what they considered their sphere even if they could not occupy it themselves, launched an expedition against Charlesfort. Coincidentally they arrived and found it abandoned a few days before Laudonniere's flotilla slipped over the bar of St. John's River and sailed upstream to build Fort Caroline. The Spanish returned to Havana, convinced the French were out of the picture.

Unfortunately for the lofty purposes of patriotism and religious toleration Spanish gold and the legend of more of it in mythical "Appalachia" was still exerting its fatal influence. Although the French this time came equipped to establish an agricultural colony, they could not settle down to working the land. Gold had to be around someplace and once again it became a preoccupation.

Meanwhile Laudonniere, who expected to find the Floridians anxious to join France against Spain instead found them courting him for alliance in their own squabbles. He had no plans to play a secondary role in Amerindian politics but he found himself supporting, first one side, then the other.

Winter brought scarcity, near starvation and rebellion. Thirteen men took a small boat and made an unauthorized dash to Cuba where they seized a Spanish prize. A few weeks later another sixty-six mutineers took a larger ship and sailed toward the Antilles where they captured a Spanish brigantine which they triumphantly sailed back to Fort Caroline.

If the pirates expected a royal reception they did not get it. Laudonniere shot the leaders and had their bodies strung from gibbets. The brigands had foolishly announced the French return to Florida and Philip II was furious. He had already authorized one of his most capable captains, Pedro Menendez de Aviles, to found a settlement in Florida. Now he ordered him to drive the French out "by what means you see fit." Menendez sailed with eighteen ships and 1,540 soldiers and settlers. His fleet was scattered by a hurricane but the captain pushed on with five ships carrying 600 people.

At Fort Caroline the settlers, after waiting over a year for relief finally found it in the presence of Jean Ribault with a fleet of seven ships. He had managed to extricate himself from the Tower and England and returned to France to drum up support for the colony. Unfortunately the same day Ribault anchored off the St. John's Menendez made landfall at Cape Canaveral and turned North where he encountered the French fleet still lying offshore. After an uneventful exchange Menendez dropped down the coast to a small harbor. He landed a party that threw up a stockade around the council house of a local cacique. On September 8, 1565, fifty-three years after Ponce first entered North America and sixty-eight after Cabot discovered it, Menendez came ashore "with many banners spread, to the sound of trumpets and salutes of artillery" to christen St. Augustine, the first permanent settlement and oldest city in North America.

Now the conflict between Christians for North America was on. Florida was hardly worth fighting about but French pirates had been harassing Spanish shipping since the time of Columbus. Spain hardly needed an unfriendly settlement where they could refit and refurbish.

Determined to attack the Spanish before they could reinforce Ribault sailed South with twelve ships and 600 men. Approaching St. Augustine he made a fatal mistake. Noticing Menendez flagship, the *San Pelayo*, was missing -Menendez had sent it off to round up what was left of his original expedition - he set off in pursuit. But it was hurricane season and just then a bad one hit.

Realizing the French ships could not soon return, Menendez marched 500 harquebusiers through the storm to Fort Caroline. Attacking the unguarded stockade "they vied with one another to see who could best cut the throats of our people," said a French survivor. Within an hour 132 French corpses littered the ground. Forty-five Frenchmen, including Laudonniere and le Moyne, fled through the steaming forrest to two small ships and set sail for France. For them the war was over.

Ribault's fleet was smashed by the storm and driven ashore near Cape Canaveral. Menendez, marching back to St. Augustine encountered the first 200 dazed survivors staggering North along the beach on the opposite side of the St. John's. The French, having no way of fording the river, outnumbered and outgunned surrendered. Menendez ferried them across in groups of ten, marched them behind a dune and put them to the sword. The process started on September 29, 1565 and continued for at least two weeks. Ribault, leading a larger group arrived at the same place on October 11. When the two antagonists faced each other Ribault is said to have offered a large ransom but his turn came like the others, on a dagger and a spike.

This event came to press immediately in England and France in le Challeux' *Discours de l' Histoire de la Florida...* But in the face of continuing religious strife it did not make much of an impact, initially at least. French Catholics were killing Huguenots themselves. What did it matter if the Spanish killed a few more. It was not until 1579 that a new edition in French came from that stronghold of Protestantism, Geneva. This time it bore the lurid title: *Brief discours... de quelques Francois en la Florida & du Massacre... que Barbarement Execute... par les Hespagnoles...*

If fell to Hakluyt, who saw the advantage of encouraging Franco-Hispanic rivalry and Anglo-French cooperation to get Laudonniere's own account printed in Paris in 1586. Where he found the manuscript he does not say, but he probably got it from Thevet, who he knew and who had recently supplied details of the colony to an Italian compiler.

Now the colorful story of massacre and brutality was rescued, as the editor put it "as from the tomb," and published at Hakluyt's expense in French and in his own translation in English. Although Hakluyt claims in the preface to the English edition the volume enjoyed some success in France it is not borne out by the facts for today it is among the rarest of books. Hakluyt goes on to say "By the malice of some too much affected in the Spanish faction [in France] it had been above twenty years suppressed," and there was a certain boldness in its revival. This boldness brought forth praise. "Monsieur Harlac, the lord chief justice of France," wrote Hakluyt, "and certain other of the wisest judges, in great choler... asked who had done such intolerable wrong to their whole kingdom as to have concealed that worthy work so long."

Another publisher, again not a Frenchman, got interested in the book, Theodore de Bry. Around 1590 he was searching out le Moyne's widow to get illustrations for his own edition of Laudonniere's account of the fate of his fellow Huguenots when he met Hakluyt who convinced him to start an Americana series with Harriot's *Virginia*. But even de Bry's sumptuous editions with their vivid engravings failed to excite much interest. After publishing Harriot and Laudonniere in English, French, German and Latin editions he found it profitable to confine the remainder of his series to the latter two languages.

Here we leave the French, peculiarly on the eve of their great colonial expansion, with apparently very little interest in or knowledge of America. It would seem as if they stumbled over it about the time of Cartier and forgot about it thirty years later. Foreigners, notably Hakluyt, de Bry and Chauveton got more information published in French than they did.

THE ENGLISH

If, after Cartier's mines produced fool's gold France thought of America largely in terms of an opportunity for religious toleration - send Protestants to live with the Devil - even more recalcitrant England had to be dragged kicking and screaming into America and Empire. Frobisher discovered it for them, by accident while he was heading for Cathay. One searches in vain for English interest in expansion before Frobisher with a single exception. A disappointed investor in Cabot's voyages and brother-in-law of Thomas More, John Rastell, wrote a play entitled: *An Interlude of the Four Elements*, produced about 1518-'19. The patriotic theme says:

> This see is called the Great Occyan,
> So great it is that never man
> Could tell it sith the worlde began;
> Tyll nowe, within this xx yere,
> Westwarde be founde new landes,
> That we have never heard tell of before this
> By wrytynge nor other meanys,
> Yet many nowe have ben there;
> And that contry is so large or rome,
> Muche larger than all Cristendome,
> For dyvers maryners had it tryed,
> And stayed by the coste syde
> Above v. thousande myle!
> But what commodytes be within
> No man can tell or well imagin,
> But not yet long ago
> Some men of this contrey went,
> By the kynges nobel consent,
> It for to serche to that extent,
> And could not be brought therto...
>
> O what a thynge had been than,
> Yf that they that be Englyshemen
> Might have ben the furst of all
> That there shulde have taken possessyon,
> And made furst buyldynge and habytacion,

A memory perpetuall!
And also what an honorable thynge,
Bothe to the realme and the kynge,
To have his domynyon extendynge
There into so farre a grounde,
The most wyse prynce the vij Herry
Caused furst to be founde...[1]

But Rastell's idea of the map was presumably the same as Cabot's. We are still talking about Asia. Nothing else significant happened until Frobisher and still it took time to understand the idea of colonies. Frobisher's ventures were not intended to plant colonies but return lucre to England. She had almost no literature about the other side of the earth and not a single printed map of her own.

As far as the printing press was concerned this failure was largely corrected by one man, Richard Hakluyt, a preacher by vocation and geographer by avocation. He is another of those figures whose life and writings are inseparable. Hakluyt was born at exactly the right time, about 1552, the year before the first successful overseas venture to Russia. Had he been born fifty years earlier he would have lived in insular England. Fifty years later he would have been a mere worker in archives. Instead his life span from 1552 to 1516 allowed him to participate in the development of a larger England that would soon stretch her fingers around the globe.

His story starts with Hakluyt's older cousin, also named Richard Hakluyt (1535? - 1591) who came to London for legal training about the time the Russia Company was formed. He became an advisor to that and other overseas ventures. He counselled Frobisher and Gilbert and wrote propaganda for Raleigh. The younger Hakluyt began in the 1580's where his cousin left off. He also did much for Gilbert and Raleigh. He was a director of Raleigh's Virginia colony and was one of four who received from King James the charter for the finally successful Virginia. He was equally active in ventures that reached East giving lavish advice to aid in the firm foundation of the East India Company among others.

The history of Hakluyt's career is in large part the intellectual history of the beginning of the British Empire. Thus the clergyman stands as one of the directing minds of a new national spirit. The *Discourse on Western Planting*, written for Raleigh's Virginia colony, is not only a statement of commercial and colonial policy but the announcement of a new nationalism. The same voice sounds more majestically through the noble narratives of *Principal Navigations*.

Presumably it was through his cousin young Hakluyt came into contact with the merchant travellers gathered around the Russia Company. He tells us in the dedication of *Divers Voyages. . .* he made the acquaintance of "merchants of credit that have lived long in Spain." He talked with Steven Borough, the most distinguished of the Russia Company captains. He interviewed Drake on his return from his journey round the world, corresponded with Mercator and formed the friendship of Michael Lok, a disillusioned investor in the Frobisher expeditions. Lok had seen much of the world as a trader in foreign parts and rather too much in the ways of speculative enterprise. The disappointed merchant would be of considerable help to the young preacher-geographer with his own undertakings.

As Hakluyt matured from youth to young man a number of significant events occurred which created a very mixed climate in England. First there was Frobisher and despite his failure to find a Northwest Passage it remained on the maps and Adrian Gilbert and John Dee soon formed a new company to look for it. Meanwhile the tale of every traveller argued fabulous treasure on the new continent and every yarn was believed, if only because the conquerors of Mexico and Peru had so little to go on. At the same time the English had been trying to cash in on New World commerce at least since 1562 when Hawkins made his first slave trading venture. Following the skirmish described in *Troublesome Voyage. . .* English "merchants" armed to defend themselves and frequently running in packs began an intense competition with French pirates for Spanish treasure. Drake brought home enough loot from his West Indies raid of 1585-'6 to provide his investors with a ten thousand percent profit.

But Piracy and slave trade would not an empire make and the unknown continent still beckoned. At worst it might be a stepping stone between England and Cathay especially in view of Frisius' and Munster's antiquated maps still coming off continental presses. At best there was the possibility of discovering, in the unexplored lands between Florida and Newfoundland a new Peru. North America could be a trade route or a treasure trove. In 1578 Humphery Gilbert proposed a Newfoundland colony for both purposes.

On the other hand there were many negatives. Frobisher's failure had bankrupted the Cathay Company. Spain had supremacy in America and a powerful Atlantic fleet to defend it which their brutal extermination of the French Florida colony demonstrated they were quite prepared to do. English ships had a good carrying trade between Lisbon and Cadiz and Northern Europe which was dependent on already strained Spanish goodwill.

It was against this background Hakluyt's publishing career began, humbly enough in 1580, with translation of Cartier out of Ramusio entitled: *A Shorte and brief narration of. . . Discoueries to the Northweast partes called Newe France.* It was done by a fellow student at Oxford, John Florio. Although his name does not appear in the book Hakluyt says in the dedication of *Divers Voyages,* "the last year, at my charge and other of my friends, by my exhortation, I caused Jacques Cartier's two voyages. . . to be translated out of my volumes." We hear the ventriloquist's voice in the preface of the *Brief Narration* addressed to "All Gentlemen, Merchants, and Pilots. . . or whosoever desirous of new discoveries." He tells them, "here is a description of a country no less fruitful and pleasant . . . than in England, France of Germany. . . which opportunities. . . might suffice to induce our Englishmen not only to fall into some traffic with the inhabitants, but also plant a colony in some convenient place."

This initial effort was followed in 1582 by another work of sixty leaves which would grow through two decades into a leviathan that would be hailed as "the great prose epic of the English nation." It bore the title: *Divers Voyages touching the discovery of America*. In his dedication Hakluyt marvels that in ninety years since America was discovered England failed to participate in its plantation. But, he continues, "I consider that there is a time for all men, and see the Portugals' time to be out of date, and the nakedness of the Spaniards and their long hidden secrets are now at length espied, whereby they went about to delude the world, I conceive great hope that the time approacheth and now is that we of England may share. . . in part of America and other regions as yet undiscovered."

He adds that England needs more space: "Yea if we would behold with the eye of pity how all our prisons are pestered and filled with able men to serve their country, which for small robberies are daily hanged in great numbers. . . we would hasten and further. . . the deducting of some colonies of our super-fluous people into those temperate and fertile parts of America," which Hakluyt points out are closer to England than any other part of Europe. Bees he explains, "when they grow to be too many in their own hive at home, are wont to be led out by their own captains to swarm abroad and seek themselves a new dwelling place. If the examples of the Grecians and Carthaginians. . . may not move us, yet let the wisdom of these small, weak, and unreasonable creatures."

He mentions a conversation with the Portuguese ambassador who professed amazement "that those countries from the point of Florida northward were all this while unplanted by Christians," and claimed the Iberian said were he younger he would sell all he had "to furnish a convenient number of ships to sea for the inhabiting of those countries and reducing those gentle people to Christianity."[2]

Painfully aware that before she could get anything started England needed to know much more about America Hakluyt set out to paint a verbal picture in *Divers Voyages*. The work is a combination of previously published material, recommendations on purposes and policies to be observed in colonization writ-ten by Hakluyt's lawyer cousin for Gilbert's colonial scheme of 1578 and some salvaged manuscript material. First he sets out to establish England's claim to America "from Florida to sixty-seven degrees Northward" on the strength of Cabot's discovery. (For Florida read South Carolina. On 16th. and 17th. Century maps the name was applied to the entire area de Soto transversed.) For this information he had to turn to Ramusio and Cabot's contemporary the London chronicler Fabyan. As if this was not enough to establish claim he got hold of Robert Thorne's manuscript book and map which had been in the hands of his executors for sixty years. In this connection he mentions Rut's voyage although Rut added no information and it's hard to imagine what he discovered. Then he picked up the mischievous Zenos who, together with recently published Frobisher material, summed up information about the frozen North. He reprint-ed his account of Cartier's two voyages then turned back to Ramusio to get Verrazano's description of the middle regions. For good measure he threw in a brief notice of the French in Florida.

This is far from a complete or critical collection of North American voyages. The Spanish are conspicuous by their absence and Florida gets short shrift. But Hakluyt was leery of lands ostensibly occupied by Spain. Discretion, even in the eyes of the colonial propagandists, was the better part of valor.

Not content to recount voyages Hakluyt adds the usual impressive list of American products which he probably intended to be the most tempting part of the prospectus. He brings up the Northwest Passage and suggests planting colonies might facilitate its discovery. His list and discussion of the passage look dubious now, but they were justified by the authorities Hakluyt cited which if not unimpeachable, were yet unimpeached.

Still, *Divers Voyages* is amusingly anachronistic. In addition to including the Zenos who should have been impugned on the mere experience of Frobisher, his inclusion of Thorne's map of 1527 and an equally archaic one by Michael Lok with its false "Sea of Verrazano" make it seem Hakluyt did not really want to hear the truth.

In June of 1583 Gilbert sailed for America to begin his first colonial experiment and Hakluyt intended to go along. But there seems to have been a swift change of plans for in autumn of that year he was in France as chaplain to the new English ambassador. He remained in that position for five years but returned to England on at least a half dozen occasions, usually in the interest of the Colonial Party. The French had hands on information about America the English needed so in many ways Hakluyt was better suited to the French post.

The year Hakluyt sailed for France Sir George Peckham picked up on the idea of America as a dumping place for dissidents. He proposed a Catholic colony in a work bearing the title: *A true Reporte of the Late Discoveries of the Newfoundlandes* and suggested a site there which would be remote from Spanish harassment. He would send settlers without cost on an outgoing fishing fleet, stowing them in space reserved for cod on the return trip. The settlers would catch plenty to eat on the Grand Banks. Once settled they would expand from fishing to more attractive industries based on the familiar list of abundant commodities: silks, dyes, Palm [!] wine, etc. which "such persons as have discovered in those parts do testify that they found." In sum it looks like a low budget scheme by somebody who did not know much about geography. It came to nothing. But it is interesting because it introduces in England the same feeling of a romantic quest that kept Spain on a roll through its glorious century with some dedicatory verses penned by poetic pirates. Frobisher offered:

> A pleasant ayre, a sweet and firtell soil
> > A certain gaine, a never dying praise:
> An easy passage void of loathsome toile,
> Found out by some and knowen to me the waies,
> > All this is there, then he who will refraine to trie
> > That loves to live abroad, or dreads to die.

And Francis Drake thought:

> Who seeks by worthy deeds to gain renown for hire;
> Whose heart, whose hand, whose purse is prest to purchase his desire;
> If any such be, that thirsteth after fame,
> Lo! here a mean to win himself everlasting name.
>
> Who seeks by gain and wealth t'advance his house and blood;
> Whose care is great, whose toil no less, whose hope is all for good:
> If any one there be, that covets such a trade,
> Lo! here the plot for common wealth and private gain is made.
>
> He that for virtue's sake will venture far and near;
> Whose zeal is strong whose practice truth, whose faith is void of fear
> If any such there be, inflamed with holy care,
> Here may he find a ready mean his purpose to declare.
>
> So that, for each degree, this treatise doth unfold
> The path to fame the proof of zeal, and the way to purchase gold.[3]

After Frobisher's gold turned itself and him into fools it fell largely to Hakluyt, with patronage from the Colonial Party, to keep the printing press going during the 1580's. We have already referred to most of the work he did during his Paris period but there had to be more. It found expression in 1589 in an 825 page tome entitled: *The Principal Navigations, Voiages and Discoveries of the English nation. . . to the most remote and farthest distant quarters of the Earth within compasse of these 1500 yeeres. . .*

The *Principal Navigations* appeared when English sentiment for American colonization was at a low ebb. Frobisher failed, Gilbert's venture turned to nothing, the first Virginia colony of 1585 faltered in both morale and supplies. It was brought home by Drake returning from his West Indies voyage. The Roanoke colony of 1587 was cut off by the Spanish war and had disappeared entirely by the time Raleigh diverted a privateer to check on them.

Hakluyt's tone is patriotism and propaganda. In the dedication to *Principal Navigations* he tells us while he was in France he, "heard in speech and read in books, other nations miraculously extolled for their discoveries and notable enterprises by sea, but the English of all others for their sluggish security, and continual neglect of the like attempts, especially in so long and happy time of peace, either ignominiously reported or exceedingly condemned." He then quoted the slighting words of a French historian who, "called the English lazy despite their superior shipbuilding and discipline. Thus both hearing and reading the obloquy of our nation. . . and further not seeing any man to have care to recommend to the world the illustrious labors and painful travails of our countrymen: myself being the last winter returned from France. . . . determined notwithstanding all difficulties to under take the burden of work."[4]

The result was a folio of at least 700,000 words intended to prove England had always been an international maritime nation and would remain one while in fact she had not yet become either. He starts with the Empress Helena (discoverer of the True Cross) then stresses the crusaders and reprints Mandeville complete. Already we are steeped in the lore of the romantic and fantastic. (Nobody even knows if there was a Sir John Mandeville.) Coming down to his own time he becomes more prosaic and encyclopedic. He printed abstracts from Admiralty instructions, pillaged the records of private adventurers such as the Russia Company and gave descriptions of countries to which English trade was carried. He provided detailed accounts of voyages to Russia, the Levant and Africa and added numerous private letters, such as those which told the story of his own and his cousin's activities. He reprinted various tracts which bore on enterprise, and for "stopping the mouths of the reproachers" cites tributes of foreign geographers to English enterprise.

The section dealing with western voyages is somewhat larger than those dealing with voyages to the South and East. He begins with Madoc then passes on to a parley Columbus had with Henry VII when he had sought backing from the monarch for his voyage of discovery. He amplified such Cabot records as he could dig up. He travelled 200 miles to interview an ancient survivor of a Newfoundland voyage of 1536 and obtained reports of Hawkins' voyages which marked the first shock with Spain as well as reports of escape by some of his captured men. (Including the fantastic David Ingram.) He included in reprint most of Gilbert's writings and details on his colony. He gave connected narratives of the Raleigh colonies adding the first book on Virginia which Harriot had just published. He detailed Frobisher's voyages and the more recent explorations of John Davis to the Northwest along with Drake's and Cavendish's glorious circumnavigations.

Unfortunately, with the exception of Drake and Cavendish, this section reads like the annals of English maritime misadventure. Henry VII was probably sorry he did not listen to Columbus when he had the chance. Cabot was lost at sea. The Newfoundland voyage of 1536 resulted in the loss of a ship and murder and cannibalism by survivors on another. Hawkins' third voyage was "Troublesome," Gilbert drown along with his colony, Raleigh's first Virginia colony foundered and the second disappeared. Frobisher and Davis were fiascos.

Still, *Principal Navigations* made good publicity for America. Reports by Peckham, Harriot, David Ingram, Henry Hanks, *et al* spoke of wealth, rich soil and friendly Indians. Although we have already heard most of these points we can let Hakluyt quote Arthur Barlow, who made a Virginia reconnaissance for Raleigh in 1584 -'85, sum them up one more time. He: "found the people most gentle, loving and faithful, void of all guile and treason and such as lived after the manner of the Golden Age. The earth bringeth forth all things in abundance as in the first creation, without toil or labor. The people only care to defend themselves from the cold in their short winter and feed themselves with such meat as the soil affordith. . . a more kind and loving people there cannot be found in the world, as far as we hitherto had trial."

To this hyperbole Barlow echoes another old theme that began with Columbus and climaxed when Indians sold Manhattan Island for twenty-four dollars: The Indians were happy to trade valuable furs for trinkets.

And, if there had been Indian troubles maybe this could be turned to advantage. Henry Hawks hints the Indians might welcome the English as allies because the Spanish "keep the Indians in great subjugation." And "They have attempted divers times to make insurrections but they have been overthrown." And if the Indians were sick of the Spanish they were just as sick of the French. To Hawkins' complaint that the French in Florida desired to live by the sweat of other's brow's Hakluyt adds Christopher Carlysle who says Cartier's seizure of Donnacona and disputes during the second winter he was there "put the whole country into such dislike with the French as never since they would admit any conversation with them."

The first edition of the *Navigations* failed to satisfy Hakluyt's passion for completeness. This resulted in a new edition in three volumes of 1598-1600 which more than doubled the original 700,000 words. Although the work bore the same title this time a couple of foreigners (including the Zeno's) snuck in. Hakluyt had to grudgingly concede in the dedication of third volume that Englishmen had not covered the *entire* world and his objective was to provide the most complete world picture possible to encourage exploration both East and West.

An interesting feature of the new edition was a greatly expanded medieval section. Although Mandeville disappears without apology Hakluyt found new narratives of medieval crusaders and pilgrims and we hear of conquests by Arthur at sea, and the size of fleets under various middle ages kings allowing these chapters to expand from about 75,000 words to about a quarter million. Wittingly or not Hakluyt seems to join hands with poets creating an English version of the romance of chivalry.

He may have encouraged them in his first edition with references to Madoc and Mandeville. In any event England's time for empire was coming and poets seemed to sense it. In Marlowe's *Tamburlaine* the Scythian conqueror tells his sons:

> Look here my boys; see what a world of ground
> lies westward from the midst of Cancer's line
> Unto the rising of this earthly globe,
> Whereas the sun, declining from our sight,
> Begins the day with our Antipodes.
> And shall I die, and this unconquered?

More interesting is Spenser's Fairyland. With the Welsh Tudors on the throne Madoc was floating all over the place. And, while the theme was not pandemic especially in face of the harsh realities of the North American experience, it lurked beneath the surface and it is impossible to separate the pastoral desire from descriptions of America. The new locales appear in Sindey's *Arcadia*, a name contributed to a portion of America by Verrazano, while Shakespeare's *Tempest* is set here and *As You like It* and *Midsummer's Dreams* are placed in fantastic or bucolic landscapes.

Spenser, seems to be seeking a once and future place, the England of yore. He is not too specific on location but Drake had already christened California "Nova Albion" and America comes shining through his verse when he explains to the Queen:

> . . . none that brearth living aire, does know
> Where is that happy land of Faery,
> Which I so much doe vaunt, yet no where show.
>
> But let that happy man with better sence advize
> That of the world least part of us is red:
> And daily how through hardy enterprise
> Many great Regions are discovered,
> Which to late age were never mentioned.
> Who ever heard of th' Indian Peru?
> Or who in venturous vessel measured
> the Amazon's huge river, now found trew?
> Or fruitfullest Virginia who did ever view?
>
> Yet all these were when no man did them know,
> Yet have from wisest ages hidden beene:
>
> Of Faery Lond yet if he more inquire,
> By certaine signes, here sett in sondrie place,
> He may it fynd.
>   - *Faerie Queene*, bk. II, 1,2,3.

Returning to Hakluyt, by 1600 he had told a noble story in which the heros are legion. No explorer, captain, trader or settler has eminence; all meet the same enemies, which are the perils of nature and the unknown. Along with heros like Drake are traders and settlers, dropped into empty spaces to face, in nonchalance, despair or riotous merriment unknown dangers of fever, frost and privation, the incomprehensible alien and possibly recover something lost.

Hakluyt's career did not end with the century. He remained active until his death but with *Principal Navigations* on booksellers' shelves England was poised on the threshold of empire. If France, still in the grip of factional wars, had apparently forgotten about America, the English, largely thanks to Hakluyt's labors, managed to keep up a steady stream of Americana from Frobisher on.

Afterwords &
Afterthoughts

APOLOGIA PRO LIBRO SUO

DURING our random stroll through 16th. Century America we seem to have drifted all over the place without drawing many conclusions. Why didn't you stick to a single subject some frustrated reader asks? What do Oviedo, Casas Pizarro, Hakluyt, Maps, Theodore de Bry and the rest have in common except for occupying the same century? The answer is obvious. Nothing happens in a vacuum. Most of our authors tended to influence, confirm or confute each other either in the interest of discovery or (more commonly) for their own purposes. The flip side of the romance of chivalry was the black legend. Characters like Pizarro and Cortez and Oviedo, the last who he frequently fought with, were the stuff of Casas. He in turn furnished material for Hakluyt's and Chauveton's colonial propaganda. Spanish accounts of natural wealth clearly motivated the English and French. Scholarly skeptical Raleigh probably got most of his naive ideas about Guyana from Gomora. (In this connection a digression, if it is not already obvious, might be in order. It took centuries for the European mind to separate the Americas. Furthermore anyone looking for North American heritage in the previous pages can find it. Our traditions hardly started with the Mayflower Compact or followed any systematic progression. Look at the govenment that immediately followed the compact or remember that two centuries later the Alamo fell to a Mexican patriot who had outlawed slavery in Texas. It started in the imaginations of Martyr and More who, to use Martyr's words, had discovered "a new born progeny." Or, more sadly, that just mentioned institution which las Casas damned, Martyr reluctantly acquiesced to and Sepuleveda found necessary, that grew up in America.)

For some relationships we have to read between the lines. For instance, what is the relationship between Casas, maps, Vespucci and the naming of America? Probably quite a bit. Casas vigorously resisted the application of Amerigo's name to the New World and insisted till his death Columbus had rediscovered the Indies of antiquity. The idea of a cut off land possibly occupied by another species was dangerous to his cause. Meanwhile the need to get Amerindians from Babble to America forced cartographers to back peddle, saying more than they knew, while speculation on Indian origins focused attention on the noble savage of classical antiquity. Although examples are abundant we can use Thevet's apparently inconsequential remark, "It would be thought if these wilde men have frequented Asia they should have learned this from the Albates..." (p.158) and his comments on subsequent pages provided a background for the noble savage while the demonic theme justified conquest. Exotic nature provided a stage set for a romance of chivalry. A different example is Jacques Cartier who, with Orince Fine's map in hand, assumed the St. Lawrence led into the heart of fabled Cathay. This made Saguenay credible. One purpose of my overlapping chapters is to suggest interrelationships during the period.

In order to give our adventures into the new a place to live I have confined myself to the most common themes in their literature. It would be presumptuous to speculate too much or assume a single imperative. Essayists have the privilege of 20/20 hindsight. Historians should not. God, Satan, Mammon, chivalry, nobility, barbarity and curiosity run through the preceding pages. None predominate, they intermingle leading to contradictions and confusion in my story but they existed within the century as they do in any period. I have occasionally used the words irony and irrationality or suggested it but our authors wrote with no sense of it. For instance describing Balboa, Cortez and Pizarro as cross bearers seems incompatible with what the history books say but Cortez exhibited evidences of piety on many occasions and Balboa built an altar on the spot he sighted the Pacific. Hakluyt, on the other hand, frequently claimed a primary purpose of expansion was extension of Christianity but he was clearly more of a patriot than a priest and the scholarly missionary Landa was a book burning sadist. Acosta for all his curiosity answered questions before asking them. But, they all had to reconcile a complex, variegated world into an acceptable picture just like we do.

In the course of typing the preceding pages I often felt like Father Acosta who, after listening to Indian myths of their history commented, "they are more like dreams than true histories." But if he had the courtesy to hear them out we should extend the same to him. In the process we learn more about the writers themselves than what they were describing. We also learn something about our own time. A primary purpose of history is to bring our own perceptions into focus and learn to take ourselves with a grain of salt. Deep down people of all periods share common yearnings and curiosities in finite consciousness. Our story is about a long forgotten time's expression of them and efforts by its denizens to reconcile the unanticipated with what they though they knew. Our era has learned to anticipate change (so had the late 15th. Century) but when it comes will we be able to absorb it with less droll results than our ancestors?

PERCEPTIONS AND AWARENESS

We have been discussing a century that had very little awareness of America. In 1597 a bibliography published in Venice by Antonio Possevino: *Apparatus ad Ommniusm Gentium Historiam...* listed only thirty titles on the Indies. Europe was occupied with its own problems, religious schism, threatening turks, provincial wars and a dramatically changing economy. Exotic lands represented a disproportionately small percentage of book production and Americana was a fraction of that. France produced more than twice as many books about the Turks, a clear and present danger, between 1480 and 1609 than the Western Hemisphere and three times as many on Asia and the East Indies. Huttich gave America about forty pages and Munster even less. Authoritative writers like Bodin could presume to describe the human race with almost total ignorance of America. Most of the best minds of Europe were somewhere else during these early years. Aside from the Spanish, whose presses were reticent at the best of times, the New World did not loom large on the horizon. But *Apparatus ad Ommniusm Gentium Historiam* notwithstanding by 1600 all literate Europe knew there was a very large land mass with some very different people in the middle of the Ocean Sea.

How it was perceived is another matter. There were anachronisms, reprints of works long out of date, efforts to organize and understand and misinformation. Best sellers like Vespucci, Staten and Gomora were read by many with the same seriousness as a modern reader peruses a novel. One only has to look at de Bry's illustrations for Staten to imagine how titillating he was. On the other hand thoughtful writers like Cieza and Acosta and, on the philosophical side, More were popular and must have given considerable pause for thought.

By the 19th. Century natural history, ethnology and comparative religion became the stuff of modern science but they did not get there by following a straight path. As awareness of America grew during succeeding centuries many of these questions and issues instead of disappearing changed and grew along with it. About the only subjects that had a vaguely straight forward progression through the century and beyond were cartography and iconography and even they occasionally took a turn for the worse. (California became an island around 1625 and stayed one for the rest of the century. Mythical kingdoms disappeared only to be replaced by new ones and an assortment of Northwest passages, some absolute hoaxes, cropped up.) Iconography improved because artists increasingly depicted European settlements and other things more easily understood back home and amateurs like Maria Meriam and Mark Catesby were fascinated with painting American flora and fauna. But when it came to the most endemic and complex feature of America, the Indian, artists continued to portray him according to their own prejudice as if they had never seen one. Rather the path was a backwards-forwards dialectic which sometimes resulted in intellectual progress and others to explanations which would make Acosta look like a 20th. Century philosopher, because for many the new has to be organized into beliefs that are important to them. Archaic ideas provided a negative side of the coin which forced fresh speculation. When the Pacific became so wide even St. Thomas could not cross it new answerers were demanded. The result was both comparative religion and new myth. Sometimes centuries old romanticism was transplanted to America. Chivalry became the Legend of the West. Other times anachronism struck. Las Casas' *Brief Relation* was printed through the 19th. Century as if his atrocities were still happening.

Less tactile issues assumed a life of their own. Most interesting are natural history, Indians and theology. The idea there might be something unique about America started when Columbus wondered why Indians in the same latitude as Ethiopia were not black. Vespucci's confutation of ancient authority and heretical discoveries could have gotten him burnt at the stake. Acosta got America back into the orthodox scheme of things at century's end and with a couple of exceptions (exclusive of Indian issues) it stayed there through the 17th. Century. America was composed of earth, air, fire and water just like everywhere else. It took the Age of Reason and Comte de Georges Louis Leclerc Buffon's *Natural History* or as it came to be known "The Unnatural History" to get that nonsense stirred up again. Buffon came up with what he thought was the original idea that American species differed from those of the Old World. (Apparently he had not read Vespucci, Oviedo or Acosta.) Had he confined himself to this simple observation he probably would not have made much of an impression but he also decided American mammals tended to be smaller and inferior. Take the lion for instance. Comparing the king of beasts to the puma he notices the American "lion" not only lacks a mane, but is smaller, weaker and more cowardly. In fact, he perceives with a sudden flash of intuition, it is no lion at all. From there the animals file past him as if they were just coming off the Ark. One by one the naturalist looks them over and denies them American citizenship. "Elephants belong to the Old Continent and are not found in the New... one cannot even find there any animal that can be compared with the elephant for size or shape," he says. The only American creature that bears a remote resemblance to the elephant is the tapir, a dwarf compared to the African Elephant, a pocket pachyderm. Llamas are just as bad. They may look like giraffes but even if one stood on stilts and strained its neck it could not match one for size. There are no rhinoceroses, hippopotamuses, camels, etc. Loathsome lower orders, like snakes and insects, flourish in the New World but mammals are much less numerous than in the Old. Buffon counts 130 Old World species and about half as many in the New. The latter not only has fewer species those it has are generally more puny. The unavoidable conclusion? "Living nature is thus much less active there, much less varied, and we may even say, less strong." Until now American nature had generally been described as abundant either by amazed spectators or propagandists. Now Buffon threw down the gauntlet. By the time he finished he had created a blanket indictment of the hemisphere. Nature itself, animals, Indians, creoles and presumably transplanted Europeans all came up wanting. Naturally Americans were outraged. A century long debate ensued which Antonello Gerbi needed 650 pages to summarize in *Dispute of the New World*. It involved everybody from Jefferson to Hegel and Franklin to Goethe.

The Puritans carried the same millenarianism into America as the Spanish. They saw the entire world in the grip of the Devil and their American haven was no improvement. Samuel Sewell sought to "expose the antick fancy of America being Hell" in his *Phaenomena quaedam Apocalyptia* (Boston, 1697) but he confesses "there is so much confusion in the discourses upon this subject, that a man cannot tell when he is in Heaven and when he is in Hell," and "so near an approach to so complete resemblance of Hell was not to be found in *rerum natura* as America." John Smith, hardly a Puritan, wrote in his book on Virginia, "The principal god of the Indians is the Devil." Meanwhile Samuel Purchas was worrying about floods and the Doubting Thomas issue but harked back to the Devil imitating God theory. It is no coincidence that the witchcraft delusion attained its dramatic finale in Salem. Even after that absurdity Cotton Mather in *Magnalia Christi Americana* tells us about biblical scholar Joseph Mede (1586 - 1638) who: "conjectures that the American Hemisphere will escape the conflagration of the earth which we will expect at the descent of our Lord Jesus Christ from Heaven: and that the people here will not have a share in the blessedness which the renovated world shall enjoy. . . The inhabitants of these regions who were originally Scythians, and therein a notable fulfillment of the prophecy about the enlargement of Japhet will be the Gog and Magog whom the devil will seduce to invade the New Jerusalem with the envious hope to gain the angelical circumstance of the people there." Mather admitted Mede's opinion was conjectural but several other writers considered it most probable. The theme ran through Americana into the 18th. Century until Satan started to fade out.[1]

A bibliography of works discussing Indian nature and origins into the 19th. Century would be longer than this book. As John Ogilby complained in 1671: "the learned dispute so much, that they find nothing more difficult. . . for whether inquiry be made after the time when the Americans first settled themselves thither, either by shipping or by land; on purpose, or accidentally; driven by storm, or else forc'd by a more powerful people, to remove from their old plantations and seek for new? Or if any one should be yet more curious, asking the way that directed them out of another country to this New World? Or else enquire for those people, from whom the Americans deriv'd themselves? He will find several opinions." [2]

During the 17th. Century science and religion started to go separate ways, but it was nearly two centuries before they stopped speaking. This resulted in a collection of crackpot ideas founded in the previous hundred years of discovery. Around mid century a Frenchman named la Peyrere resurrected Paracelsus' heresy of a separate creation, suggesting that Americans might be "pre-adamites." Following hard on his heels came Thomas Burnett who to save his soul could not figure out why God had created such a disorderly planet with mountains always getting in the way, crooked rivers that never seemed to be going convenient places, etc. His effort to get it all worked out appeared in London in 1681 entitled *Theory of the Earth*. Burnett assumed the flood made the mess and Amerindians were not necessarily the children of Noah because Providence, "we may reasonably suppose, made provisions for every continent." These wondering writers were not alone. The seriousness of the problem is suggested by the title of a book published in Mexico in 1763 by the Jesuit Father Francisco Xavier de Orrio. In English it reads: *Solution to the great problem of the population of the Americas, in which on the basis of Holy Books there is discovered an easy path for the transmigration of Men from one Continent to the other; and how there could pass to the New World, not only the Beasts of Service, but also the wild and harmful Animals; and by this occasion one completely settles the ravings of Pre-Adamites, which relied on this difficult objection until now not properly solved.* About the same time the encyclopedist, Diderot, was forced to deal with pre-adamites along with problems of biblical chronology. A few years later one of the most noted and pandemic scholars of the period, Alexander von Humboldt, speculated in his *Kosmos*, "If the animals were not taken to the distant lands by angels or these enthusiastic huntsman, the inhabitants of the continent, then they must have sprung directly from the earth; whereupon the question arises, to what end were all the animals gathered in the ark?"

The orthodox still insisted Indians had to be Noah's progeny but as Ogilby pointed out there were many opinions. Speculation ran through at least the first half of the 19th Century. The millennial-wandering apostle-Indian origin issue found tactile expression in the 1820's when Joseph Smith wrote a novel called *The Book of Mormon*. It is still rolling off presses today.

If we skip over Pocahontas the Noble Savage got a brief rest through the 17th. Century. So far as the English, French and Dutch were concerned they were dealing with the same pesky Indians the Spanish had to put up with. There are a few pastoral images from the period but they are the exception. *The Jesuit Relations* were among the most influential in trying to create a favorable impression of the Indian but they are also laced with accounts of martyrdoms and self sacrifice among the breathern. Then, in the 18th. Century, he made a dramatic reappearance. Modern literature on the subject is too complete to merit much further discussion but since we introduced him along with Martyr we cannot leave without saying goodbye. One of the cornerstones of the resurrection was Joseph Francois Lafitau's *Moeurs des Savage Americans* which appeared in 1724. Lafitau was a Jesuit who served among the Iroquois. He too was concerned with Indian origins and in an effort to prove they were descended from the Tartars prepared an encyclopedic description of their customs, religion, and social organization. Though his authority has never been questioned he added a strange twist to his argument. He placed illustrations of Amerindians side by side with plates depicting classical urns and statues. Either he did not trust his own drawing ability or sought to depict Indians as they lived before becoming contaminated by European influence so he fell back on copying plates from Bry (including one depicting Raleigh's acephalous monster, the Ewaiponoma). In any event Lafitau's engraver succeeded in making Indians look more like classical gods than Bry himself. The Golden Age strikes again.

Although the desire for the pastoral influenced Noble Savage literature of the 18th. and 19th. Centuries anti-Buffon polemic exacerbated it. Thus by 1760 Benjamin West was comparing a Mohawk warrior to the Apollo Belvedere, no less. (One sees in the savage nobleizers and attacks on Buffon the beginnings of a sense of identity and national pride in the Americas and seeds of American revolutions. Remember, the patriots at the Boston Tea Party were dressed as live free or die Indians.) When those tea tossing rascals became founding fathers portrait busts depicted them as Roman senators. By mid century the twin themes of classicism and the free Indian assimilated themselves into Miss America/ Columbia or Miss Liberty when coins and statues of her depicted a classical figure wearing an Indian war bonnet.

The New World also provided a filter for preexisting dreams. The continuing emphasis on classicism by Americana authors is an example. Renaissance classicism was hardly introduced here but writers viewing the New World through classically tinted glasses certainly rediscovered it in America and passed it on to Rousseau and egalitarian revolutions. Rousseau read and was influenced by Lafitau who depended on de Bry. He almost certainly read More and he may have seen Casas' pamphlets insisting on equality and limited rights of rulers.

As I pointed out before I have made no attempt to write an essay or trace threads. History does not lend itself to easily progressive patterns. Rather it translates into what most people think at the time. But mammoth change did occur. It forced was on us by discovery.

The Reformation did not create the diversity of religious opinion or the world view we have today; Luther was more fundamentalist and superstitious than the Pope. The Renaissance for all that it changed a format was not, exclusive of cosmological issues, a breakthrough into modern thought either. Look at any Albrecht Durer engraving or an Italian religious painting. A reshaped world map necessitated that above mentioned separation of religion and science and introduced man's revised vision of himself more than Erasmus. Vespucci and Magellan, then Copernicus and finally Einstein forced the issue more than Descartes while Oviedo by way of Acosta via Buffon and Darwin created a new sense of our race. Martyr was no philosopher but via Montaigne and Lafitau (also no philosopher) produced Rousseau. This process was hardly confined to America but Columbus and Americus were the first. It would be ridiculous to say the simple act of bumping into America was singularly responsible for the modern world but the dialogue of discovery certainly got the ball rolling.

Notes

PARTNERS IN DISCOVERY

1. Translation from Pohl Frederick: *Amerigo Vespucci., N.Y.C.,* 1944, 151.
2. Pohl, 170.

FILLING IN DISCOVERY

1. Quoted from Elliot, John H. in *First Images of America,* University of California, 1976. p. 14.
2. Martyr, Peter: *De Orbe Novo, the Eight Decades of Peter Martyr d' Anghera.* Translated and edited by Francis Augustus Mac Nutt, N.Y.C. and London, 1912. Vol I p.294.
3. Martyr: Vol. II p.7.

NATURE IN THE NEW WORLD

1. Morison, Samuel Eliot: *The European Discovery of America, The Southern Voyages.* N.Y.C., 1974. p.284.
2. Oviedo: *Natural History of the West Indies,* translanted and edited by Sterling A. Stoundemire., Chapel Hill, 1959. p.120.
3. Oviedo: 54.
4. Cieza de Leon: *The Incas.* . . Harriet de Onis translator, Victor Wolfgang von Hagen editor. , Norman, Oklahoma. 1959. p.156.
5. Cieza: p. 157.
6. Cieza: p. 257.
7. Gerbi, Antonello: *Nature in the New World; From Columbus to Oviedo.* Translated by Jeremy Moyle. Pittsburgh, 1985.
8. Frampton, John: *Joyfull Newes.* . . London. 1925, Stephen Gaselee introduction. Vol. I. Quotes from p.3 and pp. 99-114.
9. Nicholas, Thomas, *Pleasant History.* . . London, 1577. p. 2 of dedication.
10. Hakluyt, Richard: *Principal Navigations.* . . (Hakluyt Society). Vol. X., 338-431.
11. Acosta, Joseph: *Natural and Moral History of the West Indies.* Hakluyt Society, Vol. I. p. 186.
12. Acosta: Vol. I. p. 197.
13. Acosta: Vol. I. p. 245.
14. Acosta: Vol. I. p. 285.

INDIAN ORIGINS AND THEOLOGY

1. Oviedo: p. 37.
2. Gerbi: p. 312f.
3. Martyr: Vol. II. p. 116f.
4. Martyr: Vol. II. p. 284.

ALL SORTS OF INIANS

1. Morison, Samuel Eliot: *The European Discovery of America; The Southern Voyages:* N.Y.C., 1974. p. 284.
2. Pohl: 155.
3. Martyr: Vol. I. p. 102.
4. Martyr: Vol. I. p. 103.
5 Martyr: Vol. I. p. 108.
6. Martyr: Vol. II. p. 70.
7. Arber, Edward: *The First Three English Books on America.* Kraus reprint, N.Y.C., 1971. p. XXVII.
8. Morison: *Northern Voyages.* p. 288.
9. Morison: *Northern Voyages.* p. 290.
10. *The Narrative of the Expediition of Herando de Soto by the Gentleman of Elvas,* edited by Theodore H. Lewis. Printed in *Spanish Explorers in the Southern United States, 1528-1543.* N.Y.C., 1907. p. 168.
11. *The Narrative of Alvar Nunez Cabeza de Vaca,* edited by Frederick W. Hodge. Printed in *Spanish Explorers in the Southern United States, 1528-1543.* N.Y.C., 1907. p 47.
12. Lery, Jean de: *Histoire d' un Voyage fait en la terre du Bresil.* . . , Geneva, 1599. p. 119f.
13. *The English Works of Thomas Hobbes,* London, 1839-'45. Vol. III. p. 122f.
14. *The Complete Works of Montaigne.* edited by Donald M Framed, Stanford, 1959.
15. Cieza: p. 136.
16. Cieza: p. 266.
17. Acosta: Vol. II. p. 401.

THE QUEST

1. Huizinga, Johan: *The Waning of the Middle Ages.* Anchor Books ed., N.Y.C., 1954. p. 31ff.
2. Washburn, W. in *First Images,* p. 338.

3. *The Voyages of the Venetian Brothers Nicolo & Antonio Zeno to the Northern Seas, in the XIV Century.* Translated and edited by Richard Henry Major, Hakluyt Society edition, pp. 5 and 23.
4. *ibid.* p. 34f.
5. Martyr: Vol. II. p. 298ff.
6. Diaz del Castillio: *Discovery and Conquest of Mexico.* edited by Irving A. Leonard, N.Y.C., 1956. p. 190f.
7. *Reports on the Discovery of Peru.* edited by Clements R. Markham. Hakluyt Society edition. p. 8.
8. *ibid.* p. 52.
9. *ibid.* p. 55.
10. *ibid.* p. 56ff.
11. *Spanish Explorers.* . . p. 52f.
12. *ibid.* p. 114.

THE BLACK LEGEND

1. Wagner, Henry Raup and Parish, Helen Rand: *The Life and Writings of Bartolome de las Casas.* Albuquerque, 1967. p. 239.

COLONIAL IMPULSE

1. Percy Society: Vol. XXII, London, 1848. p. 28f.
2. Parks, George Bruner: *Richard Hakluyt and the English Voyages,* N.Y.C. p. 121ff.
3. Louis B. Wright: *The Elizabethans' America.* P. 121f.
4. Parks, p. 121f.

AFTERWORD

1. Mather, Cotton: *Magnalia Christi Americana.* Edited by Kenneth B. Murdock, Harvard, 1977. p. 123.
2. Ogilby, John: *America.* London, 1671. p. 11f.

Index

Acosta, Joseph: 108-117, 121-128, 134-136, 186-188, 244ff.

Alexander VI Pope: 4f, 42f, 199.

Apinan, Peter: 38, 45, 54.

Aristotle: 108, 110ff, 176f, 179.

Bacon, Francis: 96.

Balboa: 45, 199f.

Barlow, Arthur: 240.

Behaim, Martin: 41, 193.

Belleforest, Francois: 220.

Benzoni, Girolgmo: 97, 121f, 226ff.

Best, George: 72, 102.

Betanozos, Domingo de: 120.

Bodin, Jean: 126, 166ff.

Boemus, Johann: 176.

Bordone, Benedtto: 54, 88.

Brendan (St.) 192, f.

Bry, Theodore de: 75, 154f, 168, 171ff, 194, 218, 220, 231, 233ff, 243, 245, 250.

Buffon, George Louis, Leclerc: 246f, 251.

Burgkmair, Hans: 208.

Burnett, Thomas: 248.

Cabeza de Vaca, Alvar Nunez: 152f, 211-213.

Cabot, John: 21. 23, 71, 237, 240.

Cabot, Sebastian: 22, 70.

Cabral, Pedro Alvaves: 12f, 43.

Cabrillo: 51, 62.

Campananella, Thommaso: 145, 209.

Cantino: 25ff.

Cardenas, Juan de: 96, 179.

Cartier, Jacques: 51, 64, 98ff, 228, 236, 241, 244.

Casas, Bartolome de las: 121f, 126, 132, 171 ff, 211, 214-225, 243.

Challeux, Nicholas le: 225f, 233.

Charles V (Holy Roman Emperor): 50, 177.   Charron, Pierre: 168.

Chauveton, Urban: 122, 131, 226f, 234.

Cieza de Leon, Pedro: 93 ff, 119-121, 180-186, 224, 245.

Cochlaeus: 43.

Coelho, Goncalo: 12-19.

Columbus, Christopher: 1-9, 11, 14-18, 21ff, 37, 42, 207 240, 246.

Columbus, Ferdinand: 1 193f.

Contarini, Giovanni Matteo: 26 29.

Coranado: 52, 194.

Corte Real, Gaspar and Miguel: 21, 23, 60.

Cortez, Hernando: 47, 51, 86ff, 129, 144 f, 201.

Cosa, Juan de: 24ff.

Cousin, Jean: 159, 229.

Dante: 14, 191.

Dati, Giuliamo: 4-8.

Diaz del Castillio, Bernal: 201 f.

Docsborch, Jan van: 141f.

Donnacona: 99f.

Dake, Sir Francis: 131, 236, 239, 242.

Durrer, Albrecht: 143.

Eden, Richard: 47, 70-73.

Ellis, Thomas: 102.

Elvas, Gentleman of: 100 ff, 131, 150ff, 159, 223, 231.

Enciso, Martin Fernandez: 85, 173f, 207, 228.

Esdras: 41, 125, 108.

Ferdinand, King of Spain: 5f, 8.

Fine, Orince: 55-60, 244.

Fonteneau, Jean: 50.

Frampton, John: 96ff.

Francis I, King of France: 48ff, 100, 207.

Fies, Laurent: 38ff.

Frisius, Gema: 55, 60, 209, 236.

Frobisher, Martin: 71ff, 101ff, 236, 238.

Galle, Philip: 165.

Gastaldi, Giacomo: 62, 66, 122.

Gilbert, Humphery: 71f, 105, 194, 236-240.

Giocundus: 10, 19f.

Gomez, Esteban: 50.

Gomora, Francisco Lopez de: 48, 96, 106, 124, 130, 167, 169, 200f, 245.

Grijalva, Juan: 47.

Hakluyt, Richard: 73ff, 105, 150, 233-242, 244.

Hanks, Henry: 240f.

Harriot, Richard: 105f, 233, 240.

Hawkins, John: 73, 103, 106, 163, 224f, 236, 240f.

Heindenburg, Juan de: 120, 122.

Herrera, Antonio de: 111, 127, 195, 203.

Hobbes, Thomas: 164.

Humboldt, Alexander von: 24, 43, 249.

Huttich, Johann: 55, 62f.

Ingram, David, 73, 105, 240.

Jode family: 70.

Lafiteau, Joseph Francois: 249ff.

Landa, Diego de: 124, 126, 244.

Laudonniere, Rene: 73, 105, 231ff.

Lery, Jean de: 160ff, 168f, 229.

Lescabot Marc: 167.

Lok, Michael: 53, 73f 235f, 238.

Lumnius, J. F.: 124.

Madoc, Prince of Wales: 192ff, 240f.

Magellan: 47ff, 86, 110.

Magus, Albertus: 167.

Magus, Olaus: 52, 65, 122.

Mandeville, Sir John: 43, 73, 193, 195, 240f.

Marlow, Chistopher: 241.

Martyr, Peter: 8, 16, 17, 43, 46ff, 51, 83ff, 119, 129f, 139ff, 166, 177, 195, 199f, 223, 243.

Mather, Cotton: 247ff.

Matienzo, Juan de: 176f.

Maximilian I, Holy Roman Emperor: 120, 208.

Mede, Joseph: 247f.

Medici, Lorenzo de: 9ff. 13, 19.

Mela, Pomponius: 38ff, 44f, 120.

Mendez de Aviles, Pedro: 232ff.

Mercator, Gerard: 67f.

Mier, Servands Terresa de: 249.

Molyneaux: 75ff.

Monardes, Nicholas: 96ff.

Montaigne, Michael: 169 ff, 190.

Montanus, Arias: 123f.

More, Thomas: 144ff, 196, 234, 243.

Morgues, Jacques le Moyne: 231f.

Motolinia, Toribio de: 175, 223.

Munster, Sebastian: 55f, 60-62, 236.

Nicholas, Thomas: 103ff.

Ogilby, John: 248.

Ojeda, Alonso de: 11, 12, 17, 19, 150.

Orrio, Alonso de: 249.

Ortelius, Abraham: 40, 68ff, 75, 167.

Oviedo, Gonzalo Fernandez de: 8, 52, 89ff, 122, 128f, 223, 243.

Pane, Fray Ramon: 174.

Paracelsus: 120, 248.

Peckham, George: 105, 238.

Perier, Antoine du: 164.

Peyere: 243.

Pigafetta, Antonio: 47ff, 85f.

Philip II, King of Spain: 201, 207, 232.

Pineda, Alonzo de: 51.

Pizarro, Francisco: 201-206, 210f.

Pliny: 8, 81, 93, 115, 195, 128.

Polo Marco: 8, 13, 17, 27, 40, 42f, 63, 194f.

Ponce de Leon: 46, 195.

Possevino, Antonio: 245.

Postel, Guillaume: 131.

Prester John: 42, 195.

Ptolmey: 13, 15, 20f, 27, 37, 39, 111, 167, 176.

Purchas, Samuel: 247.

Raleigh, Sir Walter: 106f, 235, 240, 243.

Ramusio, Giamatista: 52, 47, 87, 62ff, 147, 150, 236.

Rastell, John: 234f.

Reisch, Gregory: 39, 48.

Ribault, Jean: 231ff.

Ringman, Matthias: 20.

Roy, Louis le: 1, 166f.

Rut, John: 50f, 237.

Ruysch, Johannes: 26, 30f.

Sahagun, Bernardino de: 121, 126, 130, 132, 175f.

Schoner, Johann: 37, 54.

Scillacio, Nicolo: 9, 81f.

Sepulveda, Juan Gines: 179ff, 187, 243.

Settle, Dionysius: 102f.

Sewell, Samuel: 247.

Shakespeare, William: 189, 242.

Smith, John: 247.

Smith, Joseph: 249.

Soderini, Pier: 10, 18f.

Soto, Hernando de: 100, 150ff, 206.

Spenser, Edmund: 241ff.

Stradanus: 190, 192.

Staten, Hans: 153-156, 164,

Tamara, Francisco: 45, 176.

Thevet, Andre: 45, 71, 147ff, 156ff, 164, 167ff, 222, 224, 243.

Thorne, Robert: 50, 73f, 238.

Torquemanda: 122, 131.

Torres, Luis de: 42, 174.

Vega, Garcillisio de la: 119, 203.

Valdes, Fray Diego: 133.

Verrazano, Giovanni da: 48ff, 52f, 60, 64, 145f, 228, 237, 242.

Vespucci, Americus: 8, 22f, 27, 43ff, 81ff, 137f, 243, 246.

Vespucci, Juan: 52.

Villegignon, Nicholas Durand: 120, 156, 229, 244.

Vopell, Caspar: 67.

Waldseemuller, Martin: 10, 20ff, 27, 32f, 37f, 45, 55.

Watt, Jochim: 44f.

White, John: 75, 103.

Wytfliet, Cornelli: 80.

Xeres, Francisco de: 202-206, 210f, 228.

Zaterini, Bolognino: 65, 67.

Zeno family: 73, 196-199, 237f. 241.

Tobacco and a man smoking a cigar from
STIRPIUM ADVERSIA NOVA by Pierre Pena
and Mathias de Lobel (Antwerp, 1574).